DOMESTIC VIOLENCE

To Dianne
Best wishes
from Clarence A. Sutton
Feb. 20, 2009

DOMESTIC VIOLENCE

AN ALTERNATIVE TO DOMESTIC VIOLENCE
PREVENTION AND INTERVENTION
WORKBOOK FOR TEENS AND ADULTS

CLARENCE A. SUTTON, MSW

Library of Congress Control Number:		2007907684
ISBN:	Hardcover	978-1-4257-8096-8
	Softcover	978-1-4257-8085-2

This book was printed in the United States of America.

To order additional copies of this book, contact:
Kochom Publishing
10409 Coyote Cub Ave.
Las Vegas, Nevada
89129
40469

CONTENTS

Understanding domestic violence is taking control of your destiny.

Introduction

The demand for the introduction of this workbook to the public is the result of psychologists, sociologists, criminologists, political scientists, and service providers who are seeking an end to domestic violence.

We believe stopping domestic violence is a race against time to prevent the spread of social and family destruction within our society. The disposition of policy makers and members of the media is to dedicate significant amounts of their time to the challenging task of stopping domestic violence.

Just as domestic violence is a learned behavior, people can also be taught peaceful methods of resolving their personal and interpersonal problems and not have to resort to violence as a means of solving their problems.

Everything can be placed on a continuum from good to the worse. In regard to domestic abuse, there are relationships for which counseling can assist victims and abusers with a new outlook on how to obtain harmony in their home.

If you believe that your partner is a person who will listen to reason, and there is a possibility that your partner can change his or her abusive behavior, by all means, seek professional assistance.

However, if the abuser will not change his or her belief system and you feel as if your home will continue to be used as a battlefield, it may be time for you to make one of the most important decisions you will ever have to make, and this is to either remain or leave the relationship. The choice to stop domestic violence in your home is your choice to make.

Our goal in creating this workbook is to empower the individual with common knowledge for the purpose of personal and interpersonal safety and growth.

Our main point of approach will consist of three categories: the individual, family, and society. The combination of "Power and Control" tactics such as physical abuse, verbal abuse, emotional abuse, and economic abuse will be thoroughly discussed.

We will also address such issues as communication skills, the cycle of violence, stress, anger, substance abuse, nonviolent behavior, conflict resolution, as well as intimacy in relationships. Children are the central members of a family; therefore, chapters will address parenting skills, as well as the effect domestic violence has on children.

Although the terms *men* and *women* will be used throughout this workbook, we are also referring to teenagers, who are involved or will be involved in situations concerning domestic violence.

The strengths of the family will also be emphasized without covering up a family's vulnerabilities to abusive behaviors. Throughout this workbook, there are written exercises in which the reader is encourâged to write down their responses.

The exercises are intended to accomplish the following:

- To assist each individual to view his or her behavior as well as their partner's behavior
- To assist the individual with understanding the consequences of not taking action against his or her abuser or batterer
- To assist the individual with understanding that stopping the abuse or battering is ultimately his or her decision
- To provide the individual with alternatives to stop or prevent abusive behavior

We also encourage readers to incorporate new theories and new research findings concerning putting an end to domestic violence as such material become available.

This workbook is not about taking legal action or a replacement for legal counseling. Therefore, seek professional assistance if you decide to take legal action or need assistance with any mental issues that you are having difficulty resolving.

We also encourage the readers to seek professional assistance when they encounter a situation in which they cannot understand and to abandon the idea that they are alone, and there is no one outside of their home who will assist them with their problem.

There is outside assistance such as getting a restraining order, children support, child custody orders, child stealing, visitation orders, child and spousal support, property issues, and other legal issues that will help victims of domestic violence.

Exercises are available in each chapter to illustrate the key concepts. These exercises will help the individual to understand their situation and to assist with developing an effective commitment to making change where they believe change is necessary.

Above all, individuals must understand that if they are victims of domestic violence, they must hold their abuser or batterer accountable for their abusive behavior and not blame themselves for their partner's violent behavior. This workbook maintains that the safety of the victim(s) will always be of paramount concern.

Attention has been paid to economic status, ethnic minorities, alternative lifestyles, and people with reading disabilities.

How to Use This Workbook

This workbook is designed to help teens and adults understand that there are alternatives to the use of violence in relationships. The chapter's objectives and questions are designed to meet the parameters for specialized domestic violence prevention and intervention. It also can be used as a guide for victims of domestic violence and should provide victims, abusers, and batterers with new insight into how to live a life free of domestic violence.

The chapters are five to twelve pages in length with easy-to-follow topics and statements. This arrangement is designed to assist each individual with gaining a better appreciation for learning alternatives to violent behavior. If used in a classroom setting, each chapter could comprise of one session.

We recommend using family- and individual-relationship videos with this workbook. The choice of videos should be a cooperative effort by you and your partner. Videos can be bought at bookstores or found at your local library.

The Questions for the Reader

The questions for the reader are general as well as personal. They can assist the reader with a variety of *directions* that they may want to explore concerning their partner's behavior as well as their own behavior. The questions are uncomplicated yet profound; they are designed to generate a sincere response from each individual.

This is an excellent approach because it should reveal to the reader their level of interest in the exercise being taught. The questions will allow the readers to recognize any negative, as well as positive views they may have about their relationship. The questions will also allow the readers to test their progress from chapter to chapter simply by how the reader answers each question.

There are at least ten questions available in every exercise. If necessary, any one question may generate a new question or a series of follow-up questions, which will lead to a particular conclusion for the reader.

Related Chapters of Interest

As you read through the related chapters of interest categories, you will notice there are titles from other chapters in the workbook. These chapters have been included to provide the individual with information suitable for additional study.

A Special Note to the Reader

This workbook is written for teens and adults who may or may not be involved in a violent relationship. It was designed to provide teens and adults with information concerning alternatives to violent behavior. The reader should find this workbook useful regardless of his or her race, educational level, or economic status.

It was designed for the reader to

- understand the destructive force of abusive behavior and how important it is to stop the violence;
- explore new areas of knowledge concerning alternatives to violence;
- get a better understanding about who they are as a person and what they want out of life.

This workbook should challenge the readers' ability to take an honest look at any outdated beliefs they may have concerning their relationship. It will give them concrete tools to change any abusive behaviors. If the reader understands the idea and purpose for this workbook and decide to make a positive change, they will discover the rewards of a healthy relationship.

This workbook was written with the understanding that the writer is not engaged in rendering legal or other professional services, which they are not qualified to provide. If legal or other expert assistance is required, the services of a competent professional should be sought.

We urge the reader to read all the available material, learn as much as possible about alternatives to violence, and tailor the information to their individual needs. For more information concerning any subject material contained in this workbook, contact its publisher or turn to the reference section in the back of this book.

This domestic violence workbook is not a cure-all scheme. The readers must expect to invest a lot of time and effort into making a positive change, to unlearn negative behaviors concerning their partners or themselves. Every effort has been made to make this workbook as complete and as accurate as possible.

However, this workbook should be used only as a general guide and not as the ultimate source of learning to stop any abusive behaviors. The reader should never stop learning new ways of working through their problems; assistance will always be available for those who are interested in make change.

Important Message to the Reader

Each chapter contains at least one self-assessment for the reader to consider what changes they must make to avoid becoming or remaining the victim of any violent behaviors in their relationship. The reader is asked to be completely honest when answering the questions and statements within this workbook.

However, the reader must remember if they decide to take this workbook home, others may read his or her answers to the statement and questions. This may put the owner of this workbook at risk for confrontations. Therefore, it is the reader's responsibility and not the responsibility of the author or agency to manage this potential problem.

Acknowledgment

Nearly all published books results from collaborations between the author and several other important contributors. This book is no exception. Although I take full responsibility for its subject matter, it would never have achieved its present form without the valuable suggestions of my friend and mentor: George Anderson, LCSW. I must give a special thanks to Diane Saxe, RN, MSN, and Danuta Paczynska, BA, for their abiding encouragement and technical support.

Chapter One

What
Is
Domestic Violence?

Chapter's Objectives:

1. To provide the reader with a brief history of domestic violence
2. To explain the basic legal and behavioral definitions of domestic violence
3. To examine certain types of abusive behaviors
4. To discuss violence against women in America
5. To advise readers of the importance of seeking professional assistance if they are a victim of domestic violence

Questions for You to Answer as You Read This Chapter:

1. How well do you understand the basic legal definition of domestic violence?
2. How well do you understand the behavioral definition of domestic violence?
3. What negative behaviors should you or your partner change?
4. Are you (or your partner) a victim of domestic violence?
5. If you or your partner is a victim of domestic violence, what steps can you and your partner take to stop the abuse?

Related Chapters of Interest:

- What Is Power and Control?
- Equality in a Relationship
- Communication Skills
- Anger Management
- The Effect Domestic Violence Has on Children

Chapter One

What Is Domestic Violence?

A History of Domestic Violence

If you were to review the history of domestic violence, you would learn that violence against women is not a rare phenomenon. Historical documents from Europe, Africa, and Asia have revealed that women were, by law, ordered to obey their partners or become subject to a variety of physical punishments.

In some cultural traditions, men would take advantage of their cultural values, myths, and beliefs to use violence to control their partners.

Many cultures appeared to have engaged in the belief that it was acceptable to rule over women, or what today's society would call "having the power to control" and cause hardship and suffering to maintain control over their partner.

In ancient Egypt, violence against women is evident through the many writings on the inside of Egyptian pyramids. It is written that a wife could legally stoned, killed, or have her teeth knocked out with a brick if she spoke against her husband.

Europe's medieval period was also an uncompromising time for many women. This barbaric period in history has proven to be a time when physical and emotional abuse against women were enormous in scale.

In many cases, the physical and emotional abuse that have been found ingrained in society during the medieval period can easily be described as absolute horror.

For example, women were lynched, burned, cut, and beaten without remorse by their abusers. This sort of behavior was the accepted norm of that bleak period in history. The grief and humiliation women had to endure became a natural and widely accepted way of life.

In several South American countries, it has been reported that a husband could kill his wife if she was found to have committed adultery. The murderer would neither be pursued nor pressured by law enforcement nor be brought to justice for his crime.

For whatever reason, there is no written history of cases where women lynched or burned their husbands for being disobedient. Certainly, this does not mean women were not violent in their relationships with their partners.

In rare cases, women would become enraged with jealousy and commit an act of vengeance against their husbands and, in a fit of enraged jealousy, kill their partner; and in such cases, women have been sentenced to death. Nevertheless, the grief that women had to suffer became a natural and widely accepted way of life. As frightful as it may have been for the victims, they had to quietly accept the abuse in order to survive.

Women in America and England's Common Law

England's common law was the law of the land in America during the seventeenth and eighteenth centuries. Historical documents describe the different methods that were used to secure control over women during this period. One such method of control was known as the rule of thumb.

Out of this *unofficial law* came the belief that a husband had the right to strike his partner with a stick no wider than the circumference of his thumb. Unfortunately, there is no known legal written document that validates this law or rule.

However, it was proven that the rule of thumb was actually a tactic employed by men who simply wanted power and control over their partners. As a result, this so-called rule of thumb had nothing to do with an established law or any part of the American justice system.

In fact, men who used this rule of thumb method of controlling their wives were breaking the law by enslaving their partners and beating them with sticks.

There are several court cases in which men were brought before a magistrate for using sticks on their wives. The magistrate ruled in favor of the woman, but nothing was done to the man for his crime.

A Dark Time in History

There is absolutely no doubt that the history of domestic violence against women represents a long dark period of domination and terror perpetrated by men.

Although the historical accounts of violence against women can be expressed in words, the countless profiles of torture and misery cannot be felt or duplicated for the purpose of truly understanding the suffering of these women.

Some men may read these words and understand the message of past abusive behaviors against women. And still, others may only use this knowledge to disguise their violent behavior against women and, through ongoing deceit, will continue to shame themselves.

People in American society are well aware of the violence in our country. We further realize that finding a remedy is extremely important. The horrors of abuse from the past refuse to remain buried. Therefore, men who abuse and batter their partner must be exposed for all to see so that we can develop ways to stop the violence.

We also need to assist where we can to ensure such horrors never find their way back into our homes. By focusing on the different types of abuse, the legislative and judicial branches of our government have redefined domestic violence. Law enforcement can now identify and target people who commit acts of violence against their partners.

Domestic violence is less publicly acceptable than it was generations ago; consequently, abusers and batterers have become more treacherous by finding new methods to continue to hold their partner and family hostage.

As a domestic violence instructor, my students were men and women who were mandated by the court to attend domestic violence classes. I noticed over the years that many of my students did not realize that poking, shoving, or keeping their partner from leaving the home is a crime.

Only after reading the legal and behavioral definition did they calm down and begin to accept that it's unlawful to make physical contact with a person who does not want to be touched.

Victims as well as abusers or batterers of domestic violence need to explore the legal and behavioral definitions listed below to learn what constitutes domestic violence. Once learned and understood, women can protect themselves in the future by avoiding anyone who displays the potential for violent behavior.

After reading and understanding these definitions of domestic violence, the reader should discover three sources of power: individual inner power (spiritual), power of freedom, and the power they allow others to have over them. While the definition of domestic violence has shifted through the years, the relationship between the person responsible for domestic violence and his or her victims remains the same.

For example, there was a time when a man could slap or punch his partner, and law enforcement would simply tell him to take a walk around the block to cool off; in many states, that's no longer the case. Law enforcement is currently arresting those who commit acts of violence.

Domestic violence has two definitions: legal and behavioral. Depending upon the laws of a particular state, the definition of domestic violence varies. The basic behavioral definition of domestic violence used by many states is any pattern of assaultive and coercive behaviors, including physical, sexual, and psychological attacks, economic coercion, as well as destruction of family property or pets.

The legal definition of domestic violence identifies those who are in a "domestic" relationship with the person committing the violent act. In most states, this includes, but is not limited to,

- people who are related by blood or marriage;
- people who are currently or were previously living together;
- people who had or are having a dating relationship;
- people who have a child in common;
- one or both partners who have been or are currently violent toward their minor child or a minor child of any of the relationships mentioned above.

In cases concerning domestic violence, it is important to recognize and consider the basic differences between the term *assault* and the term *battery*.

- An assault is the unlawful attempt, coupled with the present ability, to commit a violent injury on the person of another.
- A battery is any willful and unlawful use of force or violence upon the person of another.

Following is a list of categories of the most common physical and emotional abusive behaviors that a person can commit against his or her partner. This list should assist the reader in understanding the various terms used to describe the different types of abusive behaviors.

Exercise

Has anyone been abused in your home? Place a *check mark* next to the behavior that has been done to you or your partner (past or present).

(1)
Physical Abuse

____poked ___been shaken ___grabbed ___shoved ___pushed ___thrown ___punched ___restrained ___blocked attempts to leave ___choked ___hit with objects ___beatings ___kicked ___burned

(2)
Emotional Abuse

____controlled by using violence against children_____continued threats of violence _____intimidation through attacks against family pets _____yelling ____stalked ___isolated from family and friends

(3)
Sexual Abuse

___pressured for sex ___forced sex ___forced sex with third parties ___harmed in any way ___forced to perform degrading sex acts

(4)
Economic Abuse

____withholding of family funds ____spending family funds _____making all the financial decisions ___does not assist with the family's financial problems ____controls access to family health care insurance

(5)
The Misuse of Children

_____hostage taking of children _____physical and sexual abuse of children _____force children to engage in physical and psychological abuse of partner ____custody fights ___uses visitation to monitor partner

(6)
Destruction of Property and Pets

The destruction of property and pets can be considered as violent behavior, causing psychological damage to each member of the family. However, the law will vary from state to state regarding the criminal consequences for such violent behavior.

Destruction of property and pets can be considered as

- destroying the furniture,
- breaking windows,
- kicking or punching holes in the walls,
- destroying your partner's belongings,
- destroying any part of your partner's vehicle,
- stealing your partner's keys to the home or job,
- destroying partner's clothing,
- kicking the family pet,
- killing the family pet, and
- intentionally not feeding the pet.

Professional Counseling

Most abusers will not seek professional assistance until after they have repeatedly verbally or physically abused their partners or have been arrested for such crimes. In fact, if they do obtain professional assistance, they will usually maintain that the counseling sessions were a waste of time and did not help them with their problem. Many abusers or batterers believe that their only choice to resolve domestic disputes is through the use of violence.

This workbook is designed to assist victims as well as abusers or batterers with understanding that violence is not the answer to solving domestic disputes. However, if all else fails, it is at this time that law enforcement and the justice system may intervene to provide a remedy. This workbook is an excellent opportunity for people to understand who they are and to begin to work on not being the victim or an abuser or batterer of domestic violence.

If you are a victim, abuser, or batterer of domestic violence, you will quickly learn that abusive behavior will not hold the relationship together much longer. Take this opportunity to obtain the knowledge and skills that are necessary to have a healthy relationship.

Self-Assessment

Following are statements concerning domestic violence. Apply your personal knowledge, as well as information from this chapter, to assess the level of abuse in your relationship. It is important that you answer all the true, false, or NA (not applicable) statements as completely and honestly as possible:

1. I have been emotionally abused by my partner. ___
2. I have been emotionally abusive toward my partner. ___
3. I have been ridiculed by my partner. ___
4. I have learned to overlook unkindness and disrespect from my partner. ___
5. When my partner becomes assertive, the relationship seems to work better. ___
6. I have been physically abused by my partner. ___
7. I have physically abused my partner. ___
8. I have been called terrible names by my partner. ___
9. I have called my partner terrible names. ___
10. Property has been destroyed by a member of my family. ___

The previous list of statements is for you to assess the negative behaviors in your relationship. If you have answered *true* to any of the statements above, a change is necessary to stop the abusive behavior. Use the information in this workbook, and also seek professional assistance for any questions you may have that this chapter does not address.

Chapter Two

What
Is
Power and Control?

Chapter's Objectives:

1. To provide information concerning power and control in relationships
2. To provide profiles of the two most common types of controllers
3. To describe the tactics used in maintaining dominance in relationships
4. To assist the reader with understanding the dominating power a person can have over others
5. To encourage victims of domestic violence to seek professional assistance as soon as they are able

Questions for You to Answer as You Read This Chapter:

1. What's the motivation behind the desire for wanting to dominate a partner?
2. Can you explain why abusive behavior is considered as a learned behavior?
3. Is there a controller in your relationship?
4. What tactics of power and control exist in your relationship?
5. What can a victim of domestic violence do to stop the abuse?

Related Chapters of Interest:

- What Is Domestic Violence?
- Equality in Relationships
- Love and Commitment
- Trust and Respect
- Substance Abuse within the Family

Chapter Two

What Is Power and Control?

Dominating Others

No clear distinction can be drawn between the two words *power* and *control*. However, advocates of domestic violence who created the term refer to power and control as "one person having the ability to influence their will upon others in relationships." The idea of having power in a relationship can be summed up in a single definition: a driving force to dominate through the use of words, gestures, or physical force.

The notion of using power and control in a relationship is the idea that the controller will exercise his or her authority to create inequality to the point in which their partner will lose a fraction or total individual, social, and economic rights. In the mind of a person who takes pleasure in dominating others, the attitude is "Nothing belongs to us, but everything belongs to me, and don't do as I do, do as I say." A domineering partner doesn't feel he or she is really in control until his or her partner, or other family members, do as they are told without question or hesitation.

The attitude of a controller is to control the behavior of all family members, but what's important to remember about people who love to have power over others is that all controllers are not the same. Consider the two most common controllers: the "partial" controller and the "extreme" controller. Most partial controllers are not batterers; however, they will often use emotional abuse to control their partners.

Partial controllers will never consider committing a homicide if they believe that they are losing control or have lost control over their partner. Although they want to control their partner, they are not interested in *absolute dominance*. The partial controller will often use controlling tactics such as emotional abuse, as well as control family funds, keep important information from their partner, persistently forget special holidays that are meaningful to their partner, and most of all, lie without hesitation.

The extreme controller wants complete authority in a relationship and, if necessary, will control family members through the use of extreme emotional and physical abuse. There are cases in which extreme controllers will threaten their partner with death or resort to actually committing a homicide if they believe they are losing or have lost control over their partner.

What motivates men, as well as women (women can be controllers but not to the extent as most men) to want to control another person through the use of violence? The answer could be lack of self-confidence and unhealthy self-esteem. Of course, there are many other reasons why people would want to control others. However, lack of self-confidence and having unhealthy self-esteem top the list.

Working as a domestic violence instructor, I've come to the conclusion that many controllers view themselves as being more mentally or physically inadequate than other men or women. This sort of attitude that people have toward themselves creates a kind of deep-seated fear of the unknown. This kind of fear, in most people, can be considered as the driving force behind their jealousy, anger, and rage.

In terms of a controller's mental or physical inadequacies or both, many controllers fear that their partner will discover their inadequacies and begin looking for another partner who does not have such inadequacies. There are also cases in which some men and women may believe that their partner is mentally stronger than they are, and it makes them feel less than a man or woman. They believe that their partner is stronger in the sense that he or she has an inner spiritual strength that the controllers desire to have themselves.

Therefore, the controller will use emotional and physical abuse to break their partner's spirit, proving to themselves that they are the stronger person. After abusers have driven their partner to tears and depression, many abusers or batterers will feel a perverted thrill as they observe their partner suffer. Many controllers realize the odds are against them if they continue to use emotional and physical abuse to dominate their partner.

Controllers will realize a change is taking place when their victims begin to fight back. Fighting back does not necessarily mean using emotional or physical abuse but letting the abuser know that either they stop the abuse or the victim will end the relationship by separating or filing for a divorce.

Controlling Behaviors

The eight most common power and control tactics used by a controlling person are described in this chapter. These power and control tactics are used for the purpose of maintaining control over their partner and other family members. The controller's objective is to make family members submit to their needs through the use of mental and, if necessary, physical violence.

The most common controlling tactics used by controllers are the following:

(1)
Using Emotional Abuse

A controller will use emotional abuse to

- ♦ make his or her partner feel helpless and hopeless;
- ♦ devalue his or her partner's character by calling him or her cruel names;
- ♦ make it appear that his or her partner is unstable and confused by hiding or stealing his or her personal belongings;
- ♦ humiliate his or her partner in front of other family members and friends;
- ♦ make his or her partner feel guilty when there is no reason for him or her to feel guilty.

(2)
Using Coercion and Threats

A controller will use coercion and threats to

- ♦ create fear through threats and acts of physical violence;
- ♦ threaten to leave his or her partner at a critical time in the relationship;
- ♦ threaten to kill his or her partner and the children if he or she attempts to leave them;

- threaten to commit suicide if his or her partner leaves him or her;
- threaten to report his or her partner to law enforcement or social service for some past infractions;
- force his or her partner to drop any pending charges against him or her;
- force his or her partner to commit illegal acts.

(3)
Using Intimidation

A controller will use intimidation to

- make his or her partner feel afraid through the use of threatening body language;
- smash his or her partner's personal property;
- destroy household possessions;
- physically abuse family pets;
- display dangerous weapons for the purpose of intimidating.

(4)
Using Isolation

A controller will use isolation to

- control what his or her partner does;
- control whom his or her partner can have as friends;
- control whom his or her partner talks to;
- control where his or her partner goes;
- control what his or her partner reads;
- control his or her partner's outside involvement with others.

(5)
Minimizing, Denying, and Blaming

A controller will use minimizing, denying, and blaming to

- deny his or her responsibility for their abusive behavior;
- find ways to say that the abuse didn't happen;
- shift responsibility for his or her abusive behavior to his or her partner;

- blame his or her negative behavior on his or her fits of anger and rage;
- say that it wasn't that serious when in fact, it was quite serious.

(6)
Using Children

A controller will use the children to

- make his or her partner feel guilty about the children;
- have the children relay abusive messages to either parent;
- use visitation rights to harass his or her partner and the children;
- threaten to kidnap the children when he or she has the opportunity;
- put down his or her partner in front of the children;
- turn the children against their father or mother.

(7)
Using Male and Female Gender Advantages

Is there such a situation in which one gender has an advantage over the other? The answer is yes. Having gender advantage can be defined as having certain advantages over the controller's partner because of his or her gender.

A controller will use his or her gender advantages to

- act as if he or she "reigns supreme" in the home;
- define all the domestic responsibilities within the household;
- make all the major decisions in the household;
- treat his or her partner as if he or she were a maid or puppet;
- deny his or her partner sexual intercourse as a means of controlling his or her partner;
- become physically and mentally abusive and overbearing.

(8)
Using Economic Abuse

A controller will use economic abuse to

- control where his or her partner can be employed;
- prevent his or her partner from getting or keeping employment;

- repeatedly cause his or her partner to have to ask him or her for money;
- give his partner an allowance;
- take his or her partner's income for his or her personal use;
- not allow his or her partner access to family income.

Without provocation, a controller can suddenly reveal any one of the previously mentioned cruel and threatening behaviors. Just as quickly, he or she will claim to be remorseful for the abusive behavior. This sort of abusive behavior is known as the cycle of abuse. If you are interested in learning more about the cycle of abuse, or better known as the cycle of violence, read Dr. Lenore Walker's book *The Battered Woman Syndrome*.

Exercise

You may be living in a home where tactics of power and control are currently being used to control family members. If so, below is a list of the eight most common controlling tactics used to control others. Describe the controlling tactic currently being used in your home.

1. My partner is emotionally abusive toward me when he or she

   ____

   ____

   ____

   ____

2. My partner uses coercion and threats against me when he or she

   ____

   ____

   ____

   ____

3. My partner uses intimidation against me when he or she

   ____

   ____

   ____

   ____

4. My partner uses isolation against me when he or she

   ____

   ____

   ____

   ____

5. My partner minimized, denied, or blamed me for his or her abuse when he or she

   ____

   ____

   ____

   ____

6. My partner uses our children against me when he or she

____
____
____
____

7. My partner uses economic abuse against me when he or she

____
____
____
____
____

8. My partner uses his or her gender advantage against me when he or she

____
____
____
____
____

The previous list of controlling tactics is to better assess whether you or any member of your family are being abused. Victims of domestic violence must realize that a controller can only continue to dominate if the victim gives them the power to do so. Most people realize that if they allow an individual to take advantage of them, they will, without hesitating, continue to take advantage of the situation until they get tired, which is doubtful, or until they decide to move on to another relationship.

Profile of a Controller

The notion that suggests domestic violence only takes place in the homes of the low socioeconomic population is pure nonsense. The profile of a controller can fit just about anyone regardless of his or her race or socioeconomic status. People are abused in homes, from the rich and famous to homes of the underprivileged.

Domestic violence happens on all levels of society. However, the highest rates of reported cases of domestic violence are in the low socioeconomic population, in cities with high unemployment rates, in homes where there is overcrowding, in substandard housing, and in single-parent households.

According to data from the Bureau of Justice Statistics, when compared to their distribution in the U.S. population, domestic violence offenders are disproportionately male over the age of eighteen and from all ethnic, economic, and social backgrounds. There are nearly five hundred thousand men and women in state prisons for a violent crime, and 15 percent are there for a violent crime against a family member.

Statistics show that among domestic violence offenders in state prisons, more than 90 percent are male. Of the crimes for which domestic violence offenders were in prison, 78 percent were against females, and more than half were against children under the age of eighteen. About 90 percent of offenders in state prisons for family violence had injured their victim, 50 percent of family violence victims were raped or sexually assaulted, 28 percent of the victims of family violence were killed, and 50 percent of offenders in state prisons for spousal abuse had killed their partners.

These are some amazing statistics, particularly the statistic concerning domestic homicides. Although the demographic profile of domestic violence offenders has changed over time, this does not mean that men have become less violent, and women have become more violent. It simply means that more men are involving law enforcement in their domestic violence situations, and more women are being arrested as a result.

One extraordinary thing about many abusers and batterers is that despite their appearance, there is nothing about them in the flesh that would lead you to believe that they would be any more or less abusive than the grocery clerk who packs your bags in the local supermarket or a 225-pound heavyweight boxer. Anyone can become an abuser or batterer if he or she is allowed to do so.

Our country is overwhelmed by such people of one sort or another. The mind-set of many controllers is to demand, not ask. They want to control where their partner goes, with whom they associate, where they work, the family's income, basically every aspect of their partner's life.

Controllers often find themselves pinned between their outdated beliefs and social reality. We all must be made aware that abusive behavior is abusive behavior no matter how remorseful a person may feel after being abusive or how innocent the abusive behavior may appear.

Domestic violence is so common that many people do not realize they are being abused. However, through various resources in the community, victims of domestic violence are beginning to obtain more information about abusive behaviors in their relationships. Numerous victims of domestic abuse are beginning to move toward stopping the violence in their homes by educating their partners, as well as themselves, informing law enforcement, or simply leaving their abuser or batterer.

If controllers are given the ultimatum to stop their abusive behavior or the relationship is over, most controllers will make a halfhearted attempt to understand their moral responsibilities to their partner.

After realizing they must give up their control over their partner, many controllers will abandon any notion of stopping the abuse. For example, controllers believe that to give up control would mean that they will not get their needs met or, possibly, they will fall under the control of their partner.

This way of thinking demonstrates their lack of understanding the profound nature of their behavior. Consequently, controllers may become even more committed to maintaining dominance over their partner through a range of oppressive tactics. They will attempt to make the point that his or her control over the partner cannot just be borderline control, but total control.

A major point should be made with reference to extreme controllers. Too hasty a change in taking away their control could have disastrous consequences. For example, these sort of controllers could escalate their violence to more beatings or, in some situations, even committing suicide or a domestic homicide or both. (We will continue to mention this fact throughout this workbook, due to its serious nature.)

Of the two controllers mentioned earlier, extreme controllers are the con artists, liars, intimidators, and batterers, who take perverse pride in deceiving and harming their partners. The second controller, the partial controller, is masterful in the use of mental stealth, i.e., the victim doesn't see the abuse coming.

The mistreatment may come as an innocent gesture, followed closely by verbal abuse. The partial controller will attempt to apologize and appear to be remorseful for his or her behavior, only to repeat the negative behavior once again and often without any provocation.

This kind of controller understands that there is no law against using emotional abuse, like calling his or her partner insulting names or withholding funds from his or her partner, and will *limit* the abuse to emotional and not become physically abusive. Eventually, a victim will become mentally drained from the prolonged and tormenting emotional abuse and decide to leave the relationship.

Of course, for many victims who have children and live on a modest income, leaving an abusive relationship is not quite as simple as *just packing up and leaving*. However, no matter how unsettling the road to peace may appear to a victim of domestic violence, the road will eventually unsettle itself once the victim finds peace.

We all must be made aware that abusive behavior is abusive behavior no matter how remorseful a person may feel after being abusive or how innocent the abusive behavior may appear. Any person who believes his or her partner is a controller and believes he or she wants to become liberated must stop and take a positive view of a world without controlling person in his or her life. Once victims can see beyond their abuser, he or she will be able to envision a life filled with the benefits of peace, prosperity, and freedom.

Self-Assessment

Apply personal knowledge, as well as information from the chapter, to answer the following questions. Answer the following questions with *yes*, *no*, or *NA* (not applicable) based on the first thought that comes to mind. It is important that you answer all questions as accurately and honestly as possible.

1. Are you afraid of your partner? ___
2. Do you believe your partner is afraid of you? ___
3. Are you afraid of your partner? ___
4. Are the children afraid of your partner? ___
5. Are your children afraid of you? ___
6. Do you believe that it's possible that your partner would seriously harm you? ___
7. Do you believe that it's possible that you will seriously harm your partner? ___
8. Do you believe someone should be in control of the family for the family to be successful? ___
9. Is there a gun in your home for protection? ___
10. Has your partner ever told you that he or she would find you if you took the children away? ___

The previous list of questions is to better assess your understanding of power and control in relationships. If you believe a change is necessary in the way you are being treated by your partner, use the information in this workbook, and also seek professional assistance for any questions you may have that this workbook does not address.

No matter what has been lost in your relationship, violence will not bring it back to its former years of pleasure.

Chapter Three

Equality
in
Relationships

Chapter's Objectives:

1. To provide a definition of *equality*
2. To provide a historical view of equality
3. To provide information concerning the importance of equality in relationships
4. To provide information concerning the negative consequences of inequality in a relationship
5. To provide information concerning the positive aspects of equality in a relationship

Questions for You to Answer as You Read This Chapter:

1. Should every aspect of a relationship be based upon equality?
2. Can you give an example of a situation in which you had to be unfair to make a situation fair?
3. Why is equality important in a relationship?
4. Should children have the same rights as parents?
5. What rights does a child have in a family?

Related Chapters of Interests:

- What Is Power and Control?
- Communication Skills
- Love and Commitment
- Trust and Respect
- Economic Partnership

Chapter Three

Equality in Relationships

What is Equality?

Equality is a term used to describe equal opportunity. Equal opportunity is intended to ensure that people are not excluded from the activities of society, such as education, employment, or health care on the basis of race or gender.

We believe the terms *equality* and *family* are connected. The idea of equality in relationships would imply that all family members be treated fairly and have an equal opportunity for individual and social prosperity.

Equality suggests that a well-balanced relationship be kept free from requests of any extreme nature, which would bring guilt, shame, or danger to the lives of family members or prohibit them from obtaining education, employment, or financial success.

In order for us to understand the term *equality,* as it was meant for all Americans, we must review history. The idea of equality is not a new idea that happened within the last several years. The idea of equality dates back to the Declaration of Rights of the colonies. The first truth to be declared by the Declaration of Independence in 1776 was "that all men are created equal."

The word *men* and how it was used in the Declaration of Independence of 1776, disqualified women in terms of being created equal. In today's society, the word *men* is used in a grammatical sense, which means that in all matters, men and women are created equal.

In 1776, equality was nonexistent in American homes, and despite this proud announcement of equality for all Americans, equality still does not exist in many homes today.

Of course, this distressing reflection of American's reality is slowly changing, and one day, men and women will experience the nature of equality in relationships.

Relationships that have no extreme differences in how a partner may express his or her thoughts or opinions are said to be equal and fair. In every relationship, each partner has a right to fair treatment from his or her partner. In a relationship that is equal, both partners share in the process of household decision making or, at least, share in the making of an equal number of separate important decisions.

The idea of sharing in the equal number of separate important decisions should have a positive impact on the success of one's relationship. Decisions that involve buying a new car or home, the kind of school the children will attend, employment, and the family's future retirement plan are all decisions that are designed for family success.

There is a tremendous amount of available information that can assist partners with recognizing how wonderful a relationship can become when two people work together to make important life-changing decisions.

Inequality

In order to completely understand the nature of equality, the nature of inequality must be clearly understood. Equality is the rational characteristic of mankind, and inequality is the sinister and irrational characteristic of mankind. As we previously mentioned, to employ equality is to be fair since fairness provides opportunity for all family members.

Inequality, when applied to interpersonal relationships, is the unequal distribution of goods and services, or opportunity for advancement, and any unreasonable mental or physical treatment of a family member. In short, inequality is a person's controlled mistreatment of another person by denying him or her equality in the relationship.

In many cases, a man's physical strength and warring mind contribute to his eagerness to employ the toxic instrument of inequality. Most men will use inequality for the purpose of obtaining and maintaining dominance over their partners.

In the case of inequality and controlling partners, the controlling partner determines what is considered reasonable and equal. Their idea of equality is based upon the 80 percent to 20 percent ratio, i.e., 80 percent for the controller and 20 percent for their partner and other family members.

The remarkable aspect for such an arrangement is that many controllers believe they are being generous with such an irregular percentage, particularly when the controller is an extreme controller.

An extreme controller cannot tolerate equality. He or she will make every attempt to deny his or her partner the opportunity to expand his or her mind beyond the everyday television, movies, newspaper headlines, education, and job opportunities. The idea of equality to an extreme controller is seen as a threat to his or her ability to maintain control over his or her partner.

When inequality is acted upon with a thirst for power over others, the weapon of inequality can become so brutal that it can go far beyond an individual's quest for power and control. Through generations of extreme sexist propaganda, power-hungry controllers have used the lethal instrument of inequality with precision.

For example, for centuries, women have been seen as weaklings, mindless, and out for what they could get. This sexist propaganda has stood for generations, and if some men were approached in today's society, we would find such an attitude still exists.

Of course, we do not include all men in such menacing and irrational thinking. This fact must be made perfectly clear. We continue to insist that our country is appreciative of men who have taken the time to gain knowledge for the purpose of building positive relationships and thus have brought honor to themselves.

Making Equality Work in Your Home

The most important aspect of a relationship is equality. The most effective way of receiving equality in a relationship is to speak with your partner about issues that call for equal opportunity for each member of the family.

Exercise

Using the following statements, give several examples of how equality and inequality have affected you based upon your gender or race and how equality and inequality have affected you in your relationship.

For example: I believe I have been treated fairly on my job because my supervisor is a fair person and believes in a person's skills and not in his or her race or gender.

- As a man/woman, I believe that I am being treated fairly on my job because
 ____
 ____
 ____
- Because of my race, I believe that I am being treated unfairly because
 ____
 ____
 ____
- I feel that I am being treated fairly when my partner
 ____
 ____
 ____
- I treat my partner fairly when I
 ____
 ____
 ____
- My partner treats me unfairly when he or she
 ____
 ____
 ____
- I am unfair toward my partner when I
 ____
 ____
 ____

Review what you have written and decide if your employment and domestic relationships are equal, average, or unequal. Then, decide if you would like to speak with your partner or supervisor about making any changes in how you're being treated to balance the scale of equality. Also, you must decide if approaching your partner or supervisor is a good idea. In the coming chapters, we will discuss partners who are controllers. Controllers like the idea of inequality in their relationship; therefore, for you to approach them about making changes may cause them to feel threatened and possibly cause you more problems.

Justice, Family, and Country

Some people may ask why use terms like *justice* and *country* in a workbook about domestic violence. When people speak of justice, they are usually talking about what happens in a court of law. However, justice or fair play should not only apply in our courtrooms but also in our homes.

In a home, you will often hear couples and even children say, "It's not fair that you can go out with your friends, and I have to stay home with the children," or one of your children may come to you and say that their "brother or sister isn't playing fair." In either case, as you can see, each person is seeking fair treatment from others.

Everyone wants to be treated fairly, whether it's inside or outside of the home. If the citizens of our country expect fair play when it comes to politics (fair elections), sports events (fair play), the justice system (a fair verdict), and anything else, which involves some kind of sharing, transference of opinion, or distribution of goods and services, why shouldn't each family member expect the same treatment from other family members?

Our country, in general, believes in the ideas of justice, and when everyone understands and uses the ideas of justice, families will flourish. Our justice system, in its entire magnificent splendor, forbids crimes against all its citizens.

This includes every human being. It is obvious that women do live within the boundary of our country; as a consequence, the ideas of being treated fairly should apply to all women as they apply to all men. Is this not correct?

Considering the previous statement, should men and women have the same right to live free of violence? Do men and women not share the same feelings and emotions? Is it fair when men and women have different economic and social opportunities?

Due to centuries of prejudices, stereotyping, and prejudging, these questions may prove to be difficult for some men and women to answer. Nevertheless, these questions must be addressed and answered sooner or later.

It appears that at every turn, there are people in relationships who must struggle with some sort of power play by a partner, whether it involves sex and finances or controlling where a partner can go and whom he or she can speak with as if he or she *owns* his or her partner.

The imbalances of justice and privilege in our country and in personal relationships have improved to some degree. Our country and its people are witnesses to a new dawn of justice and greater opportunities for the independence of people in domestic relationships.

Everyone should be made aware (if they are not already aware) that everyone living in this country should be entitled to the same privileges, whether they are in a dating relationship or married.

For any controller who may be reading this material, try to understand that you will not feel less powerful or intimidated by the advancement of a family member. If you trust and love your partner, let go of your need to control him or her, and rid yourself of any gender prejudices or criticism of your partner's success. You'll barely notice that your partner is earning more money than you or is able to create better ideas concerning developing and managing family affairs.

Self-Assessment

Apply personal knowledge, as well as information from the chapter, to answer the following statements. Answer the following statements with *true*, *false*, or *NA* (not applicable) based on the first thought that comes to mind. It is important that you answer all statements as accurately and honestly as possible.

1. It's foolish to think that only men should have equality. ___
2. There will always be inequality issues concerning race and gender. ___
3. Equality does not exist in my relationship. ___
4. It is difficult to be fair all the time. ___
5. Equality is needed in our home. ___
6. Women have been searching for equality for centuries. ___
7. My relationship would improve if I were treated with respect. ___
8. The reality of power is simple: the gender with the power should control the other. ___
9. I have an excellent reason why equality is important in my relationship. ___
10. To say that men and women can never become equal in a relationship constitutes a challenge to the survival of America. ___

The previous list is to better assess your understanding of the terms *justice* and *equality* in relationships. If you believe that it is necessary for you to learn more about inequality in personal relationships, use the information in this workbook, and also seek professional assistance for any questions you may have that this workbook does not address.

Chapter Four

Emotional Abuse

Chapter's Objectives:

1. To define the term *emotional abuse*
2. To provide information concerning people who use emotional abuse
3. To discuss the negative consequences of emotional abuse
4. To discuss the negative consequence emotional abuse has on children
5. To discuss issues concerning learning how to avoid being emotionally abused in a relationship

Questions for You to Answer as You Read This Chapter:

1. What is emotional abuse?
2. Why would emotional abuse be considered one of the most destructive behaviors?
3. Why are people emotionally abusive toward their partners?
4. How can people tell when they are being emotionally abused?
5. What are the positive steps to stop being a victim of emotional abuse?

Related Chapters of Interest:

- Communication Skills
- Trust and Respect
- What Is Domestic Violence?
- Equality in Relationships
- Love and Commitment

CHAPTER FOUR

Emotional Abuse

What Is Emotional Abuse?

What is *emotional abuse*? *Emotional abuse* can be defined as any inappropriate behavior that is intended to cause psychological or physical harm to another person. Emotional abuse is designed to damage or destroy a person's self-esteem and to create doubt in a person's mental and physical abilities.

Abusers and batterers use emotional abuse to control and deprive their partners of their basic freedom—a right that is essential to their partner's happiness and sense of personal inner strength.

The following examples are behaviors that abusers and batterers use in their relationship, which can cause emotional abuse to their partners:

- Calling their partner upsetting names
- Criticizing their partner in public
- Swearing at their partner
- Falsely accusing a partner of wrongdoing
- Scolding a partner in front of their children
- Teasing their partner about a physical attribute, affecting self-esteem
- Attacking their partner's opinions
- Threatening their partner with suicide threats
- Death threats aimed at their partner or other family member
- Threatening their partner with abandonment
- Acts of cruelty toward family pets
- Telling a partner that he or she is worthless
- Telling their partner that meeting him or her was a mistake
- Telling their partner that he or she is terrible in bed
- Telling a partner about an extramarital affair

Although emotional abuse is not considered as an immediate threat to human life, emotional abuse can, over a period of time, cause a tremendous amount of psychological pain. This unrelenting psychological pain is often felt years after being emotionally abused. Many victims of emotional abuse will carry this mental pain for the rest of their lives.

Based upon the behaviors that cause emotional abuse, we have come to the conclusion that emotional abuse can be considered a cruel act of violence. Emotional abuse is cruel in the sense that victims will isolate themselves from friends and other family members, develop unhealthy self-esteem, become depressed, and can develop symptoms of mental and physical illness.

Controllers and Emotional Abuse

Controllers who are emotional abusers do not believe in equality; they believe in inequality. Their motto is "As long as I have the control, nothing can go wrong, and if something does go wrong, it wasn't my fault." To an emotional abuser, his or her partner's opinion of him or her doesn't matter, respecting his or her partner's feelings doesn't matter, and what the controller believes to be fair isn't fair at all.

All boundaries concerning fairness that were verbally or mentally set during the beginning of the relationship are no longer relevant. Within the mind of controlling partners rests the thirst for obedience, which causes their minds to overflow with anger, fear, unhappiness, resentment, and suspicion. And all who live within the controller's family must surrender their freedom, desires, and sacrifice their self-esteem to satisfy the controller's *ego*.

Contrary to what many people believe about partners who control family members, many controllers are excellent when it comes to controlling their personal feelings. A controller's emotions are disguised; a controller may be feeling cheerful but will not show it.

A controller believes that showing emotions that indicate happiness will send the wrong message. Controllers believe that if they were to show signs of being happy, they will be exploited. There is also the belief that anger, when displayed, will keep the victims in line.

Conversely, controllers may appear to be angry, but in fact, they aren't really angry at all. Skilled controllers can turn their feelings off and on with amazing accuracy. It's sort of like persons who can laugh at a joke someone has told, and they know the joke wasn't funny, but they laughed anyway; or like when someone is talking to the boss, and the boss says something that's not funny, but everyone laughs.

Their smiles and laughter aren't really what they are feeling, but they cannot tell their boss, so they fake it. Skilled controllers are the same way. They cannot tell their partner that they are afraid, or they want to show happiness for fear of losing control.

So when controllers are challenged or ignored by their partner, they will flex their power by intimidating their partner through threatening looks, raised voices, and angry gestures. This act of muscle flexing is the way a skilled controller *shows his or her fangs in situations where he or she feels threatened.*

Controllers will also flex their muscles if they believe that the victim is no longer frightened of them. If controllers believe that they have lost control over the family, they believe that they cannot accept defeat or show any remorse.

In such a case, the controllers will take their abuse to another level and become physically abusive to prove to the victim that they still have the economic and physical strength to remain in control. This can prove to be a very dangerous and frightful juncture in a domestic violence situation.

In many cases of physical abuse, the victim will decide to physically fight back. And if *she* is injured during the physical exchange and decides to call law enforcement, she should report that *she* had been abused by her partner. Many controllers will tell the police officers that they were protecting themselves, and *they had to use force* to keep from being injured.

Of course, there are controllers who are skilled at maintaining power and control over their partners without attracting the attention of friends, relatives, or law enforcement. They achieve this by not physically injuring their partner but emotionally attacking their partner's character.

Controllers can recognize, with flawless precision, the crippling effect emotional abuse can have on their partner, as well as other family members. They realize that if they do not leave any visible physical scars on their partner, people will never realize they are or have been abusive.

People who use emotional abuse to control their partner will attempt to convince their victim that there is no one outside of the family who can help them.

If the abuser repeated this particular threat often enough, many victims will begin to believe that there is no one who can help them, or there is no way out of the relationship without being physically abused or financially deprived of the means to support their family.

When the victim does decide to seek outside intervention, i.e., calling extended family members, friends, counselors, or law enforcement, the controller will hold his or her partner responsible for creating a problem because *she* has told outsiders about family business. This sort of abuse will continue for months and even years.

Once the victim begins to believe that there is a choice of remaining in the abusive relationship or finding a way out, the choice will be made to find a way out of the relationship and never look back.

The Negative Effects of Emotional Abuse

Although people can become seriously ill as a result of being emotional abused, there are no known cases in which a person has died as a result of being emotionally abused.

Of course, there are cases in which people have died as a result of stress-related illnesses or suicide or homicide. No one has proven that such deaths were the result of emotional abuse, but people can say that emotional abuse was a contributing factor.

Physicians cannot prove that emotional abuse isn't the major cause of a particular suicide and homicide, but the fact that the possibility exists should not be taken lightly or dismissed.

As a case in point, the rate of teenage suicides in this country is on the rise. If emotional abuse is a contributing cause of teenagers committing suicide, no emotional abuser will step forward to take responsibility for their death. How can an abuser be the cause of a teenager's death?

When teenagers are constantly being told by their father or mother that they are worthless, ugly, lazy, stupid, and will never amount to anything, the psychological effects can be devastating.

If a teenager is told enough times that he or she will amount to nothing, he or she begins to question his or her own identity, which can be very depressing and difficult to overcome. How can a teenager take life head-on after being told such pessimistic things throughout his or her teen years?

The same can be said for adults; we do not like being told that we are worthless as human beings. The effects of emotional abuse on adults and teenagers may be similar, depending on the individual's personality, belief system, culture, or preexisting mental condition(s).

As a counselor and domestic violence instructor for men and women, I have heard many patients and students tell of incidents, on their jobs, of being called names like lazy, fat, and stupid. While driving home from work, they had been cursed and "given the finger" by total strangers. Once they arrive home, they face their abuser, who continues to insult them with similar names like stupid and lazy.

How much of this negativity can a person take before he or she begins to say to himself or herself, "If everyone is saying and doing awful things to me, then what my partner, father, or mother is saying about me must be true"? On the other hand, we must remember that there are people who would like nothing better than to see others feel the way they are feeling.

Remember the motto "Misery loves company." Emotional abusers believe that they should not *suffer alone when they have the ability to make others feel as miserable as they do.*

Individuals who physically and emotionally abuse their partners believe that if they do not physically or emotionally abuse their children, their children aren't being harmed. This notion could not be farther from the truth.

When young children witness their mother or father being emotionally abused, many children will become anxious, afraid, angry, or depressed and will have disturbing dreams and possibly develop other debilitating symptoms.

Many children will begin to act out their anger and frustration by using some of the same words that they hear their parents use during a fight.

When children are playing with their toys and friends, they will act out their anger and frustration upon their siblings and toys. Contrary to what an abuser believes, he or she is creating problems and mental pain for everyone in his or her family—a mental pain that is so devastating that it could remain with the victim for the rest of their life.

Many emotionally abused women believe that one of their biggest problems is convincing law enforcement that they are being emotionally abused. Many women find reporting emotional abuse to law enforcement very difficult because emotional abuse doesn't leave the victim with any visible bruises or broken bones.

Therefore, if a victim of emotional abuse cannot convince law enforcement that emotional abuse is causing her pain and suffering, whom can she turn to? We suggest that victims of emotional abuse would contact someone who works in the field of domestic violence and be directed to someone who can help resolve their domestic problems.

Exercise

Are you being emotionally abused? Following are questions that can assist you with that determination. Use information from the chapter, with your personal experiences, to answer the following statements. Answer by filling in the blanks with *true*, *false*, or *NA* (not applicable) to any question that may apply to you and your family.

1. My partner and I fight a lot. ___
2. My partner seems to be angry most of the time. ___
3. My partner blames me for everything that goes wrong. ___
4. My partner is very controlling. ___
5. I feel depressed most of the time. ___
6. I am easily hurt by the things my partner say to me. ___
7. My children feel uncomfortable when my partner is in the home. ___
8. My children told me that they hate their father or mother. ___
9. My children are experimenting with drugs. ___
10. My children have become rebellious. ___
11. I do not feel as if I am being emotionally abused. ___
12. My partner and I share all family responsibilities. ___
13. My partner understands the meaning of love, trust, and respect. ___
14. I understand the meaning of love, trust, and respect. ___
15. I love to be near my partner. ___
16. My partner has a good sense of humor. ___
17. I have a happy family. ___
18. My partner and I enjoy each other's company. ___
19. My children appear to be happy. ___
20. My partner and I agree that emotional abuse in our home can affect how our children view parenthood. ___

Scales can bring reality back into one's life. Consideration of the list above will help you get a clear picture of what is happening in your relationship. Carefully review the list. If you answered *true* to three or more questions from 1 through 10, someone is using emotional abuse. If you answered *true* to five or more questions from 11 through 20 and all *false* from the first ten statements, your partner is not using emotional abuse.

Breaking Free

There are professionals in your community who can assist you with finding solutions to the problem of being emotionally abused by your partner. Although extended family and friends are a good source of comfort and support, they are not professionals.

Consequently, you must seek professional assistance to find a solution to the problems that may have developed as a result of being emotionally abused. Evidence, obtained through research, has proven that everyone who has been directly or indirectly exposed to physical or emotional abuse should receive professional counseling.

When a person has been constantly exposed to physical and emotional abuse by a loved one, the affects can continue for years after the abuse has occurred. Victims of physical and emotional abuse must familiarize themselves with positive ways of keeping abusers or batterers out of their lives.

Victims of domestic violence must learn to understand their feelings, acknowledge them, and calmly express how they really feel about being abused. Gaining an honest awareness of their feelings will reduce the risk of becoming physically or emotionally abused in future relationships.

Following is a list of ideas that will keep your relationship free from emotional abuse:

- Realize that emotional abuse is a serious problem.
- Realize that your health and safety and the health and safety of your children are of the utmost importance.
- Never allow a person to devalue your character (who you are).
- Never allow anyone to play mind games to upset or to control you.
- Never allow anyone to humiliate you in private or in public.
- Always take any threats of committing suicide or homicide very seriously.
- Never allow anyone to yell at you as a means of control.
- Never allow anyone to isolate you from your children, family, or friends.
- Never allow anyone to use violence against your children to "get even with you."
- Contact programs that assist victims of domestic violence.

> No one has to be a victim or remain a victim of emotional abuse. Once a person breaks free from a partner who uses emotional abuse to control him or her, he or she will find that there is a new and wonderful life waiting to be explored.

Self-Assessment

Following is a list of the most common tactics used by an emotional abuser. You will find a few questions that will overlap previously asked questions. What you are looking for is certainty, i.e., whether you and your children are being emotionally abused or not being abused.

It's important to stop and think before answering these questions again. Apply personal knowledge, as well as information from the chapter, to answer the following questions. Answer *yes*, *no*, or *NA* (not applicable) to the questions. It is important that you answer all questions as accurately and honestly as possible.

1. Is there anyone in your home who uses put-downs to make family members feel bad about themselves? ___
2. Has anyone threatened to commit suicide? ___
3. Have there been any death threats? ___
4. Is there anyone deliberately playing mind games? ___
5. Has anyone been humiliated in private, in front of other family members and friends, or in public? ___
6. Has there been any unnecessary use of violence against the children? ___
7. Is there anyone who leaves and stays away for long period of time and no one knows his or her location? ___
8. Is there any yelling to control a family member? ___
9. Does either partner isolate the children from the other partner? ___
10. Is vulgarity used a lot in your home? ___

The previous list is to better assess any use of emotional abuse in your home. Review the list. If you answered yes to any of the previous questions, there is emotional abuse taking place in your home. And if there is emotional abuse in your home, you should consider it necessary to discuss with your partner that he or she begin making changes in his or her behavior. Use the information in this workbook, and also seek professional assistance for any questions you may have that this workbook does not address.

Chapter Five

Using Coercion and Threats

Chapter's Objectives:

1. To define *coercion* and *threats* as they apply to relationships
2. To recognize the presence of coercion and threats in a relationship
3. To describe the fundamental nature of an abuser
4. To discuss what motivates people to do what they do and break the law by using coercion and threats
5. To discuss issues concerning the cruelty of coercion and threats in a relationship

Questions for You to Answer As You Read This Chapter:

1. Can you define the word *coercion*?
2. Can you define the word *threat*?
3. Can you give an example of a serious threat made to you by your partner?
4. Why do abusers use coercion and threats in their relationship?
5. Is it okay to threaten a child who is misbehaving?

Related Chapters of Interest:

- What Is Domestic Violence?
- Equality in Relationships
- Communication Skills
- Parenting Skills
- The Effects of Domestic Violence on Children

Chapter Five

Using Coercion and Threats

Unwanted Restraining

What are the definitions of *coercion* and *threats*? In relationships, *coercion* can be defined as using any kind of unwanted restraining tactics, dominating force, or use of intimidating remarks toward a partner. The sole purpose of using coercion and threats is to weaken and intimidate a person into doing something they do not want to do.

Following is a list of ways an abuser gains satisfaction from the use of coercion and threats:

- Forcing a partner to have sex with him or her or someone else
- Forcing a partner to commit illegal acts
- Forcing a partner to beg for what he or she wants or needs
- Forcing a partner to wait on him or her as if he or she were a servant
- Forcing a partner to lie to family and friends about injuries he or she may have suffered after a fight

A *threat* can be defined as any action or expression that is designed to make a person believe he or she will be subjected to mental or physical injury. Following is a list of ways an abuser or batterer will use coercion and threats toward his or her partner or other family members:

- Threaten to slap, punch, kick, and so on
- Threaten to kill the partner if he or she tells anyone about the abuse
- Threaten to abandon the children
- Threaten to tell others about something personal that his or her partner has told them in confidence that could have damaging consequences
- Threaten to put them out of the house
- Threaten to kill their partner or commit suicide (or both)

Couples may become stressed or depressed from time to time. However, stress or depression is no reason to force or threaten someone into doing something that he or she does not want to do. Any person who uses coercion or threats against his or her partner certainly should not believe that such behavior would make the partner love and respect him or her.

Many abusers believe that through the use of coercion and threats, their demands will not be challenged, and sadly, this may be true. Many victims who have been abused by previous partners in their past may allow a new partner to force and threaten them. At some point in an abusive relationship, many victims will eventually come to the understanding that they have choices.

After months and years of being forced and threatened by their partner, many victims will often choose to seek outside intervention (e.g., family and friends or intervention through the justice system). Gaining confidence and using the information they have received from outside intervention, victims of domestic violence will begin to believe there is hope to stop the violence and eventually move on with their life.

Establishing Dominance

The fundamental nature of using coercion and threats is to establish domination. In the beginning of a relationship, an oppressor does not show their interest in being the dominant partner. They are very skillful at convincing a potential partner that they are honest, warm, caring, and affectionate.

Of course, when a person talks about having or displaying these wonderful qualities or both, most people will believe they are not in danger of being abused and are basically out of harm's way. However, it's all part of the oppressor's game to deceive their partner into believing they are not to be feared.

As the potential victim relaxes and trusts the person, the oppressor will slowly begin to impose his or her will over their victim. People of this nature depend largely upon stealth; they will use an array of behaviors and verbal communication to deceive their victim into a false sense of security.

Abusers will also use less threatening methods of intimidation to keep their partner and other family members in line, but the use of force and bone-chilling threats are the main weapons of choice.

What would make a man or woman who uses coercion and threats any different from those who may use other tactics of abuse? We believe that there isn't much difference. The thought of becoming physically or emotionally injured by any person makes such threats a frightening experience for any victim.

Men who use coercion and threats are very dangerous people, particularly when they threaten to kill their partner or anyone associated with her. *Any threat to take the life of a partner or associate must be taken seriously.*

Collectively, men who use emotional and economic abuse are responsible for the continuing annual increase of mothers and their children becoming homeless. The most depressing aspect of this scenario is in the fact that many homeless families believe they are better off homeless than living in a home with an oppressive and dominating partner.

Exercise

The following exercise will assist with the discovery of whether coercion and threats are being used in your relationship. Use information from the chapter in combination with personal knowledge to fill in the blanks, answering all statements and questions as accurately and honestly as possible. Determine which situation is using coercion and which situation constitutes a threat. Remember any of these situations could apply to either partner.

- When my partner becomes angry with me about a certain situation, he or she will often ____

  ____

  ____

  Was what he or she said a threat____coercion______neither____?

- There are times when my partner frightens me when he or she _____

  ____

  ____

- When you were frightened by your partner, were you threatened ____ coerced_____neither_____?

- I have used force to get my partner to ______________________

  ____

  ____

- There were times when I had to use threats to get my partner to

  ____

  ____

  ____

- Have you ever used force to get your children to do something you wanted them to do? ______

- I have had to threaten my children to get them to

  ____

  ____

  ____

- Has your partner ever forced you to commit any illegal acts? ____

- Have your children ever heard you make any kind of threat toward their mother or father? ____

- Has your partner ever forced you to have sex? ____

- Do you ever feel like you are a servant? ____

Using coercion and threats for the purpose of installing fear *is wrong*. To threaten another person's life is against the law and must be taken seriously. If such a threat has been made toward you, do not wait until the person decides to follow through. You have choices to make: either leave the relationship or call the proper authorities. In either case, *caution is essential.*

Looks Can Be Deceiving

What does a person look like who uses coercion and threats? For sure, they don't have horns, glow in the dark, or have a sign on their backs that reads, "I am an abuser. Beware."

Many people believe they can tell what a person is like by the way they look—i.e., smile, walk, talk, dress, or comb their hair—or by looking them in their eyes. Some of these characteristics will tell you about a person's character, but it will not tell you whether or not they are malicious by nature.

There is no way of knowing whether a person is a controller by simply looking at them.

Consequently, what many people will do is label men or women. Many people believe that abusers and batterers are addicts and alcoholics who hang out in places that facilitate trouble, i.e., bars, clubs, and the homes of friends who are troublemakers. This may be true for some but not for all abusers and batterers.

Many abusers have no red-flag characteristics that would distinguish them from the average citizen in a crowd of people. Most abusers and batterers do not hang out or associate with negative elements of society but are hardworking men and women who appear to live a normal social lifestyle.

If most abusers live such a normal social life, then where are they? Abusers and batterers who are not currently in a relationship are concealing themselves behind a mask filled with jealously, frustration, resentment, anger, and deception. The remainder is hidden from public view.

Many of these abusers and batters are calling themselves parents, husbands, wives, boyfriends, and girlfriends. If we look inside the home of an abuser and batterer, we would find some of the most deceitful, plotting, and resourceful domestic criminals to ever grace the privacy of a home.

Let us take a look at a smooth, soft-spoken man or woman with large framed glasses. People who *know* this person will tell you that he or she has a sense of humor and poses no threat to anyone. In fact, the person is said to be *a darn good old guy or gal.*

This kind of man or woman is not out to hurt anyone and realizes that domestic violence can become physically dangerous as well as expensive in terms of legal costs and could become potentially damaging to his or her professional career.

This person realizes he or she does not have to use physical abuse to gain and maintain absolute power over his or her partner. However, what he or she does understand is how to use threats through the use of various verbal and physical expressions (body language).

This particular person is skillful in dominating his or her partner while avoiding police detection. He or she shrewdly employs a cruel, perverted attitude through a series of threats delivered so the victim actually believes they will be harmed if they do not obey.

For example, the verbal expression "You remember what happened to you the last time you made me angry" followed by a menacing stare is enough to convince most victims that what may follow will have harmful consequences. Where do you find such a scandalous person? You do not find them; they find you.

Although an abuser or batterer may find you and abuse you, and a large number of abusers and batterers are able to challenge the system and walk away without as much as a warning from law enforcement, many are caught and are convicted for their crimes.

The following is a list of ways many abusers justify their abuse toward the victims:

- They must keep outsiders (law enforcement, friends, fellow employees, and extended family members) out of family affairs.
- If they remain in control, the family will get ahead financially.
- Their children's future depends on their ability to manage the family's affairs.
- They have the skills to keep their home a safe place, and being abusive cannot be avoided.
- They want to convince their partner that there are families that are doing a lot worse than they are, and their partner should be happy and satisfied with what they have.

> The amazing aspect of a person who uses coercion and threats is that they will often tell their victims that they love them. They do not recognize that using coercion and threats isn't an act of love but an act of total selfishness.

What Motivates a Person to Become Abusive?

What motivates a person to want to dominate and control others? Is it selfishness, lack of confidence, money, power, or sex? If the abuser is selfish, then everything is about "me, me, me." In many cases, the person cares more for themselves than they do their partner. Whatever the inspiration people use to emotionally and physically harm others, their behavior is certainly morally wrong and is against the law.

Research has shown that people (men in particular) who batter their partners perceive themselves as being more intelligent than their partners and, as a result, believe they must use their assumed *superior intelligence* to rule their supposed less-intelligent partner. Of course, such an idea is absurd. If a person has superior intelligence over their partner, they would not use their intellect in such an inferior manner.

Abusers and batterers use coercion and threats against family members not because of intelligence but as a convincing tool for maintaining dominance. Use of force and threats against others is illegal and oppressive, yet abusers will continue to use violence as long as the victim allows it to happen.

Victims of domestic violence should not be blamed for wanting to make their relationship work or being too frightened to leave the relationship. Victims of domestic violence must realize that many abusers are very skillful con artists.

They will say and do whatever is necessary to make it appear as if the family is safe, even following an episode of violence toward a partner or family member. They will talk extensively about the wonderful plans they have for the family and how *sorry* they feel about becoming abusive.

Apologizing is also an important factor in a con man's performance. Some will apologize by buying gifts, and others will use an emotional display such as crying to keep their victims in line. Others will justify their abusive behavior by giving excuses for their abusive behavior toward a family member.

None of these reasons would be valid to someone who would not accept being abused by their partner. Whatever techniques abusers and batterers use, they believe that it's important to keep their victim believing that everything will work itself out in the end.

When a victim begins to develop healthy self-esteem, they will realize that their abuser or batterer is right when he or she said everything will work out in the end, but not with the same intended ending. The healthy conclusion would be to exit the abusive relationship via separation or divorce.

Solutions for Abusers and Batterers to Stop Their Violent Behavior

What can a person who uses coercion and threats do differently? The answer to that question can be answered by reading any chapter on communication and conflict resolution. If a person who uses coercion and threats is reading this chapter, he or she can begin changing his or her behavior by using the following examples:

- Do not create fear through threats or acts of physical abuse.
- Talk and act in a manner that allows your partner to feel safe and comfortable expressing herself or himself.
- Do not threaten to leave at a critical time in the relationship.
- Do not threaten to commit suicide if your partner decides to leave the abusive relationship.
- Do not force your partner to drop any charges that may be pending against you.

- Do not force your partner to perform illegal acts.
- Ask for what you want without commanding.
- If your partner tells you that the relationship has ended, leave the relationship the way you entered—peacefully.
- Understand the legal consequences of any negative behaviors.

There are lessons to be learned from every experience in life. It will take some people only once to learn the realistic aspects of a successful relationship. For others, it may take longer for them to sort out the reasons why they act the way they did toward someone who loves them.

An excellent question abusers can ask themselves is, "How can any good come from violence against a loved one?" People who use coercion and threats must make a commitment to stop controlling others.

Abusers and batterers are able to turn their lives around by searching deep within their mind to find hope and not despair, joy and not pain, forgiveness and not rage, and love without the presence of control or hate.

Self-Assessment

Following are questions to assist you with realizing whether or not you or your partner is using coercion and threats in your relationship. Apply personal knowledge, as well as information from the chapter, to answer *yes*, *no*, or *NA* (not applicable) to the following questions. It is important that you answer all questions as accurately and honestly as possible.

1. Have you or your partner ever given each other ultimatums? ___
2. Have you or your partner made each other do anything either of you really did not want to do? ___
3. Have you or your partner ever said that either of you would take the children away? ___
4. Has your partner told you that either of you would kill the other if either of you were caught cheating? ___
5. At any time in your relationship, have you ever been afraid of what your partner may do to you if you made a mistake of some kind? ___
6. Have you or your partner ever slammed the doors in your home during or after an argument? ___
7. Have you or your partner ever yelled at family members to make a point? ___
8. Have you or your partner ever done anything that would make either partner feel degraded? ___
9. Has your partner ever grabbed you by your arms and moved you in any way? ___
10. Do you and your partner understand the legal consequence of domestic violence? ___

The previous list of questions is to better assist you with understanding the term using *coercion* and *threats* in your relationship. If you believe that it is necessary for you to learn more about coercion and threats in relationships, use the information in this workbook, and also seek professional assistance for any questions you may have that this workbook does not address.

Chapter Six

Using Intimidation

Chapter's Objectives:

1. To define the term *using intimidation*
2. To discuss the characteristics of intimidation
3. To examine the mind of an extreme intimidator
4. To discuss why people use intimidation to control their partners
5. To encourage those who are being intimidated to find a solution to the problem of being intimidated

Questions for You to Answer as You Read This Chapter:

1. What is intimidation?
2. What are methods used to intimidate?
3. Have you ever been intimidated? If so, how were you intimidated and how did it make you feel?
4. Have you ever used any method to intimidate your partner?
5. If you are being intimidated and fear for your life and the lives of your children, do you know where to find assistance?

Related Chapters of Interest:

- Using Coercions and Threats
- Communication Skills
- Trust and Respect
- The Male and Female Role in Relationships
- Love and Commitment

Chapter Six

Using Intimidation

Methods Used to Frighten and Torment

Intimidation consists of a person using threatening looks, gestures, or any behavior that would cause another person to believe they will be harmed in any way.

Intimidation is any method that abusers and batterers use to bully or torment their partners and other family members. *Intimidation* can be described as any deliberate attempt to control a person by instilling fear to get a person to perform an act that they would not want to do. For example,

- threatening to use physical violence to get a person to obey, i.e., putting one's fist in the face of their partner or children;
- displaying destructive and deadly weapons for the purpose of intimidation, i.e., placing guns out in the open for others to see or pointing to a weapon as a warning for family members;
- threatening one's partner through verbal and nonverbal clues, i.e., yelling, putting one's fist through a wall, or destroying property;
- threatening to use personal wealth or social status to control what a partner does, i.e., threatening to spend all the family's finances;
- threatening to give the family's pet away or physically abusing pets.

> When an abuser harms the family pet, he or she is also emotionally harming family members who truly love the animal. Many family members view their pet(s) as part of the family and would not like their *pet(s)* to be harmed in any way.

Intimidation is a pressure tactic used by abusers and batterers who want to gain or maintain control of their relationship. Intimidation is chosen over compromise, particularly by an extreme intimidator. Extreme intimidators view compromising as a weakness that should be avoided.

People who intimidate their partners will, at times, use physical intimidation and, at other times, will employ *nonphysical intimidation*. By using nonphysical intimidation, an intimidator will often set upon destroying his or her partner's self-esteem through insults and criticism until his or her partner gives uncontrolled access to all aspects of their personal life.

Also, nonphysical intimidation will not leave any visible signs, such as marks, which can be seen by law enforcement officers should they be called.

Intimidators will develop new and even more sophisticated intimidating tactics as they feel the need, often catching their partner by surprise. This increase in intimidation by the abuser will either force the victim to leave the abusive relationship or remain and continue to be the victim of an oppressive partner.

Intimidators

What is an *intimidator*, and would you know an intimidator if you heard or saw one? The answer to that question is no, particularly if they aren't in their mode of intimidation. What is important is being able to recognize intimidators through their behavior. Consequently, we will focus on three kinds of intimidators to give you some idea about people who are intimidators.

We will first discuss people who have a tendency to intimidate but do not have the cruel heart of an extreme intimidator. This sort of person will only intimidate if their partner allows it to happen and will stop any negative behavior when asked to do so.

Our second intimidator is sort of like the first; they will intimidate if they are allowed and will continue to use other tactics to intimidate after their partner has requested them to stop. However, if they truly believe their partner is serious about terminating the relationship, they will quickly alter their behavior for fear of the consequence.

The third intimidator is an extreme intimidator. They are exceptional intimidators. Many are quick-thinking people who realize their strength to intimidate others and are very skillful with the tactics used to intimidate others, i.e., through their physical strength or financial status.

The extreme intimidator will begin a relationship by playing a cat-and-mouse game with his or her potential partner. Like the cat, the extreme intimidator will not let his or her prey get away by becoming too aggressive too soon; for if he or she becomes aggressive too quickly, he or she stands a chance of losing his or her prey and will have to go on the *prowl* again.

Consequently, during the early stages of a relationship, extreme intimidators will use his or her skills to gain the confidence of their potential partner. The person will achieve this by systematically studying their partner's behavior, behavior that will allow him or her to decide how to best approach the person to gain and maintain power and control over their partner.

The extreme intimidator may begin using abusive language to measure the response of his or her potential partner. Abusive language does not have to be directed against the potential partner; it may be directed toward someone else in other situations, such as while driving, in a store, and on the telephone, or explaining a situation that may have happened on his or her job.

As time passes, the intimidator will direct their negative behavior toward his or her partner by using cold stares or grunting sounds, and with submission or acceptance of this behavior, the intimidation will proceed to verbal abuse.

The extreme intimidator is sending a clear message that he or she is a force to be taken seriously. The cold stares or grunting sounds are alerts that negative consequences could happen if their demands are not met.

Extreme intimidators are usually men who do not believe love is a strong enough reason to hold their relationship together. This sort of person is highly confused. They believe that fear and love are one and the same; if she fears him, she will love him.

This kind of person gains enormous satisfaction from hearing their partners weep and plead for life's simplest enjoyments. Extreme controllers believe they must maintain dominance over every aspect of their partners' lives by holding their victims in a furious grip with life-threatening consequences.

If their victim decides to go against the extreme intimidator's wishes—e.g., going out with a friend, purchasing needed personal items, or simply rejecting their intimidator's request for sex—many extreme intimidators will go into a rage and become physically violent.

When a victim of such an abuser decides to strike back, it's not about money or power; it's about their freedom or mental and physical survival. Extreme intimidators will hold on to their mentally and physically dominating power and control at all costs and will defend their beliefs to the *death*. In some cases, they will take the life of their partner or of the children or both and then commit suicide.

Most intimidators would rather use intimidation than compromise, particularly an extreme intimidator. Extreme intimidators view compromising as a weakness and should be avoided.

Why Do People Use Intimidation?

Why do people use intimidation? Certain people intimidate others because they know that they have the power to intimidate. People who use intimidation know of its overwhelming power and the negative mental effect that threats can have on a person. And they also know that people do not like the idea of being threatened with the possibility of having mental or physical injury.

Of course, there are other reasons a person would use intimidation. For example, many people who use intimidation often suffer from some sort of personality problems such as anger or rage, anxiety, unhealthy self-esteem, depression, inferiority or superiority complex, and so on. Intimidators are so busy focusing on family members that they do not believe or want to believe they have mental health issues that need to be addressed by a mental health professional.

Rising Awareness

In the beginning of a relationship, one really doesn't know what the other person is like unless they *pay very close attention to their behavior*.

People are like the weather, changeable in that the sun doesn't shine all the time, and inevitably, there will be rain at some point in time. When it rains, how hard will it rain and how much damage will it cause? The same can be said for people. When a person is irritated and isn't in the mood to be humorous, is it difficult to be near that person? And when they are angry, how much damage do they cause?

Many people do not pay close attention to the behavior of a potential partner when they become angry, which is like standing in the rain during a lightning and thunderstorm. From a distance, one can hear the thunder and watch the lightning slowly approach, but is it wise to stand motionless until a bolt of lightning strikes?

The comparison between someone who cannot control impulsive anger and someone who uses his or her anger to harm others is like thunder and lightning. When abusers and batterers are out of control, they will first flash their anger, roar their disapproval, and then strike without thinking or caring about the consequences.

It's important when developing a new relationship to always look beyond the person who appears to be saying all the right words. This person could be an intimidator; look for warning signs, and *when they begin to* show *thunder and lightning, prepare to quickly come out of the storm.* Learn more about people who use intimidation and their impulsive behaviors. You may think that you have found the man or woman of your dreams and yet all you have found is a storm of catastrophic proportion.

Exercise

Following are levels of intimidation used by partners in relationships. Place a check next to the level of intensity of intimidation that takes place in your relationship.

- My partner never intimidates me. ___
- My partner rarely intimidates me. ___
- My partner intimidates me regularly. ___
- My partner always intimidates me. ___

Rate the following methods of intimidation based upon past behaviors of you or your partner. If your partner has used intimidation, place a *P* for *partner*; if you have used intimidation, place an *M* for you; and if both partners have used intimidation, place a *B* for both of you using intimidation; and place an *N* if neither of you use intimidation.

My partner has intimidated me by

- yelling, ___
- showing physical strength, ___
- stopping financial support, ___
- withholding sex, ___
- using his or her professional skills against me, ___
- going out with other men or women, ___
- threatening to tell others something personal about my past, ___
- threatening to commit suicide, ___
- threatening to kill me and the children, and ___
- threatening to take the children away. ___

> Using intimidation is an act of aggression and has no place in a loving relationship. If you or your partner is acting out any of the above behaviors, you must first talk to him or her about how you feel being treated in this manner.

If you do not get positive results after discussing this matter concerning your partner's behavior, seek professional assistance to help you find a solution to this potentially explosive problem.

Stopping the Use of Intimidation

There are simple solutions to eliminate intimidation from a relationship. Men or women who believe they must use intimidation to make a relationship work must study how successful couples cope with difficult situations. They must discover the difference between the use of intimidation and encouraging and inspiring their partners through love and understanding.

Regrettably, intervention through the legal system is the means through which many men and women come to the understanding the damage intimidation can have on a relationship.

Using intimidation to dominate and control one's partner could have long-term legal consequences. But court involvement may be the turning point an intimidator may need, allowing him or her to mature into becoming a better partner in current or future relationships.

If you know a person who uses intimidation in their relationship, they must immediately begin to learn new skills of communication, trust, and respect. This will enable them to develop a relationship based upon love and equality.

Remember, if a person believes they must use intimidation to get what they want, this is not someone who loves you. Using intimidation is a serious act of violence and should not be taken lightly. To stop being intimidated by one's partner is a decision the victim must make, and we recommend seeking professional assistance.

Self-Assessment

Following are statements to determine your use of intimidation in your relationships. Apply personal knowledge, as well as information from the chapter, to answer the following statements. Answer each statement with *true*, *false*, or *NA* (not applicable). It is important that you answer all statements as completely and honestly as possible.

1. I will never allow my partner to control me by intimidating me. ___
2. We have a gun and other weapons in my home for protection. ___
3. My partner never displays weapons to intimidate me. ___
4. My partner never shows me love and affection, but he or she would never use intimidation to control where I go or what I decide to do. ___
5. When a parent uses intimidation in front of their children, they are teaching them how to intimidate their future partners. ___
6. When I look at my partner in a certain way, he or she knows that I mean business. ___
7. My partner understands that when I intimidate him or her, I do not mean any harm. ___
8. My partner has mentioned committing suicide in the past. ___
9. I understand that abusing the children is another form of intimidation to my partner. ___
10. Intimidation could lead to physical violence. ___

The previous list is to better assess your understanding of using intimidation in your relationship. Review the list; if you believe it is necessary to learn more about using intimidation in relationships, use the information in this workbook, and also seek professional assistance for any questions you may have that this workbook does not address.

Chapter Seven

Minimizing, Denying, and Blaming

Chapter's Objectives:

1. To learn why people act the way they do
2. To define the terms *minimizing*, *denying*, and *blaming*
3. To define and discuss *ego defense mechanisms*
4. To discuss the feeling of anxiety
5. To define and discuss ego defense mechanisms and how it relates to abusive behavior

Questions for You to Answer as You Read This Chapter:

1. What is an *ego*?
2. What is the difference between one's *id*, *ego*, and *superego*?
3. What does it mean to *minimizing*, *denying*, and *blaming*?
4. What does it mean to deny one's negative behavior?
5. What does it mean to blame others for one's negative behavior?

Related Chapters of Interest:

- What Is Domestic Violence?
- Codependency
- Emotional Abuse
- Anger Management
- Communication Skills

CHAPTER SEVEN

Minimizing, Denying and Blaming

It's All About One's Ego

In this chapter, we will provide information concerning the term *ego* and how a person's ego affects his or her opinion and behavior toward others. This information is given for the purpose of learning about the way many people perceive reality and what actually is reality.

We are sure at some point that you have heard people talk about a person's ego and how their ego may have affected their judgment. Well, in many ways, they are right in their assumption concerning a person's ego.

However, there is a great deal more going on inside a person's mind than just their ego. According to the psychoanalyst Sigmund Freud, there is also the id, ego, and the superego. Freud used these terms to describe the division between our conscious and unconscious.

Simply put, first, there is our id. Our id is our subconscious. Hidden inside our subconscious is information that controls the motivation and information that's reserved by our consciousness. Secondly, our ego is concerned with our outside reality and is generally conscious, and third, the superego is our inner moral judge, which is partially conscious and is our conscience.

> What we have done is shifted from the totally unconscious mind, the *id* to the almost conscious mind, *ego,* and subsequently to the moderately conscious mind of the *superego*.

Because the ego is the "middleman" for the id and the superego and our environment, we will only focus on the ego. The responsibility of our ego is to find a balance between our subconscious drives (for pleasure), morality (right and wrong), and our environmental reality (where we live and how we live). It is important to remember that our ego must keep our id and our superego safe and happy, and anything that the ego does cannot have grave consequence.

For example, our ego must guard against stressful situations because the id doesn't like stress. To do this, the ego has what is known as ego defense mechanisms to help it with any situations that may have a conflict with the id.

For example, if the id wants to experience a certain pleasure that conflicts with reality, society's morals, norms, or even a person's morals, rules, or anything that the person knows is wrong, the ego will turn to its ego defense mechanisms. So what are defense mechanisms, and how would they apply with domestic violence?

Ego Defense Mechanisms

Sigmund Freud's theory states that people use ego defense mechanisms to reduce anything that may cause them stress, i.e., minimizing, denying, and blaming the truth on someone or something else.

The process of defending our mental state from *stress* is the responsibility of our personality, which functions on an unconscious level. The ego's defense mechanisms function *instinctively* and *unwillingly* and act in two ways to defend against stressful situations such as

- denying the truth and
- lying to cover up the truth as if lying will not expose their guilt.

Anxiety

Since the id doesn't like anxiety, let us define *anxiety*. What is *anxiety*? *Anxiety* can be described as a combination of emotions that would include fear and irritability concerning a person(s), thing, or situation.

These feelings are often followed by one or more physical sensations such as

- restlessness,
- increased muscle tension,
- trembling hands or body,

- unsettled stomach,
- rapid heartbeat,
- headaches or shortness of breath or both,
- trouble sleeping.

Anxiety is also an emotion that motivates us to act. Its function is to ward off sudden danger and send a signal to the *ego* that unless appropriate measures are taken, the danger may increase.

For example, when a partner has been verbally or physically abused, they will feel anxious or stressed. The victim may walk away from the situation, fight back, or call law enforcement to relieve the stress. The person who caused the stress will also develop tension, particularly if law enforcement has been called.

When law enforcement arrives at the home, the abuser's or batterer's anxiety builds and consciously or unconsciously, and they will say or do whatever is necessary to relieve the anxiety.

The abuser or batterer will either accept responsibility for his or her behavior, deny that anything happened, or justify his or her abusive behavior by blaming his or her partner to relieve his or her anxiety.

Our anxiety can be controlled by rational and direct methods. When our ego cannot control our anxiety by using rational methods, our ego relies on more unrealistic methods, namely, ego defense mechanisms to help cope with the anxiety and to defend against being *wounded*, which is better known as one's wounded ego.

Following is a list of the ego defense mechanisms that abusers and batterers will often use to cope with anxiety:

Minimizing

Minimizing is any attempt to understate or make light of any abusive behavior.

For example:

- I just pushed her, and she fell.
- He or she would not get out of my way, so I had to remove him or her.
- He or she is just too sensitive.

- She bruises very easily.
- If he or she listens, I wouldn't have to yell.
- I had a few drinks, and I wasn't thinking clearly.
- It's only a scratch; it could have been worse.
- Pushing him or her isn't abuse.
- He or she yelled at me first.
- Yelling at children when they misbehave isn't abuse.

Denying

Denying is stating or believing that abuse did not occur when in fact it did occur.

For example,

- I didn't touch him or her.
- I did not hit her; she pushed me.
- She hit herself and made it seem as if it was my fault.
- Calling my partner "stupid" does not bother him or her.
- Telling my partner that he or she cannot spend family income isn't controlling him or her.
- My partner exaggerates; I'll push her, and she will say that I hit her.
- I am abusive, but my children understand, and it doesn't affect them as much as people claim it does.
- I am an alcoholic and drug abuser, but it doesn't affect my family.

Blaming the Victim

Blaming the victim is any attempt to shift the responsibility on someone else.

For example:

- My partner understands how I am when I drink.
- My partner started it; what was I supposed to do?
- My partner talked me into it.
- My partner made me do it.
- He or she didn't shut up when I asked him or her to.
- My partner likes being controlled.
- I told him or her not to say another word, but he or she kept on pushing me.
- So I am abusive at times; my partner must learn to take me seriously.
- My partner knows how to push my buttons.
- Some men or women like being hit and told what to do.

When an abuser realizes that he or she must take responsibility for his or her abusive behavior, it may become personally painful and, in many cases, too painful to accept. Consequently, the abuser will minimize what happened, deny what really happened, or blame his or her partner and other family members for his or her abusive behavior.

Many abusers behave in such a way as to avoid the mental pain that anxiety will cause; this is done in an attempt to protect their ego. It is certainly easier to minimize, deny, and blame their partner and other family members than for them to see themselves as abusers.

However, if an abuser continues to behave negatively toward their partner and other family members, their problems will not go away; they will only become worse. Abusers and batterers must realize that life is filled with stressful situations, and they must learn to accept that fact or remain a very lonely and confused person.

Rationalization

When abusers or batterers rationalize, they create reasons to explain away their wounded ego. They will use any means necessary so the reality of their negative behavior doesn't cause them too much anxiety. For example, a victim of months and years of abuse decides to leave the relationship. The ex-partner will soothe his or her wounded ego by convincing himself or herself that his or her ex-partner wasn't anything but trouble.

They may go on to convince themselves that they are glad to see their ex-partner leave. Or the abuser may say to himself or herself that he or she was planning to leave the relationship before his or her ex-partner had decided to leave, believing in the notion to leave before the ex-partner will make him or her feel better.

Projection

Projecting is often used in the trusting aspect of a relationship. With projection, a person will have negative traits that are unacceptable to their ego. Often, they will project their negative thoughts and behavior on their partner when in fact, he or she is reflecting the unacceptable negative thought and behavior in him or her.

Thus, they may condemn their partner for "unhealthy behaviors" to hide their unhealthy thoughts and behaviors.

For example, a person wants to cheat on his or her partner or may have cheated. As a result of his or her feelings of guilt, he or she begins to *believe* that his or her partner is or is about to cheat on him or her. Consequently, the person will confront his or her partner and make such statements as "I know you are cheating on me, but I cannot prove it yet." In such a case, it is difficult for the person to trust that his or her partner will not cheat when the person can't trust himself or herself not to cheat if given the opportunity.

Displacement

Displacement is another negative, yet well-used aspect of domestic abuse. *Displacement* is aiming one's anger and negative behavior toward one's partner or other family member when the person who really created the negative feelings cannot be harmed or be held accountable for causing the person the stress.

For example, although an angry person would like to express his or her anger or rage toward whom or what made him or her angry, he or she will decide to pick a safer target for his or her anger or rage, a target that is less of a threat. That would be, in most cases, their partner or other family member. If their partner isn't available, they would verbally or physically abuse a friend or even the family pet.

Exercise

The following statements are basically designed for an abuser or batterer and should assist him or her with understanding ego defense mechanisms and when and why he or she may have used them. However, we all use ego defense mechanisms at some point during a given day.

Review this chapter by looking for any ego defense mechanisms you or your partner may have used in the past or are currently using, and then read and answer the statements.

Minimized

My partner or I have minimized negative behaviors in our relationship by

____

____

____

____

____

Denied

I have noticed that my partner or I have denied taking part in any negative behavior in our relationship by

____

____

____

____

____

Blamed the Victim

When my partner or I was proven to be wrong, my partner or I would blame the other person by

____

____

____

____

____

Rationalization

The last few situations my partner or I used rationalization was when he or she

____
____
____
____
____

Projection

The last time my partner or I used a situation to project our feelings on the other person was when he or she said or did

____
____
____
____
____

Displacement

The last time my partner or I displaced personal feelings on the other person was when my partner or I

____
____
____
____
____

> These statements appear to be designed only for an abuser or batterer. However, if you're the victim of domestic violence, do not take on any guilt or shame that doesn't belong to you. Remember, every human being will use these defense mechanisms to protect himself or herself from being harmed.

Resistance to the Truth

As human beings, it is essential for us to understand human nature, our place in the social environment, and why we act the way that we do. The fundamental question of this chapter is "Why do most people have difficulty facing the truth when they have been found to be wrong?"

One possible answer would be that some people have a fear of the truth, particularly if the truth will cause them mental stress or physical harm.

For example, a person is on trial in a court of law and is asked to swear on the Bible. "Will you tell the truth, the whole truth, and nothing but the truth, so help you God?" Do you think this person is going to tell the whole truth if they thought for one minute that they will go to jail if they told the truth?

We believe a very large percent of our population would not tell the truth if it meant the consequence for telling the truth will cause them pain and suffering. We aren't saying that everyone is a liar. What we are saying is that our subconscious mind (id) doesn't like stress and depends upon our ego to do whatever it takes to defend against being stressed.

When we tell the truth and it causes us stress, our egos will find some way to rationalize, minimize, deny, or blame something or someone for causing us to tell the truth. Let us once again take a look at the statement "So help you God."

If a person believes that God would actually punish him or her if he or she told a lie, he or she would probably tell the truth, because a person may believe that to be punished by God would be a lot worse than any punishment that man could bestow upon him.

Of course, we could argue this point for years about God, man, and truth and how many would lie and how many people would tell the truth if they were pushed into a corner. Consequently, the question still remains, if you were pushed onto a corner, would you lie or tell the truth?

Would you tell the truth if there were severe consequences?

Self-Assessment

The following statements should assist you with understanding our ego defense mechanisms and how and why we use them. Apply personal knowledge, as well as information from the chapter, to answer *true*, *false*, or *NA* (not applicable) to the following statements. It is important that you answer all statements as accurately and honestly as possible.

1. I have never lied. ___
2. I understand the term *ego*. ___
3. Our ego defenses are a part of our personality. ___
4. Denial is one example of an ego defense mechanism. ___
5. I will only lie when I feel threatened. ___
6. Many of us lie to keep from being hurt. ___
7. I have a fear of the unknown. ___
8. I understand the term *anxiety*. ___
9. I have never minimized my negative behaviors. ___
10. I take full responsibility for my actions. ___

The previous list of statements is to better assist you with understanding human ego defense mechanisms and how and why we use them. If you believe that it is necessary for you to learn more about ego defense mechanisms, use the information in this workbook, and also seek professional assistance for any questions you may have that this workbook does not address.

Chapter Eight

Economic Abuse

Chapter's Objectives:

1. To define the term *economic abuse*
2. To describe the mind of an economic abuser
3. To discuss the effects of economic abuse in a relationship
4. To discuss any relevant issues concerning the abuse of family finances
5. To discuss methods to protect against economic abuse

Questions for You to Answer as You Read This Chapter:

1. What is *economic abuse*?
2. Do I trust my partner with managing the family's finances?
3. How do I protect myself from being economically abused?
4. Do I need more than two credit cards?
5. How much do I know about managing the family's finances if something were happen to my partner?

Related Chapters of Interest:

- What Is Domestic Violence?
- Economic Partnership
- Trust and Respect
- Parenting Skills
- Setting Reachable Goals

Chapter Eight

Using Economic Abuse

Misuse of Family Income

What is *economic abuse*? *Economic abuse* can be described as the misuse of family income by abusers to gain and maintain power and control over their partner and other family members. Economic abuse isn't much different than any other controlling tactic that an abuser will use against his or her partner.

The noticeable difference between the other controlling tactics and economic abuse is that economic abuse causes emotional abuse and deprives family members of needed goods and services. Although unwise spending of family income can be considered as economic abuse, try not to confuse unwise spending of family funds with misuse of family funds for the purpose of controlling family members.

Following are examples of economic abuse for the purpose of controlling a partner and other family members:

- Forcefully taking their partner's earnings
- Create situations in which their partner must ask or plead for money
- Preventing their partner from getting or maintaining employment
- If they allow their partner to obtain employment, the abuser will control where their partner becomes employed
- Giving their partner an allowance to control what they can and cannot afford to purchase
- Using family income to make unwise investments, purchasing illegal drugs, gambling, and any other situation that depletes family income
- Placing the family in debt by not paying bills
- Depriving their children of needed resources, e.g., clothing, proper diet, and shelter
- Depriving their children of funds for their future, e.g., education

> Any of the above examples of economic abuse can cause emotional abuse. Economic abuse has gotten many families in overwhelming debt and is at the top of the list for the failure of many relationships.

Money Is Power

It's a proven fact that to have money is to have power. There are situations in which having money or not having money can be the difference between life and death or living lavishly or becoming homeless.

For example, let's take a look at health care. There are certain hospitals and other health facilities that would not give health care services to a person who does not have funds or some kind of resource to pay for medical services. The question is, what does this have to do with economic abuse?

Many economic abusers are so caught up in the idea of controlling their partners that they fail to realize the personal and social dangers of not maintaining adequate family income. And if controllers do realize the dangers and do nothing to protect their family, they are more of a danger to their family than their family realizes.

And it's not that the victim of economic abuse doesn't understand the power and the influence of money; it's that some victims do not care about the influence that money has. Many victims do not care how much money their family has.

What many victims of economic abuse care about are feelings, and as long as their family is happy, they are happy. They want to love and be loved; they want to care for their family and have their family care about them.

The sad aspect about being a person whose only concern is to love and care for his or her family and others is that many of them will fall victim to social and domestic parasites, the enemies of America, i.e., the con men and crooks.

Domestic con men and crooks will exhaust a family of not only their money but also their pride. We regard domestic con men and crooks as nothing less than pirates and the common enemy of a family's growth and success.

The depressing aspect of being a victim of domestic piracy is that there isn't a law against it. The justice system appears to have no interest in apprehending and punishing a person who economically abuses his or her family.

Up until today, our justice system appears to have more serious fences to mend, such as spousal abuse, child abuse, elder abuse, and so on. In all these cases, you will find that money, in some way, had something to do with the abuse. Money is no different than any other instrument of power. In the right hands, good things can happen; in the wrong hands, bad things can happen.

Bad things happen when money is placed in the hands of an economic abuser. An economic abuser has a craving to control his or her partner through the use of money, and that craving can be very intense.

It is their desire to control their partner that can often take them from being loving and caring to becoming a yelling, out-of-control maniac. When a controller controls all the household financial decisions, *they have the power* to pave the way for a major family financial disaster.

For example, when many controllers believe they are in the process of losing control of their power over their victim(s), they will plunge their family so far into debt that the chances for their partner to recover from such debt will seem impossible.

There is one other fact that must be made known to a victim of an economic abuser: some economic abusers know how money works. This is not in the sense that they have the skills to properly invest family finance to become financially stable or rich, but that they know how to keep the family on the edge of financial ruin by barely making ends meet.

For example, many abusers will foolishly spend money on drugs, alcohol, or gambling, but not to the point of becoming completely penniless. They know how to control their foolish spending and know the value of a hard-earned dollar. This may sound contradictory, but if you think about it, to economic abusers, money is a means of communication.

And what they are saying in essence is, "If a person allows me to control him or her through the use of money, I will." Their ultimate goal is to always know how to obtain enough money to keep their victims in financial bondage.

However, controllers realize they must be able to obtain enough money to continue to finance their bad habits. And if their relationship fails, they can continue to live comfortably and have a sort of income that would prepare them for their next victim.

Victims of an economic abuser must realize before it's too late that an abuser is a misguided con artist whose mind is filled with illusions and tricks. Everything a controller says and does has an ulterior motive attached. Many economic abusers masquerade themselves as this all-caring boyfriend, husband, father, girlfriend, wife or mother.

At the same time, they are selfishly thinking about themselves and not the financial future of their family. By the time the victim discovers his or her partner's true identity and his or her motives, the victim will have nothing left but his or her clothes, automobile, household furniture, and bad credit rating; and they are deep in debt.

Exercise

Before reading any further, answer the following questions with *yes* or *no* to determine whether or not there is economic abuse in your relationship.

1. Does your partner have control of the family's finances? ___
2. Do you have control of the family finances? ___
3. Does your partner forcefully take your earnings? ___
4. Does your partner or children have to plead for money? ___
5. Are you forced to stay home and not become employed? ___
6. Does your partner control where you can become employed? ___
7. Do you or your partner use family income to make unwise investments? ___
8. Does your partner make all the financial decisions without consulting you? ___
9. Do you or your partner purchase illegal drugs or gamble? ___
10. Do you and your partner seem to always argue over money issues? ___
11. My partner and I discuss all financial matter. ___
12. If your partner has control of the family finances, is he or she open-minded and honest in how he or she spends the family's income? ___
13. Do you and your partner have an allowance to manage family income? ___
14. Do you and your partner barely make ends meet? ___
15. Does your family have a family budget? ___
16. Does your family have the proper health and automobile insurance? ___
17. Do you and your partner buy affordable gifts for each other? ___
18. Do you and your partner know when an agency is trying to "cheat" your family out of the family's income? ___
19. Are you pleased with your current financial situation? ___
20. Are you and your partner financially preparing for the future? ___

If you answered *yes* to five or more of the first ten questions, there is a possibility that there is economic abuse in your relationship. If you answered *yes* to five or more of the last ten questions, you may be in debt and have other financial problems, but there is no sign of economic abuse. Remember, it doesn't necessarily mean that a person is economically abusive because they manage the family's finances.

Financial Survival

In the beginning of a relationship, both partners *assume* that each person will be rational with the idea of how their family will survive the world of family finance. They are hopeful that each person will work hard and achieve the basic common goals that they have set for their family's financial survival.

Common financial goals include purchasing a home or a nice car and being able to buy personal items they can enjoy and still have enough money to send their children to college. Of course, many of us realize that we are taking a chance when we assume what another person will or will not do.

Nevertheless, we are hopeful that our partner will live up to their part of the agreement that the family will be able to achieve their financial goals. But what choice do we have? We cannot read a person's mind or force someone to hold up his or her end of a deal. So once again, we rely on blind faith because we know very little about a person's true past, and we certainly do not know what they will do in the future.

There are people who are fortunate enough to meet someone who will take family finances seriously, and there are those of us who are not as fortunate. Those of us who are not so fortunate will meet and fall in love with someone whose personality will, later on in the relationship, bear resemblance to the personality of Dr. Jekyll and Mr. Hyde. For a while, the person who is managing the family income will ensure that all family members' financial needs are met.

After a period of time, and without telling their partner, the person managing the family income will begin spending money he or she does not have, i.e., overcharging credit cards, gambling, or loaning money to extended family and friends.

Another problem arises when one partner notices that the other partner is spending money, and he or she decides to spend money as well. They believe that if their partner can spend money, why can't they spend money on some of the things they like to buy? Consequently, both partners will go on wild spending sprees and plunge their family deeper into debt.

Following are other reasons couples will suddenly have the urge to spend family funds:

- Hasn't learned to trust each other
- Become depressed and believe that if they bought themselves a few items, they will feel better
- Will loan money to an extended family member or friend who doesn't repay the loan
- Cannot resist going for quick-money investments
- Has not learned to recognize a rip-off in a store offering a sale
- Believes they must buy their family members expensive gifts for their birthdays and Christmas
- Does not have the willpower that it takes to save
- Does not have short- and long-term goals
- Has short- and long-term goals but are not excited enough to want to achieve their goals on time

> There are many reasons couples find to spend family income. Try to think of other reasons couples are having financial problems.

Breaking the Cycle of Economic Abuse

As we mentioned before, trying to convince an extremely controlling partner to change their behavior without professional assistance is a waste of time and energy. The reason is that an extreme controller is driven by a negative belief system, a negative belief system that's fueled by selfishness that is so powerful that he or she cannot seem to resist the temptation to control his or her partner.

The extreme controller's urge to control the family income is so strong that he or she believes if he or she were to relinquish their power and control, he or she would not be able to function as a strong member of the family. Many partners believe that if they plead to the extreme controller's sense of fairness, he or she will listen to reason.

Well, pleading with an extreme controller to share in the financial decision-making process hasn't helped the family in past financial discussions, and it's not going to happen now. An extreme controller cannot see any reward in relinquishing control or sharing financial responsibility.

Therefore, many victims of economic abuse would believe a quick solution to the problem would be for them to simply leave the relationship. Although that may be the simplest solution to the problem, it's not a realistic solution. Any victim of economic abuse who is not employed or does not have adequate income to support their children will find it extremely difficult to live a normal financial life. At least that's what many victims believe.

Becoming a single parent and supporting two or more small children will be difficult but not impossible. It's always in a victim's best interest to learn as much as possible about the available *resources in their community,* as well as his or her *legal rights,* concerning his or her children and themselves.

There are agencies in the community that will assist single parents with expenses and explain in detail their rights as a single parent. For victims who are in debt, there are laws to assist the victim against rude debt collectors. Having debt problems is a concern, but not an immediate concern for someone who is trying to start over.

Many debtors will allow a person to get back on their feet by allowing them to pay the minimum amount due. However, always remember to read the small print concerning paying the minimum amount due.

Depending on the amount of your debt, paying the minimum amount due could keep you paying some bill(s) for years. Many of these agencies could not care less about your domestic problems; they want you to "show them the money." Also remember that a single parent's immediate responsibility is making sure the children are properly housed, fed, safeguarded, and protected.

If you are living with a controller who will listen to reason, you're in luck. This sort of controller has been controlling the finances because you have allowed him or her to do so. The fact of the matter is that there are people who allow their partner to control the family's income for different reasons. For example, they may believe their partner can better balance the family budget, or they would rather have someone else worry about bill collectors.

In any case, if you believe that you would like to become more involved in how the family income is spent or you would like to manage the family's income, you must let your partner know that you would like to take a more active role in the family's finances. Of course, your partner will want to know why you have a sudden interest in the family's income, but that's to be expected.

Simply tell him or her why you are interested. There shouldn't be any arguing or fighting because this sort of controller is not a fighter; he or she has been in charge of making sure the bills have been paid and nothing more.

Millionaire Status

What are the odds that you and your partner will become millionaires in your lifetime? We would say the odds are enormous that you or anyone else reading this book will become a millionaire in their lifetime. We're not saying that it's impossible; we are saying that it's improbable.

Once we come to the conclusion that we will not become millionaires, what's next? Living on a lower, middle, or upper income economic status? Yes, that's exactly what we are saying. For those of us who will not make it to millionaire status, all we would like to do is at least live a comfortable lifestyle.

In order for us to live comfortably, we must become more money conscious, learn how to control our spending, and learn to save. One of our goals should be to secure future employment, because that's where the money comes from and not the dream of hitting the lottery or winning a million dollars in a casino.

Anyone who calls me on the telephone or walks up to me on the street and suggests that they can show me how I can make a million dollars is a fraud, particularly if they aren't rich themselves. I am sure you have heard the saying, "There is a sucker born every day." That's a con man's motto. Do not fall victim to that motto. Nothing is free; there is a price we pay for everything.

There is only one way for many of us to earn money; we must find gainful employment. Gainful employment for many of us would be an annual income of $30,000-$40,000 a year. For a family of four, that may not seem like a good-paying job, but if both partners are working, it adds another $25,000.

Now you will have an annual income of $55,000-$65,000, and that's not bad at all. If you were to think about it for a moment, although we may not get a lump sum of a million dollars, a family who earns (together) more than $55,000-$65,000 a year for thirty years will have earned nearly a million and a half dollars.

Now that we have this information and have decided to stop wasting family income, what's our next step? We will begin by having you take a look at various consumer strategies that will reduce spending, but will not affect your standard of living. We will do this by setting financial goals.

Exercise

Following is an exercise to assist with setting and reaching financial goals.

Name three or more short-term financial goals you and your partner would like to achieve. (A short-term goal is a goal that can be achieved within several months to a year. For example, finding a good-paying job, beginning a savings account, and saving for birthday gifts and gifts for other important days of the year.)

1. ______________________________
2. ______________________________
3. ______________________________
4. ______________________________
5. ______________________________

Name three or more long-term goals you and your partner would like to achieve. (A long-term goal, in this case, is a goal that would take several years or more to achieve. For example, buying a home, purchasing a new car, and saving for your children's college.)

1. ______________________________
2. ______________________________
3. ______________________________
4. ______________________________
5. ______________________________

The Budget

Now your family needs a budget. A budget will allow you to determine how much money you have to put toward your short- or long-term goals. Listed below are the basic steps that should be taken to organize a family budget:

- Your family's monthly total family income ____________
- The family's monthly necessities and the cost of each ____________
- Rent or house payment ____________
- Food ____________
- Clothing ____________
- Utilities (gas, electric, telephone) ____________
- Car payments (gas, insurance, and repairs) ____________
- Insurance (health and life) ____________

- Savings ____________
- Miscellaneous ____________

Now total up all your expenses and fill in the following:

- My family's total monthly income is ____________
- Subtract expenses ____________
- What's left after subtracting expenses ____________

Now you know how much money you can set aside each month for saving toward your goals. Now you and your partner can make a plan. The key to reaching any goal is consistency. Always stick to the plan; if an emergency arises, take care of the emergency and return to your plan.

Self-Assessment

Following are questions to assist you with discovering whether or not economic abuse exists in your relationship. Apply personal knowledge, as well as information from the chapter, to answer *yes*, *no*, or *NA* (not applicable) to the following questions. It is important that you answer all questions as accurately and honestly as possible.

1. Do you understand the term *economic abuse*? ___
2. Do you believe you or your partner is an economic abuser? ___
3. Do you believe that if you make the money, you make the rules? ___
4. Have you ever gambled away the family's income? ___
5. Do you pay your bills on time? ___
6. Are you currently employed? ___
7. Do you argue with your partner over money matters? ___
8. Is there enough money coming in to raise healthy children? ___
9. Do you invest in anything that will increase your financial worth? ___
10. Have you begun to save for your children's college education? ___

The previous list of questions is to better assess your understanding of economic abuse in relationships. If you believe that it is necessary for you to learn more about economic abuse in relationships, use the information in this workbook, and also seek professional assistance for any questions you may have that this workbook does not address.

Chapter Nine

Economic Partnership

Chapter's Objectives:

1. To explain the term *economic partnership*
2. To address the issues concerning family finances
3. To discuss today's economic environment
4. To discuss the importance of having and maintaining an excellent credit rating
5. To explore the idea of investing family income

Questions for You to Answer as You Read This Chapter:

1. What does *economic partnership* mean to you?
2. What are some of your future financial goals?
3. Are you currently in a relationship where all financial decisions are made by both partners?
4. Do you believe in saving for the future?
5. What are several good investments for the average-income family that are sure ways of receiving a return and could assist you with keeping your family financially secure?

Related Chapters of Interest:

- Economic Abuse
- Communication Skills
- Equality in Relationships
- Conflict Resolution
- Trust and Respect

CHAPTER NINE

Economic Partnership

Family Finances

What is economic partnership? Economic partnership is the act or relationship of a couple working together to make the best family financial decisions possible. Any decision that has the potential of determining whether there is a loss or gain of family finances, the opinions of both partners is advised.

For example, when a partner decides to have children, change professions, or buy a new car or home, both partners should have their opinion heard before the actual transaction or transition has been finalized.

Economic partnership does not necessarily mean that either person isn't capable of making their own decisions. What it simply means is that a couple who make decisions together will frequently make the best decision. Economic partnership is extremely important when there are children in the home. When there are children involved, the way a family spends their money will change dramatically.

Before a couple's first baby arrives, couples usually spend money as they see fit. However, once their new baby arrives, the way a couple spends their money should change dramatically. Couples with a large annual income rarely will have a problem spending money on the finer things in life when their first baby arrives.

On the other hand, if you are like millions of couples whose income barely allows them to make ends meet, you and your partner will have to focus more on the needs of your baby than on personal spending. Young adults who are considering having a family must realize that having money for the basic needs of the family or not can affect every aspect of their relationship.

Your children are no different than you were when you were a child. You depended on your parents to provide you with your needs, and now your child is depending on you. Up to a certain age, children will eat anything sweet and call it breakfast, lunch, or dinner and wear any clothing and call it appropriate.

For example, take breakfast cereal. If a child likes a certain breakfast cereal, the child will eat their favorite cereal for breakfast, lunch, and dinner and wouldn't complain. The same can be said for clothing. If they like a certain dress, a pair of pants, pair of shoes, or shirt, they will wear it every day until they cannot wear it any longer.

Children will accept any excuse their parents give them when it comes to food and clothing because what else can a child do. They cannot and will not take their parents to the side and say to them, "Now, Mom and Pop, I need better food, clothes, and an assortment of toys to play with. Now stop making excuses."

Small children will not talk to their parents in such a manner; they accept life the way it is handed to them. The message concerning economic partnership is that not many relationships can succeed in today's *money-oriented society* when there is no financial cooperation between partners. And you can take that fact to the bank.

Money Talks

If there is anything to the motto "money talks," you have better listen and listen well. The first profound statement that money will make to a couple with their first child will be, "If you want to know how powerful I am, need me and not have me." If money really could talk, it will suggest that a parent's first priority is to *always* keep money available.

Parents should make sure that they have enough money available that will provide their family with the proper food, clothing, shelter, transportation, and for any emergency that may arise. Money will also suggest that if parents are spending family income on grown-up toys, social functions, gambling, or drugs, they must change their spending habits.

Parents must reconsider how they spend their income or the consequences could be so financially devastating that it could take the couple years to recover.

Some people would add that having money is a good thing, and others would say, "Money isn't everything."

What they are trying to say is if a family is happy with what they have, isn't being happy what having a family is all about? We agree with both issues concerning money. Having money doesn't necessarily bring happiness to a family, but not having money when it's needed will often ensure moments of frustration, sadness, anger, and many sleepless nights.

What does money have to say about the cost of having children? Of course, the statistics concerning raising children will vary over the coming years. According to the U.S. Department of Agriculture, a middle-income family can expect to spend more than $160,000 to raise a child from birth to age eighteen.

For higher-income families, the total is closer to $234,000. These figures are greater for middle- and higher-income families because they can afford to spend that amount of money on their children. But what about the lower-income families (the poor)? What can they expect to spend on raising a child from birth to age eighteen?

A family who earns less than $30,000 a year will spend less than $72,000 in eighteen years to raise a child. In today's society, what can a family of five expect to do with $30,000 a year?

Despite what society believes about many American families, it's not easy to live in the better neighborhoods, buy the best foods, clothing, transportation, heath care, or the best education with an income of $30,000. So what should a couple do under such circumstances?

First, they can educate themselves about the current and future job market by finding a *realistic trade* that truly interests them. Secondly, they can obtain the training necessary to get a job that will make available the kind of income needed to provide their children with the best or, if not the best, as close to the best as their money will allow. After all, don't our children deserve the best that we can offer?

Third, keep your job as long as you can, that is, at least twenty years. There are great rewards in keeping a job and *retiring from that job* with excellent benefits.

Exercise

How important is money to you? Are you earning enough money to support your family the way you would like? Are you willing to lose everything because of money problems? Answer the statements below to find out. Place a check mark next to *True* if you agree with the statement. Place a check mark next to *False* if you disagree. When you have answered all the statements, you'll have an idea whether you are heading for financial success or for financial ruin.

1. I have no problem saving for my family's future. ___
   True False
2. Having an excellent credit rating means a lot to me. ___
   True False
3. I dislike not being able to buy the things I want, but it's worth it in the end. ___
   True False
4. One of my goals is to find a job in which I can earn a good salary and someday retire. ___
   True False
5. My marriage is going bad, so I am going to spend every penny so my partner doesn't get to take it. ___
   True False
6. My partner and I work, and we make all family decisions together. ___
   True False
7. My partner and I are not interested in get-rich schemes. ___
   True False
8. My partner and I save money so that our children can go to college. ___
   True False
9. My partner and I look for items we can buy on sale. ___
   True False
10. My partner and I believe in paying as we go. ___
    True False
11. I have no problem owing others money. ___
    True False
12. I work hard for my money; therefore, I will spend my money as I see fit. ___
    True False
13. I have no problem taking out a second mortgage to go on vacation or to buy a new car. ___
    True False
14. I overuse my credit cards, so what. ___
    True False

15. My partner and I have more than seven credit cards between us, and we use them all. ___
    True False
16. One day, I will hit the lottery or a jackpot in a casino; it's a good investment. ___
    True False
17. Children do not need to go to college to make it. ___
    True False
18. I am not interested in investing my money. ___
    True False
19. I don't like it when people try to tell me what to do with my money. ___
    True False
20. Tomorrows aren't promised to anyone; "spend it while I have it" is my motto. ___
    True False

The first ten statements should assist you with determining if you are heading for financial success, and the last ten statements should assist you with determining if you are headed for financial regret.

Today's Economic Environment

The story of a family having financial problems is a familiar one in today's society, especially in homes where money is in short supply. Financial problems can develop when one or both partners believe they must wear the latest fashions, eat at the finest restaurants, buy the latest electronic devices at unbelievable prices (with a warranty) like cell phones, and overuse credit cards. Anyone who spends money in such a manner is only asking for trouble, and the trouble goes by the names of Mr. or Mrs. Deep in Debt.

The important thing to remember about Mr. or Mrs. Deep in Debt is that you can run, but you cannot hide. (To run means to relocate, change your name and so on.) You cannot run or hide because the people that you owe money to have your name, date of birth, place of birth, social security number, and even you mother's maiden name.

So where are you going to hide? No matter where you live, those to whom you owe money will find you. What we are trying to say is do not play with money as if it grows on a tree in your backyard.

Remember, your future, the future of your relationship, and the future of your children is at stake. Nevertheless, if you decide to play this high-stake game by overspending, you will soon realize that you are in over your head. You will find yourself so far in debt that it would take a decade or more before you can break even after paying your bills. This is one game that doesn't end until you have paid back every penny you owe.

Effectively managing family income does not have to be a mystery, nor does it have to take years of training on how to save and spend family income wisely. After all, many couples with low incomes have bought new homes, automobiles, and other wonderful things because they have taken the time to research and develop ways to invest and save their earnings even if it means working two jobs until they reach a certain financial goal.

Couples who manage their money wisely use a mixture of personal and interpersonal skills. When you understand these skills, it will be possible to assess your financial strengths and weaknesses and develop a plan for improving your money-management techniques.

One excellent rule to remember is to keep your debt level under control and keep away from agencies with bad reputations who promise to save you money. They aren't in the business of saving people money; they are in the business of earning themselves money. We must mention that there are honest agencies with good reputations that will help you get out of debt, but what will it cost you in the long term?

We have mentioned how credit cards can cause financial problems if people aren't careful how they use them. Nevertheless, credit cards do have their advantages when the balance is paid in full each month. If a couple must have a credit card, it has been recommended that two credit cards are all a couple will need. Also, stay away from cash advances.

With two credit cards, you can use one credit card for buying day-to-day items that you can pay the balance each month, and another credit card can be used for buying more expensive items. As far as the larger items are concerned, try to save and pay with cash or check, and try not to get into the habit of using your credit card.

The interest on a credit card will break you faster than you can imagine. And just think, between you and your partner, there must be seven credit cards. Now take a moment and think about the interest rates on the use of four of those cards. By the time you finish paying the interest on those cards, you'll be lucky if you have enough money to buy a pack of chewing gum.

In today's economic environment, you do not have to reinvent the rules of family finances. All you have to do is learn the basic rules and follow them.

Fraud, Scams, and Cons

Because con artists are everywhere, it would be in your family's best interest to learn who these people are and what rock they will crawl out from under. We cannot give you a detailed description of all the different kinds of scams that are out there to take your hard-earned money. The best thing for you to do is to read the *Great Book of Cons* or read *The Complete Idiot's Guide to Frauds, Scams, and Cons*, or both. Both books will give all the information you will need to protect you and your family from falling victim to these *merciless money grabbers*.

Also remember that many of these con artists work inside the law, so it's up to you to know when to walk away or hang up the telephone. Yes, your telephone. They have passed laws now that allow these con artists to *invade* our homes. Telephones will ring in many homes more than twenty to thirty times a week, and there will be someone on the other end of the line telling the couple that they have the answer to all their money problems. Be very careful of people who tell you that they have the answer to all your problems.

We must also mention the fact that couples must be careful with spending their money on high-tech products. The world of technology has taken over. A couple will spend thousands of dollars for a big-screen television or car with all the new technological advances, only to find out that they have brought a high-tech piece of junk.

Along with the high price for the product, they must spend large sums of money to repair it. We recommend that everyone do their research on ever-expensive high tech products before buying a product you know nothing about.

For example, your family has saved for several years to purchase a big-screen television for $2,000-$3,000. The repairs on a big-screen television can range from $400 to $1,000 or more. This is a poor family's nightmare. Research is the key to not being swindled because once you have bought the product, it belongs to you, and so do the repair bills.

Shared Decision Makings

Sharing in the decision-making process will allow a couple to organize their information and consequently, obtain needed resources from their money. For example, buying nutritional food for the family, an affordable home, a new car (or making repairs on the old car), and a family health and life insurance are all decisions for which both partners should have an opinion.

These sorts of decisions will allow a couple to feel comfortable about the future of their family and reinforce the idea of communication and trust in their relationship. It is important to remember that both partners should be completely satisfied with the final decision to purchase or not to purchase a certain item.

As a family, there will be times when buying what is necessary will be more important than spending money on personal pleasures such as buying nice clothes or going out of the town.

There are people who refuse to see family income in such a realistic way. These kinds of people are so carefree with their spending habits, and before they realize it, they have plunged the family deeply into debt.

These kinds of people go looking for con artists to save them. In some cases, they will avoid paying their bills by simply not paying their debts or file for bankruptcy. They either do not realize the negative consequences of such an irresponsible financial decision or simply do not care about the consequences.

Couples must learn the basic skills of spending and saving. Once couples have learned how to manage their family's financial responsibilities, they will begin to develop a good credit rating. A good credit rating is a must for those who would like to purchase a new home or a new car. Words for the future of economics will be "How is your credit?"

Following are a few basic rules to developing an excellent credit rating:

- Never spend more than you have.
- Learn the difference between wise spending and wasteful spending.
- Remember credit cards are the same as money, and using them comes with a heavy price tag (interest).
- Make all payments on time. (This will also save money on late fees.)
- Never hold back from paying a bill because of a possible error. Pay the bill and then discuss the problem.

> In the not-so-far future, your credit rating will be the difference between getting what your family needs and doing without.

Investments

Everyone would like to become debt free and reach millionaire status, but how realistic is it to become a millionaire? Most of us aren't gifted athletes or will find the lucky numbers to win the million-dollar lottery. So how can a couple become financially independent and not have to worry about the monthly bills that exhaust their bank account?

If your goal is to become financially independent, then you must once again do your research to find the answer to that question. This workbook or this particular chapter isn't about providing you with information about becoming a millionaire.

This chapter is about economic partnership and how a couple should make decisions together so they can get some of the things they desire or do more than *just survive* on the modest income they earn.

However, if a couple has control of their finances, i.e., free from debt, there are ways they can earn money beyond their weekly paychecks. They can invest some of their earnings. There are risks in investments, so be careful.

A couple must be very careful how they invest their money. Many investments are no different than going to Las Vegas or Atlantic City and sitting down at a poker table or slot machine and believing that you will walk away with thousands of dollars.

A very large percent of us will only walk away with our hands in an empty pocket and a sad look on our face. Banks, investment agencies, and casinos didn't build those enormously beautiful buildings by losing money or giving away money.

Remember one fact about large investments: the larger the investment, the larger the risk. If you and your partner decide to invest, choose an investment that has less risk of you losing all your money.

The following is a list of investments for the average-income family that are sure ways of receiving a return and could assist you with keeping your family financially secure:

- Real estate
- Bank certificates of deposit
- U.S. government bonds and notes

There are greater risks when you invest in:

- U.S. corporate bonds
- Foreign corporate bonds
- Blue-chip common stocks
- Common stocks
- Coins and stamps

People work hard for their money but do a poor job of investing it. Sure, there are people who will make large sums of money from blue-chip common stocks, foreign corporate bonds, and common stocks. But there are those who lose everything with these investments. Anytime you think about these investments, think about Las Vegas, Atlantic City, and other places that have gambling and the odds of you walking away a winner.

There are many ways to invest money, but only one *sure method* of getting a return on your investment. That's to invest in your children's future through education. Do everything you can to ensure your children get the proper education and, consequently, a great profession.

No matter which of the investments you choose, always remember to keep your money safe so it will be there when the family needs it. Purchase only investments you and your partner understand.

For example, you and your partner understand how certificates of deposit and real estate work, but do not understand very much about futures trading, currency hedges, buying on margin, or taking a short position on an Internet stock. If this is the case, do not tamper with what you do not understand and invest only in what is *perfectly clear* to you and your partner.

Remember to never take a person's word when it comes to money; *get it in writing*. When you have a contract with any company, *always read the small print* because many agencies will use small print to hide important facts.

Self-Assessment

The following statements should assist you with determining whether or not you are having an economic partnership in your relationship. Apply personal knowledge, as well as information from the chapter, to answer *true*, *false*, or *NA* (not applicable) to the following statements. It is important that you answer all statements as accurately and honestly as possible:

1. I understand the term *economic partnership*. ___
2. My partner and I never fight over money matters. ___
3. My partner and I use our credit cards sparingly; and that allows us to keep cash in the bank. ___
4. We pay our bills on time to avoid a lot of late fees. ___
5. My partner and I have planned for our children's future. ___
6. I will look into how to better invest my money at some future time. ___
7. I am happy with the way things are going financially in my family. ___
8. My partner and I have a household budget. ___
9. I need help with investing our/my money. ___
10. My partner pays the bills with the money we earn, and he or she is doing a great job. ___

The previous list of statements is to better assess whether or not you have an economic partnership in your relationship. If you believe that it is necessary for you to learn more about economic partnership, use the information in this workbook, and also seek professional assistance for any questions you may have that this workbook does not address.

Chapter Ten

The Effects Domestic Violence Has on Children

Chapter's Objectives:

1. To give examples of acts of violence
2. To discuss the idea of domestic terrorism
3. To discuss the most common injuries to children
4. To discuss strategies to prevent and eliminate injuries to children
5. To discuss how important it is to stop domestic abuse

Questions for You to Answer as You Read This Chapter:

1. How does watching and reading about violence affect children?
2. After a domestic battery, who are the victims?
3. In a violent home, what feelings will most children experience?
4. When children witness violence in the home, what are some of the negative consequences?
5. What are the most common injuries that happen to children during a domestic fight?

Related Chapters of Interest:

- Parenting Skills
- Communication Skills
- Conflict Resolution
- Self-esteem
- Anger Management

Chapter Ten

The Effect Domestic Violence Has on Children

Acts of Violence

Before discussing the negative physical and psychological effects domestic violence has on children, we would like to review the term *violence.*

People know when they have been physically or psychologically abused, but they do not know or understand the legal definitions of the term *violence.* After reading this chapter, the reader should be able to know what act or acts of violence have been committed against them.

So what is the legal definition of *violence*? *Violence* is any act of aggression and abuse that causes or intends to cause injury or harm to oneself or others and (by some definitions) animals or property. In some cases, violence may be a criminal act.

For example, there are two forms of violence, random and systematic or coordinated violence. Random violence is unpremeditated and can happen on a small or large scale. When violence is premeditated, it can be considered as being systematic or coordinated, which can also happen on a small or large scale.

Random violence can be perceived as violence that has not been arranged. This definition can be sort of confusing, but when you think about it for a moment, it's really not that difficult to understand.

For example, if a person is living with an abuser or batterer, the abuser or batterer may be comforting one minute and, without warning, will become indiscriminately violent the next. In other words, if the random abuser or batterer uses violence to make a point, he or she will do so without thought or hesitation.

The systematic or coordinated abuser or batterer has a method to his or her madness. This particular perpetrator has a well-thought-out plan as to what he or she will do, and how he or she will perform his or her act of violence.

In essence, the systematic or coordinated abuser or batterer has a predictable irrationality about his or her violent behavior. The idea behind this sort of person's irrational behavior is not surprising because of his or her violent personality. This sort of behavior can be seen in the behavior of the extreme controller or intimidator.

Following are definitions of various kinds of violence perpetrated against a child or other family members:

- abuse: Emotionally or physically used wrongly or improperly mistreated
- aggravated assault: Fatal assault with the use of a weapon
- assault: An unlawful physical attack upon another; an attempt or offer to do violence to another
- assault and battery: An assault with an actual touching or violence upon another
- battery: An unlawful attack upon another person by beating, wounding, or touching in an offensive manner
- cruelty to animals: A cruel act upon an animal
- murder: Killing of another human being under vulnerable conditions
- destruction of property: The damage to one's property, e.g., breaking of things, burning, or harming in a devastating manner
- rape: The unlawful compelling of someone through physical force or duress to have intercourse

These acts of violence are perpetrated by abusers and batterers on a daily basis. No child should have to grow up under any of the above-mentioned conditions. The life for all children should be fascinating and innocent, not filled with fear and uncertainty.

Domestic Terrorism

Terrorism is a term used to describe certain acts of violence or threats of violence. Many Americans believe the greatest danger facing our country today comes from religiously inspired terrorist groups that are developing weapons of mass destruction for use against our civilian population. We disagree. We believe America's greatest danger lies within our boundaries, i.e., domestic terrorism.

The terrorists we are referring to are abusive parents who often employ terrorist tactics to control and mangle the minds and bodies of members of their families. Many of the physical and emotional injuries children suffer daily are nothing less than domestic terrorism.

The weapons that are used against our country's children are the spoken words of anger and hate, fists, knives, and guns. The mental and physical injuries recorded by counselors, psychologists, public schools, law enforcement, and hospital emergency rooms are beyond belief.

Although many homes are a safe place for children, numerous others aren't. In fact, the notion that all households are a safe place for children is a dangerous illusion and consequently a massive cover-up of what actually goes on behind closed doors.

The reality of domestic terrorism is that some parents actually believe they can get away with being abusive, particularly when, for one reason or another, they consistently get away with crimes perpetrated against family members. Statistics demonstrate shocking numbers of children who are victims of serious physical injuries while living in a home filled with emotional and physical abuse.

Domestic terrorism will continue as long as perpetrators of domestic violence continue to believe that violence works and as long as many Americans ignore the call for help as America has been doing for centuries.

Children are younger and have less experience and knowledge than adults. However, they are still our children as well as our companions. Therefore, we must give our children every possible opportunity to experience a healthy family life. It is our responsibility to make sure our homes are safe and understand that safety should never yield to violence. Children should be given the benefit of our wisdom and not the negativity of a parent's anger.

The Most Common Injuries to Children

For many children, the most common types of injuries are

- fractures,
- cuts,

- displacement of bone,
- internal injuries,
- concussions,
- punctures,
- dental injury,
- internal bleeding,
- nerve damage.

> The psychological effects are at times apparent but in many other children, not apparent until later in the child's life (delayed response to trauma). The annual unreported cases of psychological and physical injuries to children suffered during episodes of family violence can run into the millions.

Children are exposed to acts of violence through movies, books, and television, which are designed to frighten and to entertain, but not terrorize. The violence children watch on television or read in books is quite different than the violence children witness at home.

Children can realize one very important fact between the two. Children realize that watching a movie about violence will not send them to the hospital with physical injuries. And when they become weary of watching or reading about violence, they can easily turn the television off or close the book and the violence will end.

What children cannot turn off or close is the violence that was committed by an abusive parent right before their eyes. Unlike the television set, a violent parent(s) cannot be turned off by remote control.

Exercise

Following are statements that can assist you with determining if your children have been affected by violence in your home. Apply personal knowledge you have gathered through watching and listening to your children, as well as information from the chapter, to answer the following statements.

Answer with *true*, *false*, or *NA* (not applicable) to any statements that may apply to you and your family.

1. My children seem depressed most of the time. ___
2. My children are too young to understand violence. ___
3. My children blame me for everything that goes wrong. ___
4. My children are very controlling. ___
5. My children are easily hurt by the things my partner and I say to them. ___
6. My children feel uncomfortable when my partner is in the home. ___
7. My children told me that they hate their mother or father. ___
8. My children are experimenting with drugs. ___
9. My children have become rebellious. ___
10. My children disrespect their mother or father. ___
11. My children don't hug or kiss my partner or me without either of us first kissing them. ___
12. My children don't laugh and have fun like they used to. ___
13. One of my children was accidentally injured during a family argument. ___
14. At least one of my children is having nightmares. ___
15. My children appear to be angry all the time. ___

Use the above scale to determine whether or not violence in your home has affected your children. If you believe that one or more of your children has been affected by violence in the home, seek professional assistance.

Most parents are blind to the effect their abusive behavior has on their children. They cannot seem to understand the mental suffering they bring into the lives of their children because of their negative behavior. Many abusers and batterers believe that their role as parents gives them the legitimate right to use verbal or physical abuse to keep a child obedient. From a child's point of view, this kind of attitude casts a dark shadow over the abusive parent.

Many children see their abusive parent as their worst enemy, worse than the schoolyard bully. Children see them as abusive persons, not as parents, but someone to avoid. An abusive parent is much more than a person who is occasionally cruel and destructive; he or she is truly confused.

Psychologists have concluded that one unquestionable fact emerges true and clear: children mimic the behavior of their parents, and consequently, the violence continues as the child becomes an adult. It's the responsibility of parents to make sure their home is made safe for their children to grow into healthy, responsible, and cooperative adults.

Parents must remember the safety of their home should never be reduced to a place of violence, whether the violence is directly or indirectly imposed upon their children. We hope this chapter will assist abusers and batterers with replacing their children's fear of being physically and psychologically injured with optimism and hope.

Strategies to Prevent and Eliminate Injuries to Children

The flood of information concerning the nature of domestic violence and the injuries to children suggests a plan that, when used, could eliminate injuries to children. Begin by understanding your role as a parent to guide your children in the right direction.

Be consistent by

- keeping parental issues between the parents and away from children;
- never using verbal abuse under any circumstances;
- never using physical abuse under any circumstances;
- never smashing or throwing things;
- never beating your children;
- teaching your children about acceptance and fairness, not revenge;
- remembering that your children are always learning from your behavior;
- being predictable and letting your children understand your feelings about certain matters and never overreacting to impress others;
- never displaying manipulative behavior;
- never displaying weapons;
- taking time to talk to your children;
- listening to what your children have to say;

- being honest and open when talking to your children;
- treating them as children and not adults;
- making promises you can keep.

The previous list consists of behaviors that children have a right to expect from their parents. Practice them with great care. Yes, children are younger and have less experience and knowledge than their parents; however, they are still children. Therefore, parents must give their children every possible opportunity to experience a healthy home environment.

It is the parent's responsibility to make sure their home is safe and understand that safety should never yield to violence. Parents should always give their children the benefit of their wisdom by teaching family togetherness.

Self-Assessment

Following are questions to assist you with understanding the effects of domestic violence on children. Apply personal knowledge, as well as information from the chapter, to answer *true*, *false*, or *NA* (not applicable) to the following questions. It is important that you answer all questions as accurately and honestly as possible.

1. Do you believe children can be affected by constant episodes of yelling and fighting between father and mother? ___
2. Do you believe that children harbor resentment toward an abusive parent(s)? ___
3. Would you consider your home a safe place for your children? ___
4. Do you believe spousal abuse can affect a child's ability to concentrate? ___
5. Do any of your children act out in school? ___
6. Do your children act nervous when you or your partner are present? ___
7. Have you ever pushed, punched, yelled, and threatened, your partner in front of your children? ___
8. Can you compare domestic violence with terrorism? ___
9. Do you think your children misbehave in school and in their community because of their negative experiences at home? ___
10. Can domestic violence cause a child to develop problems with anxiety, depression, and nightmares? ___

The previous list of statements is to better assess your understanding of the effect domestic violence has on children. If you believe that it is necessary for you to learn more about correct parenting, use the information in this workbook, and also seek professional assistance for any questions you may have that this workbook does not address.

Chapter Eleven

Communication Skills

Chapter's Objectives:

1. To learn to improve communication skills
2. To understand effective and ineffective ways of communicating
3. To understand the importance of sending and receiving messages
4. To recognize the methods that controllers use to control their partners
5. To encourage the reader to seek additional methods to learn better ways of communicating

Questions for You to Answer as You Read This Chapter:

1. Why is it important to be effective in the way people communicate with others?
2. Are people born good communicators?
3. What are the negative consequences of ineffective communication?
4. Is there an extreme or partial controller living in your family?
5. What would you like to improve in your communication skills?

Related Chapters of Interest:

- Anger Management
- Using Intimidation
- Using Coercion and Threats
- Trust and Respect
- Love and Commitment

Chapter Eleven

Communication Skills

Communicating

What is communicating? Communicating is the process of sending and receiving messages. The communication process begins first with a thought and continues as we send or receive verbal or nonverbal messages from others. Whether we're talking to someone else or thinking and talking aloud to ourselves, the key to being a good communicator is being able to send and receive messages effectively.

Many people do not realize it, but everyone has some sort of message to send whether he or she realizes it or not. The phenomenon about sending messages is that everyone sends some sort of message to people who are watching them, whether he or she realizes it or not.

As long as someone is watching us or we're watching them, both individuals are sending and receiving some kind of message. When we initially see someone from a distance, they are sending us a message about themselves, i.e., their race, gender, height, weight, hair color, behavior, and so on.

With the message we receive from the person we see from a distance, we will come to some kind of conclusion about that person. Maybe the person could care less about what people think regarding their race, gender, height, weight, hair color, or how they are behaving and will go about their business. Nevertheless, they will have told us something about themselves.

The point we are making is that when two or more people see each other or are together, they must communicate whether they want to or not. Whether we're walking, sitting, standing, looking, or listening, everything we do or not do has some kind of message attached.

When people are trying to send a message, unlike the two people mentioned earlier, we want the listener to hear and understand what we are saying and, consequently, send us an *appropriate response*. When this happens, we call this effective communication.

What is effective communication? Effective communication consists of having the ability to send a message so the person receiving the message will be able to interpret the message and consequently provide the sender with an appropriate response.

Sending and receiving messages may sound easy enough, but it's not as easy as one may be led to believe. Speaking and listening may be something that comes natural. However, speaking and listening so others can understand doesn't come natural. To become completely effective when communicating with others is a skill that takes time and plenty of practice.

Although people realize the importance of effective communication, most couples in relationships do not take the time to learn to communicate effectively with their partners. There is an old saying, "It's not what you say; it's how you say it."

In some cases, this motto may be true, and in other cases, this motto isn't true. There are many words and statements that no matter how you say them, someone's feelings could be hurt or could make someone angry.

Most people are very sensitive when it comes to how others talk to them. And certain words, if misused, can hurt them emotionally, whether the person speaking intended to hurt the person or not.

For example, not to take one's partner's feelings into account when giving him or her bad news or to respond negatively to someone who has given us bad news may not be the wise thing to do. Another example is if a person is upset because his or her partner may have forgotten their birthday, he or she may confront their partner with words such as, "How dare you forget my birthday, I hate you!"

This kind of behavior is considered as aggression, and the receiver of the message may respond with aggression, and consequently, an argument may ensue. A better way to approach this situation would be to say in a calm tone, "Sweetheart, my birthday is today. Did you forget?" This approach does not sound like an attack, and the person receiving the message will respond with an appropriate response.

Let us take another situation in which a couple is having a conversation regarding a certain topic, and each person believes he or she is right but has a different opinion. The effective way to end this discussion without it turning into an intense and disruptive argument would be to allow and respect the other person's opinion.

After further discussion, both individuals will see that they are both right, but have approached the topic of conversation from two different points of view. Arguments take place when one person or the other does not want to be proven wrong when in fact, both individuals could be right in their view of the situation.

Another problem in communicating arises when someone wants to dominate a conversation and ignores his or her partner's point of view. When this happens, there is either an argument that could develop into a contest of pushing and shoving, or one partner or the other will become silent and simply pretend to listen.

As you can see, communicating effectively is a give and take, i.e., I will listen to you, and you will listen to me, and subsequently, both of us will be happy that we had this conversation.

There are methods we can use to enjoy talking and listening to our partner, and they can enjoy talking and listening to us. Following are ways that can help a person to become more effective in communicating their message:

- Face your partner.
- Make sure you have your partner's complete attention.
- Maintain eye contact.
- Think about what you are going to say before speaking, i.e., what your thoughts are and what point you're trying to express.
- Your words should not be a collection of confused mumbling, grumbling, or whispering.
- Do not allow outside noises to interfere with what you are saying.
- Try to be specific, and use words that your partner understands.
- Make sure you are using the tone of voice you intend to use because your tone of voice reveals how you are feeling.

- Avoid raising your voice.
- Know that what you are saying is based upon facts and not presumptions.
- When sending your message, make sure you are direct and to the point.
- Do not manipulate the truth.

Remember these basic methods for future communication with your partner to improve your ability to make positive changes in your relationship.

Social Interaction

When two people meet for the first time, they convey their thoughts and feelings through their body movements and words. This social interaction, through the exchange of information, allows each person to determine certain characteristics about the person with whom he or she is speaking.

This exchange of information also assists persons in determining whether or not they feel safe enough to take their initial meeting to another level. After serious observation of the other person's words and behavior, the two people will decide to become either friends, girlfriend and boyfriend, or eventually become husband and wife.

During this time, our basic human need for intimacy will determine how quickly we become intimate; in this fact, is its danger. What is it about the exchange of information that makes us want to become more involved with a person we hardly know?

Is it the romantic words and gestures, how well-groomed they are, financial stability, sex appeal, or maybe it's because the person has a good sense of humor, i.e., they can make us laugh? All these qualities are wonderful to experience during a dating period, and they all are a means of communicating.

A person may say all the right words have a wonderful sex appeal and may be financially secure. However, the question remains. Behind the façade of romantic words and financial stability is still the question, is this person really safe enough to be trusted with one's feelings?

Or how long will it take before these persons' true character emerges and they begin to show the negative side of their personality? Will their romantic words change to a daily barrage of vulgarity and their behavior become aggressive? Initially, we do not know the answer to these questions, so we move forward with the relationship based on the information we have received.

Once the person's personality and behavior do change, then we will begin to ask ourselves, "Why didn't I see this coming?" "What was I thinking?" "He or she deceived me," "It has turned out that this person is not the person I thought they were. Now what should I do?"

Any person who is faced with this kind of situation has two basic options. He or she can choose to leave the relationship or stay in the relationship, and of course, either choice has its consequences.

The question, was I deceived? is a very important one. In many cases, people will enter into a relationship with the intention to deceive the other person for one reason or another. But in general, most people enter into a relationship believing that the relationship will last, and everyone will be happy.

Let us take a relationship that did not work out for the best, but it lasted between three months to several years. What questions should we ask ourselves about why the relationships we thought would work doesn't? Should we ask ourselves the relationship didn't work because there was a mutual lack of communication skills?

That could have been a part of the reason, but not the complete reason, one may decide their relationship didn't work. Financial problems, sexual difficulties, and physical and emotional abuse could have played a major role in the relationship going bad. In any case, having good communication skill is the most important aspect of maintaining a healthy relationship.

Good communication skills allow a couple to address their personal concerns whether they are financial problems, sexual difficulties, physical or emotional abuse.

In the case of financial problems or sexual difficulties, by having good communication skills, the couple can find ways to address their concerns and come to a positive resolution. In some cases, the same can be said for physical and emotional abuse. The simplest solution for physically and emotionally abusing others is to stop the abuse.

The key to maintaining a lasting relationship is *communicating how much we care for and love others mainly through the things we say and do.* Can two people live together and not have good communication skills? Yes, they can.

Couples have lived together for decades and were ineffective in communicating with each other. Of course, this sort of an arrangement will create a stressful environment; but they live through their stress, for the most part, by ignoring each other. Their kind of relationship may be uncomfortable at times, but for one reason or another, they continue to live together.

Many couples who live under such conditions are living together not out of love, but out of necessity. They may be living together for the sake of their children, financial reasons, or for fear of being alone.

In any case, people who believe they must live under such conditions are very unhappy. And many are waiting for the day they can escape from such unhappiness. For those of us who want to be happy in our relationship, we must learn to communicate effectively with our partners and not have to live year after year in mental solitude.

Exercise

Before continuing, answer the following statements:

- My communication skills are ___excellent ___good ___need some improvement.
- My verbal and nonverbal communications skills are appropriate for each situation. ___yes ___no ___I don't know
- My body language, tone of voice, and physical contact send the message I intend to send. ___always ___sometimes ___never
- When I have something important to say, I wait for the right time and place to approach my partner. ___always ___sometimes ___never

> Your partner cannot read your mind, and you cannot read your partner's mind; therefore, you must make sure the message you intend to send is the message your partner receives. When you communicate with your partner, you must use messages that have the best chance of being understood.

Effective Communications (Receiving the Message)

Effective communication consists not only of sending messages but also includes receiving messages. When we receive a message, we must listen carefully to what has been said by the person sending the message. Listening, another factor in effective communication, does not come naturally.

To become a good listener, one must be able to hear and understand what has been said before responding. In relationships, good listeners must know when to listen and know when to respond. When to listen and not respond simply means that there are situations in which a response is not necessary.

For example, your partner has had a difficult day at work and would like to have someone to listen to how his or her day has gone. They are not asking their partner to *fix* things or to *give advice.* Their partner may want someone to *just listen,* so they can process their feelings concerning a situation that took place on their job.

In all conversations, good listeners allow the person speaking to complete their thought and make their point, regardless of the issue, without interrupting. Good listeners pay close attention to what's being said and do not assume or attempt to read between the lines.

Assuming or reading between the lines is a fifty-fifty proposition, a proposition that often leads to assumptions. Of course, if the listener's assumptions are wrong, his or her assumptions could lead to a serious misunderstanding.

A good listener will avoid reading between the lines and focus on what is actually being said. After listening, the person will think about what has been said and consequently provide an appropriate response.

For a person to become a good listener, it's important to understand these basic guidelines:

- Stop what you're doing and focus on the person who is speaking.
- Face the person and make eye contact; this will demonstrate that you are listening.
- Look for basic facial expressions behind their words. This will alert you to how the person is feeling concerning the subject in which they are speaking.
- Show them that you are paying attention by a simple nod of your head.
- If you must ask a question, ask well-developed and clear questions.
- Wait until your partner has completed their thought and made their point before responding.

Remember to exercise *patience* as you develop your skills to become an effective listener. Listening is very important in the developing and maintaining a healthy relationship.

Ineffective Communication

What is ineffective communication? Ineffective communication can be defined as any message that was intended to achieve a purpose but did not achieve its intended purpose.

Basically, ineffective communication is simply the opposite of effective communication. Unlike effective communication, ineffective communications can and will often produce frustration, anger, stress, and resentment in a relationship.

Ineffective communication is the reason most relationships fail. For one reason or another, couples will live together for ten, twenty, and even thirty years and not talk *to* each other but talk *at* each other.

Men and women who live in a home in which there is poor communication often live a lonely day-to-day existence. Let us take for example, conversations where there are constant interruptions by someone who are supposed to be listening.

Interrupting someone while he or she is speaking can be considered as ineffective when communicating with others. Interrupting someone while he or she is speaking can be seen as being rude. Or it could make the speaker believe the listener wasn't listening or isn't interested in what they have said.

How does it feel when you are trying to explain a situation that really bothers you and the person you are speaking cuts you off and starts talking before you have completed your thought and made your point? It would cause some people to think, *What's the point of talking with this person when they have their own agenda? Either they are not interested in what I have to say, or they think that they have all the answers.*

There are also partners who will use the passive-aggressive approach to interrupt their partner, i.e., they interrupt with their body language. For example, when their partner is speaking, the person who is supposed to be listening may disagree with what is being said and will roll his or her eyes, cross his or her arms, or turn his or her head and look in the other direction.

Each of these gestures signals to the speaker that the listener either disagrees with what is being said, or they're not interested in what is being said. Consequently, the speaker may feel rejected or resentful because the listener was not courteous enough to listen to what was important to the speaker.

Now it's the listener's turn to speak. Do you think the person who is now the listener is going to pay close attention to what the speaker has to say? Perhaps or perhaps not.

Interrupting someone when he or she is speaking is one of the many reasons conversations fall apart; and someone leaves the conversation feeling frustrated, angry, and resentful. As a consequence, no one will get their point across or get their needs met. And if a partner doesn't get his or her needs met often enough, other problems will develop, creating future domestic conflicts.

One of the most destructive aspects of ineffective communications is dishonesty. People who are in the habit of controlling their partners, appear to have developed a skill at telling lies. *Their ability to lie is amazing*, and their reasons for lying are just as amazing as the lies they tell.

We understand their ability to tell the truth is interrupted by their overall desire to control situations that may prove to be embarrassing or if they believe they stand to lose something by telling the truth.

Consequently, how do you have a conversation with someone with whom you know for a fact will lie as soon as he or she is asked a question, particularly if the question may put him or her on the spot? The fact of the matter is that you can have a conversation with a liar, but the conversation will be ineffective at best.

The amazing aspect about a lair is that liars do not like being lied to and will seem to come completely apart if their partner lies to them. As far as habitual liars are concern, being a good listener will largely depend on what's being said so that they can keep their lies believable. And if they are a good listener, it's because they want to keep their lies straight. And if they aren't good listeners, it's because they do not care to listen.

If a liar decides to listen to what their partner has to say, their response may sound appropriate to a question or statement, but may not have anything to do with the truth of the matter being discussed. Also, many liars has told so many lies during the course of the conversation they can become confused. Many liars can also become confused if their partner addresses several different issues during the conversation.

The liar may have told a lie concerning each subject their partner may have addressed, and the only way out of their discussing is to start an argument. Usually, the argument is totally off the subject mentioned by their partner. The liar's goal is to shift the attention away from himself or herself and subsequently to their partner.

We have to remember that many habitual liars are quick thinkers when it comes to lying. It appears as if they have answers already planned in their mind and is waiting for the moment to spring their prearranged lies upon their partner.

And then we have the forgetful liar. They will have forgotten an earlier lie they had told their partner, and to cover up their forgotten lie, they will create a fight to divert attention away from the question.

Then we have the pretender. These are people who like to hear themselves talk and pretend to listen. They never seem to get the speaker's message; they simply do not want to hear what the other person has to say. If they do decide to respond to a person's statement or question, their response seems remote and unrelated to the issue.

This kind of liar will *pick* at certain words (selective listening) and formulate an entirely new thought. They will respond with a surprisingly bizarre statement that will leave the listener puzzled and unable to respond.

This kind of communicating can become very frustrating. Consequently, the listener will simply stop communicating with their partner, realizing that it's useless and a waste of time and energy.

There are many different reasons why a person's message isn't received. Following are examples of situations in which communication will probably be ineffective:

- The person is not interested in the message being sent. For example, people who are liars, batterers or abusers, alcoholics, or drug users do not want to hear someone tell them they need to stop lying, being abusive, or abusing drugs.
- The person believes they know it all. For example, a person who has an answer for everything when in actuality, they know very little.
- The person is long-winded. For example, he or she goes on and on about a subject and appears that he or she will never reach the point he or she is trying to make.
- The speaker does not have the person's complete attention. For example, the person was busy doing something at the time; he or she is not focusing on what the speaker is saying or is persistent on having it his or her way.
- The message is a collection of "I need" statements. For example, going from issue to issue, e.g., "I need you to cut the grass," "I need more money," and "I need more time to myself."
- There is also senseless shouting. For example, shouting from one room to another, shouting obscenities, and shouting at the children.
- There are outside noises that interfere with a person's ability to hear. For example, the television is on, the radio is playing, or children are playing in the same room where you're trying to have a conversation.

> These examples can be considered ineffective ways to communicate. As a result, the listener may get the wrong idea, and once again, a problem may develop.

Do you know how a liar feels after getting caught in a lie? They do not feel remorse; they feel as if they have been cheated. A habitual lying partner can cause so much damage to a relationship after getting caught telling lies that the possibility to trust such a person would seem impossible, particularly when it concerns an extramarital affair (cheating).

The Family Dominator

(The Extreme Dominator)

In an earlier chapter, we discussed three kinds of controllers. (Remember, a person can be controlled by their partners but does not view their controller as being domineering.) In homes where there is domestic violence, there is someone who believes in controlling as well as dominating everyone within the home.

In this chapter, we will discuss two such dominators: extreme and partial dominators. Like the controllers, the extreme and partial dominator are communicators, but in a negative sense.

The thing to remember about extreme and partial dominators (controllers) is that, although they are good at making demands on family members, they cannot tolerate being told what to do. A controlling person does not like a partner who has excellent communication skills. For example, extreme dominators do not like a partner who seems to have all the right answers, because it makes them appear weak and not in control.

Extreme dominators do not like to be questioned or be proven wrong. They will become verbally or physically abusive (or both) toward a partner who would even suggest that they stop using drugs, wasting family finances, or spending the weekends with the family.

Of course, these kinds of negative means of communicating could have a tragic ending for the victim: emotional abuse, physical abuse, or a possible homicide. If this is the case, how can a partner communicate their feelings?

More importantly, how can partners get their partner to listen to their opinion on family issues if they believe that they will be abused if they attempt to voice their opinion?

It must be made perfectly clear that like the extreme controller, the extreme dominator is not interested in their partner's opinions or feelings. If they truly cared about their partner's opinions or feelings, they would listen to reason and love and trust their partner enough to never verbally or physically harm him or her.

Contrary to what people may have heard or believed, talking to an extreme dominator about how they are feeling will not build intimacy in their relationship. Statements such as "I feel hurt" or "I feel disappointed" basically informs the dominator that emotionally, they have their partner in the position they want them, i.e., feeling weak and helpless.

What can people do in such a miserable situation? We recommend they speak with a marriage and family therapist about their problematic relationship and allow them to assist the victim with finding a reasonable solution to their problem.

A good therapist will assist the victim with obtaining a clear perspective. However, if the victim decides to leave the abusive relationship without consultation, they must develop a plan of action that would not put them or their children in physical danger from their abuser or batterer.

Victims of domestic violence must take any threat of physical violence made by the abuser or batterer as a serious matter, particularly when the abuser or batterer has made a threat to kill the victim if he or she decides to leave the relationship. Countless lives have been lost because men and women thought their partner would not follow through on their *threats of violence.*

An extreme dominator's number 1 fear is his or her partner meeting another man or woman and planning to take the children and leave the relationship. Subsequently, how does a victim of domestic abuse communicate to an extreme dominator that he or she will leave the relationship if he or she continues to be abusive?

The answer to this question depends mainly on how well the victim understands the extreme dominator's attitude and behavior. Many extreme dominators will ponder their options and attempt to behave appropriately for fear of losing their partner and the children. Other extreme dominators will become hostile, believing that if they escalate their violent behavior, it will scare the victim into believing there is no way out of the relationship without some sort of negative consequence.

For this reason, the victim and his or her children must have a well-thought-out plan as to how they will approach this person. If the victim has the *slightest idea* that danger awaits them, *outside intervention is absolutely necessary.*

Keep in mind that with a well-thought-out plan of action, each new day brings with it the opportunity for a victim of domestic violence and his or her children to break away from an abusive partner.

The importance of getting professional help cannot be stressed enough. And remember, it's all about how we communicate our wants and needs, particularly to an abuser or batterer.

The Partial Dominator

The second kind of dominator is stealthier (sneaky). Their negative behavior isn't obvious to the victim at the onset of the relationship; the victim never sees it coming. The same can be said for the extreme dominator, but the extreme dominator is a great deal more careless with his or her frustrations, anger, and behavior.

When the partial dominator is in their stealth mode, they will say and appear to do all the right things to conceal their true nature. They will say all the right things to convince their victim that they are safe to be near. They will have a sense of humor, spend money as if they have money to burn, and speak of the wonderful plans they have for the future of the relation.

Their optimistic world would make most men or women want to become their partner. Their behavior fills the soul with hope. Their potential partner finds it hard to believe that they have met the person of their dreams.

Of course, the same can be said for extreme dominators, but their behavioral changes are usually unexpected and uncompromising. The partial dominators, on the other hand, limit their abuse; their abuse seems to be well-timed and limited. Their partner will catch them in what appears to be harmless lies but not often. Lying is their greatest asset.

Partial dominators will lie when lying isn't necessary, when in fact, it would have been much easier for him or her to tell the truth. The partial dominator is, in essence, a very scared person who rarely feels safe in a relationship. Safe in the sense that they believe their partner will leave them for someone else, and they are powerless to do anything to stop it from happening. Although they will lie to their partner, they will always ask themselves the question "Was lying to my partner really necessary?"

Many people believe there are times when telling their partner a lie is necessary. There are lies people may tell when they do not feel like discussing a particular issue that may create an argument. Or they may arrive home late from work, and their partner may ask them, "Why are you late coming home?" Without thinking, they may respond, "I was caught in traffic," when in fact, they decided to talk with a friend at work, and time slipped away. Is that not a lie, when in fact, they were not caught in traffic? There is a great difference between this kind of lie and the lies the partial dominator tells.

Like the extreme dominator, the partial dominator will lie without thinking twice to cover up the truth although they do not like lying to their partner.

If partial dominators believe they have to lie about their past and current wrongdoings—i.e., extramarital affairs, finances, how they spend their leisure time—they will use many different tactics to manipulate the truth. The disheartening aspect regarding manipulating the truth is that they actually begin to believe the lies they tell, and that's how they can live with their lies.

Although the partial dominator's behavior may not be as extreme as the extreme dominator's, they will attempt to control the relationship through continued put-downs, criticisms, or ridicules. As oppressive as these controlling tactics may appear, they are still a distorted means of communicating.

However, when correctly approached, the partial dominator will give in and listen to reason if they believe that their partner is serious about making change.

Of course, there are partial dominators who will not stop being abusive due to the fact that they have forgotten how to be loving and caring, or believe being abusive is the way to keep their relationship from falling apart.

In any case, a victim of either the partial or extreme dominator must decide when they have had enough of their lies and deception and move on with their life. All victims must keep in mind that there is a better life beyond a dominator's lies.

Self-Assessment

Following are questions to assist you with finding out your weak areas when communicating with your partner. Apply personal knowledge, as well as information from the chapter, to answer the following questions. It is important that you answer all questions as accurately and honestly as possible. Answer *yes*, *no*, or *NA* (not applicable) to the following questions.

1. Would learning to communicate better help your relationship? ___
2. Is your partner willing to learn to communicate more effectively? ___
3. Are you willing to learn to become a better communicator? ___
4. Do you feel uncomfortable talking to your partner? ___
5. Does a simple conversation turn into an argument? ___
6. Has there been any physical violence after an argument? ___
7. Is your family afraid to talk about personal problems? ___
8. Do you believe everything would have a better outcome if you and your partner could communicate better? ___
9. Do you understand the importance of having good communication skills? ___
10. Are you a good listener? ___

The previous list is for you to better assess your communication skills. Review your answers to the questions, and if you find it necessary to learn more about communicating, use the information in this workbook, and also seek professional assistance for any questions you may have that this workbook does not address.

Chapter Twelve

Trust and Respect

Chapter's Objectives:

1. To discuss the importance of trust and respect in a relationship
2. To discuss trust versus lies in a relationship
3. To discuss any relevant issues that affect trust and respect
4. To discuss trust and the idea of spirituality
5. To discuss trust in oneself and others

Questions for You to Answer as You Read This Chapter:

1. What does *trust* mean to you?
2. Can you explain how it must feel to not be trusted?
3. What does *respect* mean to you?
4. Can you explain how it must feel to be disrespected?
5. Can you love someone you cannot trust or respect?

Related Chapters of Interest:

- What Is Domestic Violence?
- Equality in a Relationship
- Emotional Abuse
- Conflict Resolution
- Love and Commitment

CHAPTER TWELVE

Trust and Respect

Freedom from Suspicion

What is trust? Trust can be defined as having faith or confidence in someone or something. Trust in a relationship is built on the values of mutual respect, fairness, responsibility, genuineness, faith, and freedom from suspicion.

Trust is a very important factor in maintaining individual, family, and social stability. Family members must believe that when another family member is having a personal or social problem, they should come together as a family to assist the family member with their problem.

When family members trust each other, it takes on the primary meaning of loyalty. Loyalty inspires *family members* to feel secure and enables each person to say and do what's in the best interest of the family.

Although trust is one of the most important values of a relationship, achieving and maintaining trust appears to be one of the most difficult and the most challenging aspect of a relationship.

A relationship begins when two people exchange information concerning their past and future expectations based on their perception of the truth. However, what most people tend to do in a discussion concerning their personality and their past experiences is to tell the other person what's good about themselves and not mention anything that may cause the other person to become unease or disinterested.

In other words, they are telling the other person half of the truth about who they are and leaving out anything they believe might be an embarrassment.

This leaves us with the question, can a person who does not tell the complete truth about themselves be trusted to be totally honest in the future of a relationship? Of course not! If a person begins a relationship with half-truths and lies, how can they be expected to be truthful throughout their relationship?

Using an example of a person who didn't tell their future partner about issues concerning unstable employment history, drinking, drugs, anger management issues, or infidelity (cheating), how will they cope when their partner finds out that they are using drugs, having extramarital affairs, or cannot maintain employment? Many will continue to lie to cover up the truth because of their original deception.

What people tend to do in the beginning of a relationship is to expect from the other person a kind of *blind trust*. Some people can *feel* when someone isn't being completely honest but cannot prove it and therefore decide to accept what the person has told them. However, this approach will only open the door to suspicions about the person's honesty and, consequently, will cause future trust issues.

Think about this question for a moment. When a person meets someone for the first time and they want to develop a relationship, do you think they are going to tell the other person negative things from their past?

Would people dare reveal to a new acquaintance that they abused or battered their previous partner, cannot keep a job, like to fight, drink alcohol until they pass out, spent time in the penitentiary for a serious crime, have on several occasions contracted a sexually transmitted disease, or that they are slightly psychotic?

Most abusers and batterers will share information to satisfy the other person's curiosity but will not share enough information for the other person to leave or to consider not having a relationship with them.

A list of possible deceptions at the start of a relationship is very long, if not endless. Who can we trust to tell us the truth, and how can we tell that a person is telling the truth? We are not going to attempt to answer these difficult questions, so we will leave it up to you to decide what method one can use to determine if someone is telling the *whole truth*. People say, "You cannot go through life not trusting anyone." How would you respond to that statement?

Exercise

Following is a list of common ideas concerning trust in your relationship. Answer each statement that would apply to you and your partner. It is important that you answer all statements as accurately and honestly as possible.

1. I trust myself more than I trust anyone else because
____
____
____
____.

2. Trust means everything to me because
____
____
____
____.

3. There are situations in my past that I keep to myself because
____
____
____
____.

4. My partner can be confident that I can be trusted because
____
____
____
____.

5. I cannot love a person I can't trust because
____
____
____
____.

6. I trust everyone without question because
____
____
____
____.

7. If a person loses my trust, I can *never* trust them again because
____
____
____
____.

8. I honestly trust my partner because
____
____
____
____.

9. I have a difficult time trusting my partner because
____
____
____
____.

10. I need my partner to trust me because
____
____
____
____.

This list of statements is for you to assess your level of trust. Go over your answers and determine how important or unimportant trust is to you. Is trust as simple as some people think it is, or one of the most complicated values in a relationship?

Truth and Lies

In a discussion concerning lies versus truth, there are many questions that we may have a difficult time answering. For example, why is telling the truth so difficult for some people? Do you know of anyone who has *never* told a lie? And would you tell the truth if you knew the consequences would be severe?

Depending upon the person and his or her belief system, these three questions may vary in difficulty. Existing in a society where telling lies and half-truths are a part of life, who can be trusted not to tell an occasional lie?

For example, can you trust a merchant in the process of selling you a used car, household appliance, or home to inform you that you have purchased a piece of soon-to-be-useless item?

When we go to the voting polls, are candidates going to do what they promised once elected? *We must also clarify that all merchants and candidates running for a political office aren't liars.*

On a personal level, not all people but *most people* will lie for personal gain to keep from being harmed and, in other cases, because that's all they know how to do. Who can be trusted not to stretch the truth or tell an outright lie regardless of the consequence?

There are people who may have never told a lie. Those who truly believe in a higher power, and live an honest lifestyle may have no reason to lie. Conversely, there are some people who are incapable of telling the truth. Having lied for so long, they do not know where the truth begins or where their lies end.

So what does a person who has lied throughout their relationship do when they want to tell the truth? Do they take the risk of telling their partner the truth about themselves and be labeled a liar, or do they continue to lie to maintain their status of being a liar?

What about habitual liars? How do they remain in a relationship and not get caught in their lies? Many habitual liars will conceal the truth by telling half of the truth and covering up the truth by not answering certain questions directly. Their belief is, *what my partner doesn't know will not hurt him or her*. Most habitual liars do not find it difficult hiding behind a curtain of deception.

However, sooner or later, their partner will unknowingly open the curtain to finding nothing but lies. When this happens, trust in the relationship will be shattered. When we trust someone with our feelings, future, or with something we hold dear and they violate our trust, we can become extremely frustrated and hurt.

Couples involved in a trusting relationship will not conceal information from their partner. They will begin the relationship trusting their partner on all levels. However, unless we have lived the perfect life, we must be realistic with regards to concealing and not concealing information from a potential partner. Technically, we believe everyone has the right to keep confidential information as long as the information does not directly or ultimately harm their partner.

If opening old wounds about past experiences will create mental pain and the secrets don't interfere with the tranquility of their current relationship, in essence, they are not being deceitful; rather, they are actually protecting themselves as well as their partner.

When a woman decides not to tell her partner that she was sexually assaulted earlier in her life, is she being deceitful? Is a traumatic event something that a partner needs to know if there is belief that it would destroy their relationship? In the final analysis, it is a matter of an individual's choice and circumstance whether the person should or should not discuss painful information.

Exercise

Following are questions you can ask yourself concerning sharing your past or your partner sharing his or her past and family trust. Write *yes*, *no*, or *I'm not sure* to the following questions:

1. Do you believe that a person has the right to keep their past a secret? ___
2. Is there anything about you or your past that you must never tell your children? ___
3. Do you believe that your partner has been completely truthful about his or her past? ___
4. Have you ever asked your partner or children to trust you when you have a problem trusting them? ___
5. Have you ever broken a promise to your partner or children because you thought it would be in their best interest? ___
6. Have you ever caught your partner or children in a lie? ___
7. Is it acceptable for you to tell "little white lies"? ___
8. If someone lies to you, will you be able to trust him or her again? ___
9. Are there times when it is absolutely necessary to lie? ___
10. Have you ever lied to your partner? ___

Your answers will demonstrate that telling the total truth isn't easy, particularly when telling the truth will disturb the peace in one's family.

Trust in Ourselves and Others

What does it mean to have trust in oneself? Trusting in oneself is the ability to have self-confidence and self-respect in what one thinks and does. Trusting in oneself also means having faith in the ability to achieve and to become successful in ways that are in the best interest of oneself, family, and society.

What about trusting other people? To have and display trust in others simply means that a person approves of and appreciates people with whom they feel safe and secure. Demonstrating an ability to be open and genuine without hesitation and believe that the other person will be open and genuine can be a wonderful feeling.

When your partner trusts in you, he or she rests firmly on the belief that it's safe for him or her to be who he or she is as a person, without shame or guilt following the disclosure of honest feelings and beliefs.

This is particularly true for men and women who truly care about their partners. When people believe that they have been betrayed by their partner, it may be very difficult for them to trust that person again.

Earning back the trust and respect once lost may not be easy depending on the situation. There is a tremendous difference between lying about why you're late coming home from work and lying about having an extramarital affair. Having an extramarital affair is absolutely unacceptable behavior.

How can we trust others outside of the family, say, a close friend? There is a certain amount of doubt when it comes to trusting others with our feelings, money, or time. The reason behind not trusting others with our emotions, money, or time can be summed up in three questions:

- How many times have you trusted someone with your emotions, and they either ignored your emotions or continued to do things to hurt you?
- How many times have you loaned someone money, and they took their time returning the money or possibly never repaid you?
- How many times has someone wasted your time with foolishness or with some ill-thought-out ideas?

> People can accept a lie when there is nothing at stake; the difficulty comes with being lied to repeatedly. Continued deception can lead to the decision to stop trusting.

Letting people you can't trust go is a positive action because you can always trust in yourself and those who have proven that they can be trusted. Trusting in oneself, one's higher power, and others who have proven their reliability are basically all that one needs to enjoy life!

Trust and Spirituality

The belief of and trust of a *higher power* is an individual's preference. Therefore, we are not asking anyone to believe or not to believe in a higher power. What we are speaking of are people who have found their spirituality or are in the process of seeking it.

People who are spiritual or believe in a certain religion have confidence that their spirituality allows for them to have and maintain a well-balanced commitment of trust and love toward others.

Most people believe that it takes everything they can muster to be able to survive in today's society. Therefore, people who are in love want to do more in a relationship than merely survive. Far beyond the idea of just surviving and prospering are the goals of having a happy family life, making progress on their job, becoming successful in college, and *living the American dream.*

Many people also realize that it takes more to survive than just believing in a higher power. They realize that it's important to understand and practice the *moral virtues* learned through our parents and grandparents, those important individuals who taught us the difference between right and wrong.

We were taught about the values of faith, kindness, honesty, beauty, and happiness. We were told that living a life filled with positive virtues will serve as stepping-stones to success and that trust is one of the many treasures of a relationship. We were also taught that trust should not be lost or abandoned because of a bad day on the job, a bad drive home, unpaid bills, disagreements, or a quick extramarital affair.

For many, spirituality serves as a foundation that allows people to eventually solve their problems without being prejudged or punished.

Negative Outside Influences

Marriages are not immune to outside negative influences. Either partner can be affected by negative moral values from extended family members, immature friends, fellow employees, and other associates. These outside influences may or may be reflective of what a moral value is or even care enough to learn the importance of having moral values.

It is important to note that trust, being as valuable as it is, has little meaning to some people as long as their needs are met. For example, there are people who trust no one, yet they expect people to trust them.

Often people who trust no one have a difficult time with relationships. They are quick to suspect their partner of wrongdoings, and quick at providing others with information on how to *fix* or *terminate* a marriage. The problem in this particular case is that such a person rarely have a clue as to how to maintain their relationships.

These misinformed individuals can turn out to be the worst that a couple could rely upon for assistance in time of need. We call these people the *misery society*, as in *misery loves company*. They are similar to those known as *jailhouse lawyers* who enjoy giving other inmates advice about how to beat the law but haven't attended one day in law school and are doing five to ten or fifteen years to life.

People do not need anyone to explain how to destroy a relationship. Many couples understand the process of working through missed opportunities, how to learn from their mistakes, and how to move on without falling completely apart. No married couple needs anyone to spoon-feed them with *poisonous morality*.

People in relationships must learn to resolve their own problems unless they come to a stalemate and need to seek professional assistance or spiritual advice. Avenues of advisement can be found in professions such as marriage and family therapists, psychologists, and licensed social workers to assist couples with their problems. Do not be afraid to seek assistance to keep your relationship together.

Respect

What is respect? Respect can be defined as showing admiration or having a high opinion of oneself and others. Respect in relationships isn't determined by obedience or who exercise the most power but is determined through one's attitude and behavior. Therefore, it is safe to say that respect in relationships is based on the moral values of love, honesty, trust, equality, and compassion.

Research demonstrates that the level of respect that people show toward each other varies from either having or showing no respect (which may constitute emotional abuse in domestic situations) to having and showing considerable respect.

The respect we have for our family members should be immeasurable. The respect we have toward law enforcement officers, judges, and others may exist in a lesser degree depending on the attitude of the person.

To take that statement a step further, it's *not necessary* for us to have admiration for a law enforcement officer or a judge of the court in order to respect them. However, citizens are required by law to respect the law enforcement official or judge's position of authority.

If people are told that they are required by law to respect someone (law enforcement officer's or the judge's position of authority), there is a certain degree of resentment because most people do not like to be told how to feel.

At first contact, there is a certain amount of respect that people expect from others. However, when an extreme controller meets and develops a relationship, respect for their potential partner is merely a façade cover-up.

The extreme controller's potential partner is led to believe that he or she is respected and will continue to be respected. The controller will behave in a manner that would appear respectable, but his or her controlling tendencies are concealed behind deception. He or she will continue his or her deceptive behavior until his or her true personality, demands a return to being who he or she really is, i.e., controlling, demanding, and disrespectful.

Consequently, how do we know the person we are thinking of developing a relationship will eventually disrespect us? The hard truth is that we do not know if or when a person will disrespect us, which leads us to the question, who can we respect?

First, we were taught that we have a moral commitment to others, respecting those who respect us. Second, how can we respect someone who wants to control us? The simple answer would be that abusers and batterers don't deserve our respect.

Initially, we don't realize that the person we are dating at the time is an abuser or batterer. It's not until weeks and even months into the relationship, and only after the victim has developed intense feelings for his or her abuser or batterer that he or she begins to realize that a real problem exists. This is one of the greatest problems potential victims have to face when developing a new and meaningful relationship.

Many victims of domestic violence carry with them suspicions from previous abusive relationship in which they trusted and respected their partners only later to become victims of abuse. Victims of domestic violence are conditioned to believe that caution must be exercised in regards to trust and respect to prevent being victimized in another abusive relationship. The lesson they have learned is respect is not easily given; it is earned.

Self-Assessment

Following is a list of common ideas concerning respect. Apply personal knowledge, as well as information from the chapter, to answer *true*, *false*, or *NA* (not applicable) to the statements that apply to respect. It is important that you answer all statements as accurately and honestly as possible.

1. I honestly respect my partner. ___
2. I respect everyone whether they respect me or not. ___
3. I only respect those who respect me. ___
4. I do not "just give" people my respect; they must earn it. ___
5. My partner and I call each other bad names all the time, and we still respect each other. ___
6. I need my partner to respect me. ___
7. I only disrespect those who disrespect me. ___
8. I disrespect a lazy person. ___
9. I disrespect people who are rude to me. ___
10. I am disrespectful to others at times. ___

The previous list of statements is for you to better assess your level of respect and disrespect. If you believe that it is necessary for you to make any needed adjustments in your level of respect and disrespect of yourself and others, use the information in this workbook, or seek professional assistance for any questions you may have that this workbook does not address.

Chapter Thirteen

Love and Commitment

Chapter's Objectives:

1. To discuss the meaning of love
2. To discuss love in relationships
3. To discuss the meaning of commitment in a relationship
4. To explore the positive aspects of romance in a relationship
5. To have the reader do a self-assessment to determine the level of love and commitment in their relationship

Questions for You to Answer as You Read This Chapter:

1. How would you define *love*?
2. What do you look for in a person before selecting them to be your partner?
3. How do you feel about romance in a relationship?
4. What does commitment in a relationship mean to you?
5. Can you explain parental commitment?

Related Chapters of Interest:

- Communication Skills
- Trust and Respect
- Equality in Relationships
- Parenting Skills
- Anger Management

Chapter Thirteen

Love and Commitment

Love

For centuries, some of the wisest poets and novelists have written about love and the wonderful feeling love possesses. Most of us, like poets and novelists, realize that men and women equally crave the idea of loving someone and being loved in return.

Some people may say that they will never fall in love. However, the problem with such a statement is that everybody needs love whether they realize it or not. And once a person has experienced the feeling of love—and for one reason or another, their love for a certain person has been lost—the person who has once loved will search to find someone else to love.

We asked one hundred men and women in several domestic violence classes how they would define love. Twenty percent of the class defined the term *love* as what they believe the word *love* meant to them. The other 20 percent of the class could only give examples of people and things that they love but could not define the word *love* or explain the feeling of love.

For example, many said that they love their partner, mother, father, sister, and brother in different ways. There was no surprise at the answers that we received in view of the fact that love and the many ways one can express their love has baffled mankind since the beginning of time.

Defining the word *love* may have its mystifying qualities. Being in love and being loved in return are still conditions all of us aspire to achieve in our lifetime. Can we actually define *true love*? If we were to attempt to define *true love*, where would we begin? Perhaps with one or all the terms often used to define love, such as having a deep affection, devotion, passion, or desire for a person or thing. Yet can any of those terms be considered as true love?

People were also asked the question, could they remember their first love? Most students admitted having wonderful memories of their first love and stated that they fell in love for the first time when they were thirteen or fourteen. An inquiry was also made as to the difference between falling in love as a teenager and falling in love as an adult.

The emphasis was on finding out the differences between how teenagers love and how adults love each other. Many stated that their first love introduced a new feeling beyond any they have ever experienced before.

The description of the feeling they had at the time included having an intense indescribable spiritual closeness *each time* they saw, talked, or held hands with the person.

Others stated that their first love was unlike their love for family members because family members use the word *love* so freely that the word *love* appeared to lose its true meaning.

For many, there was a noted difficulty in making the connection between love and punishment. For example, their parents would say that they loved them, yet for any small infraction, they would be punished. Love for them became a *ball of confusion.*

Consequently, when they found someone their age who said that they loved them, it wasn't crammed with confusion and doubt but instead was clear and meaningful. Yet now that they are adults, the feeling of love has once again become crammed with confusion and doubt.

As an adult, many people speak of loving their partner dearly; however, they do not achieve the same spiritual closeness, that they felt when they were teenagers.

Because of the mistrust, disrespect, male and female suspicions, *old baggage* from an old relationship, and the inability to communicate cause them conflict.

All of us have loved someone at some point in our lives, and for most of us, the teenage years may have been when love was in its purest form. We didn't measure love for the other person by the kinds of gifts; we were able to buy them or through rehearsed poetic words.

Loving someone during adulthood has become much more complicated. Many of us have problems trusting, and many of us are filled with suspicions—suspicions of whether our partner will inflict pain like the last person did, whether our partner still love the last person they were with, whether our partner cheats on us, and so on.

Loving feelings are very difficult to develop when a person's mind is filled with suspicion and doubt. In today's society, it seems incredible how some people can roll the word *love* off their tongue with such ease. For instance, two people meet today; and within days or weeks, the words *I love you* have been heard repeatedly.

Many people believe if the word *love* can be used so loosely, then it cannot be real. The person who uses the word love so loosely must be using (it) as a means to an end, possibly as a result of being lonely or a need for sex, companionship, or financial support. One or all these reasons could lead one to become suspicious of the nature of their love.

Suspicions don't always complicate a relationship, but complications do happen with a large number of people who want to find love but, for one reason or another, have had a difficult experience in previous relationships. So can a person who has been abused in several previous relationships overcome his or her negative experiences and find love?

Some people may forget that God did not put people on earth to be alone. It follows that when we are patient enough to wait for the right person to come along, we will eventually find the love we need.

However, if a person isn't patient and settles for any man or woman he or she meets as a potential partner, he or she may be leaving himself or herself open for more pain and suffering.

Many people who find themselves *alone* believe that they *need* someone in their life right away, not the special person of their dreams, but anyone will do because of their loneliness. This is destined to be a problem, and if people aren't careful with whom they choose as a partner, they will surely not find love but, once again, find a ball of confusion.

To clarify, some of us must return to the way we once loved—that intense indescribable spiritual closeness we felt as teenagers. Take a moment and reflect upon your first love. Can you remember the innocence and the spiritual closeness? Is it possible to revisit that innocence and spiritual closeness once again?

People want to be shown and not just told that they are loved. We enjoyed being loved as teenagers, and we enjoy being loved as adults. There is an innate belief that there will always be someone whom we can love and who could love us without *the drama*.

Most people will never enjoy being alone. Of course, there are people who like having *their space* on occasion, but they will never learn to accept being lonely.

Romance

What is romance? Basically, romance is the idea of entertaining loving thoughts of affection for another person and acknowledging the need for love and companionship. Romance is also *displaying* acts of affection.

The idea of showing affection is to make the other person feel good about developing and maintaining a healthy relationship and to give both individuals a sense of self-awareness, emotional safety, and expectations for the future of their relationship.

Within the medieval tales of princes and princesses or knights in shining armor, which we read as a child, were the inspirations for many romantic childhood dreams. Talking on the telephone for hours at a time, carrying a young girl's books, or going to the local theater to watch a movie were romantic acts of affection. Those acts of affection lead to many teenagers both giving and receiving their first kiss.

Everyone has a desire for the warmth of intimacy and the security of a long-term loving relationship. Some people believe that it is extremely difficult to find love and romance in today's society, which is filled with frustration and anger.

With certainty, once a person begins to realize the true nature of love, they will experience insights into life and understand the reasons behind the words *love* and *romance* and the enormous similarity between the two.

It would be difficult to touch someone's heart through romance if they have never experienced love. Yet there are people who have been in love and still await the opportunity to experience the wonders of romance.

The following exercise is for you to help a friend to decide whether or not he or she should become involved with a person they have recently met. The examples below are information given by your friend about a person he or she is considering for a relationship.

Exercise

Read each example carefully and determine which person would best suit your friend's personality (your friend's personality closely resembles your personality). Put a check mark next to the decision your partner should take concerning this person, your advise would be for your friend to keep away, become friends, or try for a love connection.

Example 1: Your friend has been talking to a coworker, and they have become close. They see each other every day in the work setting and after work hours. This person is single with no children, great looking, very intelligent, has an excellent sense of humor, and is very good to him or her.

Your friend is interested in developing a relationship with a fellow coworker. After a few weeks, the coworker becomes slightly irritated when your friend stops to talk with other men or women on the job. Your friend thinks that it's sweet for him or her to show a *little* jealousy. The coworker, at times, will visit your friend's home unannounced with flowers or other gifts.

What kind of advice would give your friend and why?

Keep away	Become friends	Try for a love connection
____	____	____

Why?____

____

____

____

____

Example #2: Your friend has met an old high school boyfriend or girlfriend (first love) who is *trying* to recover from a difficult divorce. The person has a child from his or her previous marriage. The person is somewhat in debt and consequently has very little money for entertainment.

The person is still very nice, and your friend has never seen him or her get angry even though becoming angry would have been the appropriate feeling at the time. He or she has earned a college degree and has the potential of a great career ahead of them. The person is very supportive of your friend, and they have been dating off and on for several months. They still have feelings for each other.

What kind of advice would give your friend and why?

Keep away   Become friends   Try for a love connection

____   ____   ____

Why?____

____

____

____

____

Example #3: Your friend has met a person who is of different race and culture. The person is nice looking, well educated, has good income and is very friendly toward others. He or she is divorced with two children and has both a dog and cat as pets. The person owns a beautiful large home, is very religious, and can be trusted to do the right thing.

The person believes that a man should be head of the household but also believes in sharing the responsibilities of raising a family with his partner. Everything with this person is "black-and-white" with no ands or ifs. This person has a problem understanding American culture but deals with it.

What kind of advice would give your friend and why?

Keep away   Become friends   Try for a love connection

____   ____   ____

Why?____

____

____

____

____

Example #4: Your friend has met a person who has had a difficult past. The person is a good person 80 percent of the time and can be difficult 20 percent of the time. Your friend and the person he or she has met have a great many things in common. They like the outdoors, traveling, music, holding hands in public, snuggling together, and watching television.

The person is very assertive and at times will not take no for an answer. Every so often, this person will become upset over small situations and will use profanity to process his or her anger.

What kind of advice would give your friend and why?

Keep away	Become friends	Try for a love connection
____	____	____

Why?____

____

____

____

____

Example #5: This person is much older than your friend. He or she is single with no children but loves children. Although the person isn't good-looking, he or she is kind and gentle have a great personality and is very trustworthy.

He or she is a good communicator and will provide and support your friend whenever possible. He or she lives on a modest income but does well for himself or herself. He or she drinks alcohol and likes being with his or her friends on the weekends. He or she is not romantic but will never forget a birthday.

What kind of advice would give your friend and why?

Keep away	Become friends	Try for a love connection
____	____	____

Why?____

____

____

____

____

From these five examples, select the person you believe would be the best choice for your friend to "try for love connection." Our point in presenting this exercise is not to understand why two people become partners but to understand what captures a person's attention, and consequently, they "try for a love connection." And also how to recognize the *warning signs* that would make a person aware of negative behaviors that would tell them to "keep away" as this person has the potential of becoming emotionally or physically abusive.

Love and Disappointment

There are millions of men and women who are searching for the *perfect loving* relationship. What are the odds of them finding the perfect partner? The odds are enormous.

Consequently, people who search and believe that they have found the perfect love end up disappointed. Some will argue that there is no such thing as a perfect relationship, and others believe that if one delays jumping into a relationship, he or she will eventually find that perfect partner.

We believe there is a *higher power* that has designed life so that people can have the opportunity to experience everything life has to offer from the imperfect to the perfect. Nothing on earth was left half finished. What we are trying to say is, why would a high power create something that it loves to be partially complete?

Everyone has the choice to select a partner from either end of the spectrum. But many people will *settle* for a relationship based on the belief that the person they have met is as good as it's going to get for them. As a result, they try to make the best of it, or they believe that they can change the person to become what they want. The last idea is a disaster in progress. People do not want someone to change them; they want their partner to love them the way they are.

Equally important is for couples to understand that there will be ups and downs during the course of their relationship. Couples who understand these ideas will use their personal and interpersonal skills to make their relationship work. Couples will be successful in their relationship if they have faith, patience, and the ability to communicate. Their relationship may not be perfect, but it's as close to perfect as most of us will ever experience.

A relationship filled with mistrust, conflicts, and inconsistencies can become extremely disappointing. The love the couple thought they had probably wasn't love at all but rather, a need to feel close to someone without giving love an opportunity to develop.

Writers and poets speak of those who have been hurt by love. A songwriter once wrote, "Fools rush in where angels fear to tread." Obviously, this image of love takes on an eerie feeling. The songwriter must have believed that *to fall in love is to hurt*, and for some, happiness may or may not be possible because of a personal attitude toward love.

A controlling person who claims to be in love is another example of a disaster in progress. Their obsession to control their partner has priority over love. This kind of so-called love moves in the opposite direction of true love. In essence, the person is self-obsessed and does not have love for their partner, but an obsessive need to control.

Commitment to Family

We often hear people use the term *commitment*—commitment to excellence when used in sports events or business ventures. People use the term to encourage men and women to do their best toward the achievement of a particular goal.

In regard to commitment to one's family, commitment comes from the firm belief that a healthy family is of paramount importance and that both partners will contribute to the well-being of their family.

From infancy to adulthood, children are depending upon their parents and older siblings to teach them the importance of commitment through the ideas of faith, loyalty, and honesty. Many parents understand that commitment to family means everything. If you want to truly understand the term commitment, take a very close look at the animals in nature. Lions with cubs, a female bear with her young, birds with chicks, dogs with puppies, cats with kittens, even the creatures in our oceans are committed to the survival of their young. It's simply amazing the things animals will do to feed and protect their young. With some exceptions, people share those same commitments.

Fortunately for us, we do not have to go out each day and hunt for food or fight to the death to protect our young. Yet we must be committed to getting up each morning with a dedicated effort as parents to provide our family with the necessary things they need to grow and become mentally and physically healthy as adults.

Being committed to providing our family with the necessary things they need to grow and become mentally and physically healthy, our responsibility as adults and parents will, at times, come with a heavy price.

The heavy price many of us will experience will be at the hands of those who are seemingly focused on bringing us down, i.e., angry and overall negative people. Angry people are everywhere, and such negativity can be overwhelming for those of us who believe in peace and coexistence.

In regard to people who like to see others fail, let us refer back to the saying "Misery loves company." Using the example of two people sitting alone in jail the feelings of anger, loneliness, and depression continue as long as they sit alone. Once communication begins with another inmate and they begin to talk to each other about their situation, they begin to laugh and joke, and for a moment, being in jail isn't so overwhelming.

It is possible to become comfortable in a negative situation. Those who have served time in jail get out of jail saying that incarceration taught them other antisocial behaviors. People who think this way will have future problems with the law and will create new victims. Their jail term should have taught them to do the right thing and avoid breaking the law.

Despite the example given above, people who are committed to achieving the best for themselves and their family should always try to keep negativity where it belongs—outside of the relationship.

Those who are committed to achieving something positive have no need to *become comfortable* with outside negativity that will hinder their family's success.

Stressful situations placed upon our relationship by everyday life situations will often work themselves out. We must learn to avoid what we cannot change (holding it close for reference) and focus on what we can change.

Many social tensions and pressures will have very little negative effect upon a person if they are committed to maintaining a well-balanced attitude toward life in general and their life experiences.

Remember, the idea of dedication in one's relationship is developing a well-balanced commitment that offers all family members feelings of security and optimism for the future of the family.

> What a couple loses during times of stress will return in even greater abundance when they have *total commitment* toward each other, and other family members.

Self-Assessment

Following are questions to assist you with discovering whether or not you are involved in a romantic relationship. Apply personal knowledge, as well as information from the chapter, to answer *yes*, *no*, or *NA* (not applicable) to the following questions. It is important that you answer all questions as accurately and honestly as possible.

1. Do you have love and commitment in your relationship? ___
2. Do you see your relationship lasting more than twenty-five years? ___
3. Do your children understand the meaning of love? ___
4. Would you like your partner to be more romantic? ___
5. Do you believe that to love is to hurt? ___
6. Do you believe it's too late for romance at this stage in your relationship? ___
7. Do you believe that if there is no love in the home, it's time to leave the relationship? ___
8. Have you become frustrated with the way your relationship is going? ___
9. Are you and your partner willing to work to make your relationship better? ___
10. Do you teach your children about loving others and being loved? ___

The previous list of questions is to better assess the love and commitment in your relationship. If you would like to learn more about love and commitment, use the information in this workbook, and also seek professional assistance for any questions you may have that this workbook does not address.

Chapter Fourteen

The
Male and Female Role
in Relationships

Chapter's Objectives:

1. To understand the importance of being an excellent parental role model
2. To examine society's beliefs about the male and female role
3. To examine the role of mothers and fathers
4. To examine the importance of positive role models
5. To examine negative behaviors concerning role models

Questions for You to Answer as You Read This Chapter:

1. Who was your role model(s) when you were growing up?
2. When you were growing up did you think your father or mother were good role models? (yes or no) Why?
3. How are you similar or different from them now that you're an adult?
4. How does society influence gender roles in relationships?
5. Do children have a particular role in the family?

Related Chapters of Interest:

- Love and Commitment
- Trust and Respect
- Equality in Relationships
- What Is Power and Control?
- Communication Skills

Chapter Fourteen

The Male and Female Role in Relationships

The Role of Mother and Father

During the late fifties and early sixties, a typical television sitcom presented a stereotypical image of husband and father roles. The sitcom portrayed the man as head of the household, kissing his wife good-bye every morning before heading off to work in a two-piece suit and tie to provide financial support for his wife and children.

After work, the father would arrive home to a smiling wife wearing an apron who would be either in the kitchen cooking or on her way to the kitchen. The various sitcoms made it appear as if it was the mother's responsibility to cook and clean. And it was the father's responsibility to politely discipline the children.

Occasionally, the television sitcom would show the father playing catch with one of his three sons, then the scene would shift to the father who would be teaching his sons about the "Birds and the Bees." The marital relationship with his wife appeared to be nothing more than one person serving the other.

During those years, there were no sitcoms in which unmarried couples lived together or married couples lay nude or half nude in bed engulfed in an act of sex. You never saw fathers venturing outside the marriage for extramarital affairs or leaving their wives home alone to do the cooking and cleaning.

When boys become men and girls become women, they begin to realize sitcoms usually exaggerate the truth about relationships. Young adults today are moving away from the past and present stereotypical attitude toward men and women roles.

Many are beginning to understand and are experiencing real-life versions of married life. It is a common experience for a father to go to work each day to provide for the family, and mothers as well must find employment to earn money.

Today's young adults are also recognizing that although money is vital in a relationship, having money isn't what bonds a relationship, but rather the fulfillment of a basic need to support a successful relationship. Young adults are learning that a relationship between two people can be extremely complicated, perhaps more than they once imagined.

Many are beginning to understand the old saying that, "What brings two people together, such as love, sex, money or personal appearance, as one entity will never be enough to hold the relationship together." Many understand that it's essential to have and maintain a balance between good communication skills, love, sex, money, personal appearance, trust, respect and on.

Society's Idea of Male and Female Roles

What is the male's and female's role in a relationship? The male's and female's role in a relationship is a culturally determined pattern of behavior. Specifically, a person who occupies the status of *mother* or *father* is expected by their sons and daughters to behave in the manner universally developed for all parents by the society in which they live.

Society's ideal parental role model is to have the ability to communicate effectively by showing love, commitment, fairness, and honesty and to provide encouragement and praise to all family members. If this is society's idea of a parental role model, where does it all begin, i.e., when do we begin to learn about becoming a good role model? Let us begin at the stage of infancy.

Infancy to Preschool

Erik Erikson, one of the ten most celebrated psychologists of all time, believed that a person begins to develop their male and female role at *birth*. Erikson believed that infancy is the most important period of personal and social development.

An infant is unaware of their role. Consequently, while using all their human senses to explore their environment, they will go about their daily life looking, hearing, tasting, touching, and smelling everything within reach.

This is what infants do; their role is to learn about their environment. They are extremely curious. They will go about their day probing and searching to find out what's safe and what makes them happy. Infants learn very quickly how much influence they have over their parent's by crying when they are unhappy about a certain situation and laugh when they are pleased.

When infants are hungry, they will cry, and the parents will respond by feeding them. If the infant doesn't like what the parent has given them, they will show their dissatisfaction by continuing to cry until they are satisfied. The same thing can be said for movable and immovable objects.

Infants enjoy looking at shapes and colors of various objects and listening to the different kinds of sounds that an object will make. If the object that they see and hear pleases them, they will show signs of pleasure by laughing and moving about, and if they are displeased by what they see or hear, many infants will cry.

According to Erik Erikson, during *preschool* years, children will continue to establish their role through what they can and cannot control in their environment. They are forever being told not to touch things, to take things out of their mouth, to put things down, and to take a nap when it's nap time. But nothing seems to stop them from finding out what they can or cannot put into their mouths or what they can or cannot touch.

They are learning at an early age about what gives them pleasure and what pleases their parents. Their roles as little boys or girls will change dramatically as they play with various toys and interact with other children their age.

When you find the time, take a closer look at the cartoons children watch and the different kinds of toys children play with throughout the course of a given day. Try to determine what kinds of messages the cartoons relay to your children.

Are the cartoons about morality—i.e., good and bad—or is there a lot of violence in the cartoons they watch? Does the boy play with cars, trucks, boats, toy guns, daggers, or other knives? Does the little girl play with dolls and kitchen sets or wear her mother's shoes and dress up in her clothes and jewelry?

The cartoons children watch and the toys they play with will play a large part in developing the kind of person they will become. Consequently, the personality and role of the child continues in a certain direction.

A child's personality and social development also depends on being accepted by other children their age. For example, a child's self-esteem can be affected by the children they play with each day. Children who are accepted by the other children and enjoy one another's company will have healthy self-esteem. Their interaction among other children will help them to develop and improve their social skills as they grow older. Children who are left out of activities will feel alone and unwanted. The feeling of abandonment could cause a child to develop unhealthy self-esteem.

According to Erikson, during *childhood* (ages five to twelve), children continue to learn about their role as they play with other children. When children feel good about themselves and their ability to please other children, they will develop a sense of achievement and comfort. Their ability to please themselves and others will become a major factor in their continued role development.

A child's ability to achieve is a result of parents and teachers reinforcing the child's idea of believing in their ability to achieve. Parents and teachers achieve this by *encouraging* and *praising* the child. Children who receive little to no encouragement and praise from their parents or teachers will doubt their abilities.

Following are ways parents can encourage and praise their children:

- In homework situations, take time to review what they have achieved. Tell them, "Great work," and how proud you are of them for doing such excellent work
- During the process of a game they are playing, tell them about their mental and physical potential and compare them to someone proficient in their profession who plays that particular game.
- Sit down or cuddle with your children and allow them to talk about how good or bad their day has gone.
- Search for a subject that your children find interesting and discuss it with them.
- Take your children for special rides one at a time or all together.
- Always compare them to someone great.
- Tell your children that they will become great someday.
- Teach them about their personal appearance.

- If you have to punish a child, make sure that the reprimand fits the misdeed.
- When your children fail at a task, tell them that they can only beat failure when they continue to try to succeed.

These methods do wonders for a child's self-esteem. If not currently in use, employ these methods. Children will realize that it's okay to talk with you about their personal affairs.

At this point, you may be asking, this may be good information to know about childhood, but when do we begin to learn about becoming a good role model? As children begin to take a larger view of their social environment, they will begin to search for role models.

The search for a role model usually begins at home. First, they look toward their parents; second, they will look for a role model in cartoons, television programs, and action heroes.

Back in the day, many of the boys in my neighborhood had various cartoon characters as their first heroes. As we grew older (nine to twelve), we looked for our role models in sports, the music industry, politicians, military, religion, as well as in academics.

There were boys in our neighborhood who also found their heroes in the criminal world. Of course, these boys who found joy in the world of crime didn't find it as joyful as they imagined once they were caught, convicted, and sentenced for their crime.

Young boys and girls of today aren't any different than we were as children. However, today children have excess to multimedia efforts to look for their role models through cartoons, comic books, movies, video games, and the Internet.

In terms of searching for a role model in comic books, television programs, and video games, things have drastically changed. The sex and violence, which children have access through reading comic books, television programs, and video games is creating a different generation of role models.

Many children who watch sex and violence do not seem to understand the negative influence these things can have on them. So whom should children follow? Who should be their role models?

Mothers and fathers should be their role models and heroes, not the neighborhood bully, classroom clown at their school, or a science-fiction character on television or in a comic book.

There is nothing wrong with reading comic books, watching cartoons, or having childhood fantasies as long as a child can distinguish the difference between fantasy and reality. A well-balanced blend of fantasy and real life will allow a child to develop their creative mind and will enable them to distinguish the difference between a figment of their imagination and reality.

When children read traditional legends and stories or fairy tales that are handed down from generation to generation, they are further developing and expanding their minds. Stories about heroes displaying courage and distinguished valor by defeating villains and restoring peace is a great start for building healthy self-esteem and instilling personal moral values.

Let's not ignore the cowardly villains in movies and comic books who have been riddled with shame because they choose to bring harm to others. How many children want to become the villainous character that's often beaten, shot, or imprisoned?

The answer is not many; but many children can wind up beaten, shot, or imprisoned because they didn't fully understand personal and social moral values, which are instilled by good role model(s).

What are *moral values*? Moral values are a code of personal and social *ethics*. Ethics are rules of personal conduct, or the way a person behaves in a certain situation. A child's ethics can be seen in what a child thinks of himself or herself as well as how he or she perceives the world in which they live.

Perhaps the most challenging aspect of learning about personal ethics is when a child is exposed to fictional characters in epic stories concerning physical and emotional violence. Although many fictional characters in stories provide children with enlightening tales of love, wealth, misfortune, hardship, death, and violence, the difficulty arises when a child *chooses* to imitate the violent character in a particular story.

The child may be easily influenced by reading these stories, which could lead to a totally unrealistic view of the world. Of course, we do not believe all little boys and girls develop warring minds as a result of watching and reading about sex and violence. What we do believe is that stories of sex and violence can contribute to the negative behaviors seen in most children with behavioral problems.

This can be seen in children who believe that using violence will get them what they want. Children witness sex and violence every day. They see the bad guy or girl make large sums of money and get the beautiful girls or handsome boys; and they also see them get shot, beaten, and imprisoned. So why would a young boy or girl take the risk of being shot, beaten, or going to prison when they realize that the bad guys or girls always get caught? Ask yourself this question and think about it for a while, and wait and see what answers you create.

From Boys to Men
From Girls to Women

As we have stated, children begin to learn from their parents at an early age. Children watch their parents carry out many of the different household duties that they themselves will have to perform when they become adults.

Parents who share in all the household obligations teach children the idea of shared responsibility. For example, parents who share in the responsibilities of cooking, cleaning, and making sure their children are kept bathed and clean and communicate effectively are teaching their children how to maintain domestic harmony.

When children reach *adolescence* (ages thirteen to twenty), hopefully, their parents have given them a great deal of affection, encouragement, and praise. If mothers and fathers have performed their role as loving, trusting, and respectful parents, their children will have learned from their guidance.

Their children would have developed the necessary skills that will help them on their journey toward becoming morally healthy adults.

Most teenagers will take the knowledge parents have taught them and develop a desperate need for personal independence. They will develop a strong urge to see and experience the world outside of their immediate environment.

If you have teenagers in your home, each teenager will want to go their separate way to exercise their mental and physical strengths. This does not replace teenager's need for continued parental assistance, yet they do have the need for a certain amount of self-rule (autonomy).

Parents who are good role models must understand their teenager's need for independence, which can often be terrifying to some teenagers; but they will survive.

We use the word *most* when describing teenagers and personal independence because there are teenagers who would rather live at home until they are thirty years old, rather than try to make it on their own.

While most parents have fulfilled their responsibilities as good role models, many teenagers will continue to ask themselves questions like, who am I? And where am I going in life?

As a teenager explores the outside world, it may become confusing. In many cases, they will find out the world isn't like what they read in comic books and magazines or saw on television. Also they find out that having a good attitude could be the difference between getting what they want or not.

Many teenagers will realize very quickly that a good attitude can take them a long way, and a bad attitude can stop them in their tracks. Many will quickly realize what their parents have been teaching them about how one's attitude can have positive or negative effects on their life.

They will quickly realize that having a bad attitude will keep them from finding an excellent-paying job and deny them the opportunity of finding a good partner.

Teenagers whose parents were bad role models and were unsure of themselves when they were a child—and they did not receive encouragement and praise from such parents—will continue to be unsure or remain confused about their future and their ability to achieve.

However, many teenagers who are unsure of themselves will eventually learn how to achieve and will become successful after experiencing a lot of difficulty through trials, errors, and drawbacks.

Young Adults

Adolescents dream of the day when they will become twenty-one and are recognized by society as an *adult.* You have probably heard your children repeatedly say, "I can't wait until I am grown." Well, here they are! At this stage in their personal and social development, they should be anxious to explore new relationships with young adults their age and older.

Erikson believed that it's very important that young adults develop endearing and loyal relationships with people they choose to share their time. Young adults who are fortunate enough to meet people with healthy attitudes and well-developed positive ideas are able to avoid many of the difficult days that lay ahead.

At the age of twenty-one, young adults are naturally curious about life roles and are constantly searching for their identity. Most teenagers are thinking about becoming an adult and the responsibilities that come with being an adult. They are trying to find out who they are and where they are going in life. At this stage of development, teenagers *are searching for stability.*

Teenagers will read books designed to educate, encourage, support, and comfort them during this growing period in their lives. They have learned that people in general have many of the answers they need.

They believe that they are able to speak freely and respectably with mature family members, friends, and fellow employees, or, at times, with a total stranger to obtain many of the answers to their questions.

Young adults who grow up well nurtured by parents consistent in their behaviors *will learn to be consistent themselves.* Young adults who have listened and learned from the advice their parents has given them during their adolescent years will have the ability to appropriately answer many of their own questions.

Questions concerning life, their role in life, and their destiny will be difficult to answer at times; but eventually, they will find the answer after taking time to think seriously about where they have been, to where they intend to go.

Conversely, young adults who are unable to maintain a certain amount of consistency in their behavior or find appropriate answers to questions concerning their role in relationships will always doubt their true destiny.

Adults are often faced with doubts about who they are or where they are headed in life and will often create a destiny filled with cruel and unforgiving acts of antisocial behaviors. These young adults will often become domestic abusers and batterers.

If young adult males or females decide to take on this role, their way of thinking and behaving will be inappropriate for the development of serious and loving relationships. They will exist in a world of their own, where social rules, morals, and values are not seen as something good, but as obstacles. If the young adult's abusive behavior goes unopposed by law enforcement, they may continue to act out through acts of violence. Our communities, prison systems, and cemeteries are filled with young adults who share this attitude.

Where would a young adult get the idea that our social rules, morals, and values are obstacles that should be avoided? These ideas are often derived from bad role models at home, violent movies, books and the advisement of both young and older adults with inappropriate belief systems.

Many of these outdated belief systems are slowly fading. Those men and women who refuse to give up the idea of changing their outdated beliefs will continue to try to *outsmart* everyone with whom they come into contact. They will try to control those believed to be weaker than they are looking to gain love, sex, or money.

Exercise

Following are examples of the negative beliefs some men and women have concerning male and female roles in domestic situations. Read each statement and answer with *true* or *false*.

1. A woman's role in a family is to cook, clean, wash, iron, feed, and cloth their children. ___
2. Women who were physically abused in the past have learned to accept being abused. ___
3. Women are terrible decision makers and therefore must support the decisions of their partner whether the decisions are right or wrong. ___
4. Men are the providers and should control what happens in the home. ___
5. Women are slow in their thinking and consequently make too many costly mistakes. ___
6. Women act helpless to manipulate men. ___
7. Jealousy is proof of love. ___
8. Men are better at earning family income than women. ___
9. Women are uneconomical and like to waste money. ___
10. Women have children to trick men into marrying and supporting them. ___

> Opinions like those above are shared by men and women who actually believe them to be true. Many, if not all, of these negative beliefs will usually continue unchecked and will be handed down from friend to friend and from father to son.

Following are examples of positive beliefs concerning male roles in domestic situations:

- A man's role is to assist in the protection and caring of the family.
- Men and women are equally capable of raising children when they have the necessary parenting skills.
- Men and women have different skills in certain areas of the relationship, and each should be allowed to exercise those skills.
- Decisions are a shared responsibility between partners.
- Men are forever learning and growing along with their partner.
- There is no "boss," only a partner who must take the lead when it becomes necessary.
- Jealousy is one of the most destructive forces in a relationship.
- There is no monetary price you can put on a healthy relationship.

- It's understood that if a relationship doesn't work out, either partner should have the right to separate or file for a divorce, without the fear of being harmed.
- Love and commitment to self and family is of paramount importance.

The positive beliefs mentioned above are only a few of the many beliefs couples should learn to understand and accept.

Self-Assessment

Following are statements to assist you with understanding the idea of the male and female roles. Apply personal knowledge, as well as information from the chapter, to answer *true*, *false*, or *NA* (not applicable) to the following statements. It is important that you answer all statements as accurately and honestly as possible.

1. I understand my role as mother or father. ___
2. I am my family's champion and protector. ___
3. The male and female roles are first taught at home by parents, who understand the social and emotional development of boys and girls. ___
4. Men should assist in every aspect of family life such as cooking, cleaning, washing, and caring for the children and their partner. ___
5. My partner and I share in making all household decisions. ___
6. I have a deep love and respect for my family. ___
7. The image of the male role in America needs to be improved. ___
8. My partner and I will read and understand the ideas concerning childhood development. ___
9. My partner and I will seek professional assistance for anything we don't quite understand about ourselves and our children. ___
10. My children are the future. ___

The previous list of statements is to better assess you with understanding your teenager. If you believe that it is necessary for you to make any needed adjustments in the way you treat your children, use the information in this workbook, and also seek professional assistance for any questions you may have that this workbook does not address.

Chapter Fifteen

Parenting Skills

Chapter's Objectives:

1. To address the social concept of family
2. To provide information concerning the stages of infancy, childhood, and adolescence
3. To discuss issues concerning the positive and negative aspects of parenting
4. To address the important personal and interpersonal skills parents should teach their children
5. To address domestic violence in the family

Questions for You to Answer as You Read This Chapter:

1. Why do children behave the way they do?
2. What could a baby smell in the home that could have a negative effect on their mental development?
3. Who has the most influence on children, their parents or friends?
4. Do you understand your parental responsibility?
5. What is the best age to begin to teach your children to think things out for themselves?

Related Chapters of Interest:

- Communication Skills
- Economic Abuse
- Economic Partnership
- Substance Abuse within the Family
- The Effect Domestic Violence Has on Children

Chapter Fifteen

Parenting Skills

The Family

There are two basic definitions of a family: a group of persons of common ancestry and a group of individuals living under one roof, usually with one head of household. Individuals living under one roof can consist of a two-parent family, single-parent family, foster family, stepparent family, or gay-and-lesbian family.

The family has always been the building blocks of a society. Yet only within the last two decades has society realized the importance of family unity. Society has begun to recognize family members for who they are and not what society would like them to be.

Society is also beginning to realize that it doesn't matter whether a family member has an IQ of 150, mentally ill, mentally retarded, physically handicapped, or gay or lesbian. All that truly matters is when people come together as two or more individuals, they are considered as a *family*. As the saying goes, "Friends will come, and friends will go, but a *family* is forever." That statement is so true. When a man and woman who have children divorce and become single parents, they may lose their status as husband and wife, but they will forever be connected to their children and their family of origin.

Although everyone has a family before he or she is married, a new family is created when two people meet, fall in love (or not fall in love), and eventually have children. Once a couple has children, the children will continue the family's ancestry to another generation.

Like their forefathers, this new generation of boys and girls will eventually become men and women—men and women who will not only continue their family's bloodline but will also continue the family's traditions through their beliefs and behaviors.

It is a family's beliefs and behaviors that can be the difference between success and failure of a family. When we speak of the success of a family, we are speaking specifically about a family's mental, physical, economic, and marital success. We must also add that to become a successful family, no family member has to be perfect.

Due to the fact that no one is perfect, consequently, no parent is perfect. Every man and woman who become parents will make *mistakes* along the path of parenthood. Once young adults with a newborn baby understand their role as parents, their lifestyle as parents will take on an entirely new meaning. As parents, they will quickly realize what they did as a child and as an adolescent will no longer be as important as becoming a good nurturing parent.

Young adults who have children must understand their role as parents and realize that their children will someday become young adults. They must realize that it's their responsibility to be good role models and teach their children how to survive, prosper, and become respectful and responsible adults.

The question is, can any parent be positively sure that their children will grow up and become respectful and responsible adults? Parents cannot be absolutely sure that their children will grow up and become a respectful and responsible adult. Like their parents before them, the choice for any child to become a respectful and responsible adult will be their own choice to make. Their personality and the skills they have learned over the years will determine whether or not they will become supportive and gentle or mentally or physically abusive toward their children. The choice will be theirs to make, and the choice they make is one that they will have to live with for the rest of their life.

Those of us who have a family can think back to when we were children. Many of us never imagined how mentally and physically draining it was for our parents to nurture us into becoming well-adjusted adults.

Infancy

Couples who haven't had children as of yet *must realize* that there is a lot more to giving birth than buying a crib, clothes, a new stroller, and looking at the baby and going *gi-gi gugu*. Young parents must realize long before their baby arrives that they must be committed, caring, and patient with their newborn at all times.

They must also realize that as their baby grows, as parents, they will come into contact with new problems and questions, but there is no reason for them to panic. There is always someone who can assist young parents with their problems and questions.

For example, there will be questions like, why does my baby keep crying after I have done everything that I can to stop him or her from crying? What should I feed my baby and how often? What should I do when my baby will not eat? What should I do when my baby cannot sleep? How do I handle a tantrum? How often should I take my baby to the doctor's office? And what should I do when I become overly stressed?

We are not going to attempt to provide parents with answers to these questions. We recommend parents who have questions about their infant to seek *professional advice* to assist them with maintaining a stable and loving environment for their child.

We know for a fact that learning about caring for a baby is a serious affair, and learning about the needs of a baby through *trial and error is definitely not the answer*. One other point we would like to make concerning your baby: friends who have children may be good for sharing parental experiences.

However, all children aren't the same, so think twice before following a friend's advice about caring for *your* baby. Friends will tell you to first try this, and if that does not work, then try something different. This is your baby you're experimenting with, and if your baby becomes even more ill, it's not your friend's problem; it will be your problem.

Always seek professional assistance when problems arise that you do not understand how to solve. It's much safer for your newborn as well as for your emotional stability. It is therefore important that parents learn about their newborn baby so their child will have an opportunity for excellent mental development.

Although we will not provide information concerning any illness of an infant, the following are a few of the basic facts a parent must accept to assist their infant in his or her mental development:

- Touching your baby is important. It is critical to understand the difference between rough treatment and gentle treatment of your baby.
  For example, if you traditionally believe that roughhousing is the correct method to make a baby tough, you are sadly and tragically mistaken. Babies love a soft touch.

- When talking to your baby, use soft voice tones.
  For example, babies understand the difference between a positive and negative tone of voice and will react accordingly. Talking softly and singing to your baby will keep your baby calm.
- Caring what your child observes and smells.
  For example, babies love small things that have color and move. Cigarette and marijuana smoke, strong perfumes, colognes, alcohol, and household chemicals all can have a negative effect on the child, particularly those with intoxicating aromas.
- Communicate with your child's needs and wants; it is the parent's responsibility to read these messages with parental interest and act accordingly.

For example, when your baby is hungry, sleepy, wet, or needs to be held, do not wait until the game is over, a television show ends, or you have finished cooking. Remember, when a baby cries, he or she is not crying to get on your nerves; he or she is crying because that's how he or she communicates.

Although the local library and Internet have volumes of information concerning the mental and physical development of infants, we believe parents should always contact their child's doctor for answers to any questions concerning their infant's mental and physical well-being.

We cannot stress enough the importance of each parent obtaining the best information possible to properly care for his or her baby. Also remember it's not the responsibility of friends, other family members, or neighbors to provide information on the health care of newborn babies.

Exercise

The following exercise is to test your knowledge concerning infant care. Answer the following statements with *true* or *false*:

- Young adults know all the answers and have all the skills to care for a newborn. ___
- Young adults must learn the skills necessary to care for a newborn. ___
- Babies like to be touched with hands that hold him or her gently. ___
- Babies communicate by crying. ___
- Babies have two kinds of cries: one when they are hungry and one when they are hurting. ___
- It's okay when a baby sneezes, hiccups, or coughs. ___
- If a baby constantly coughs, parents should consult the baby's physician. ___
- A baby's environment needs to be safe. ___
- Babies are fast learners. ___
- Babies learn by playing with appropriate toys. ___

The above statements are a very small percent of what parents should know about newborns. If you have any questions about the care off your infant, contact the baby's physician.

Childhood

Childhood is between the ages five and twelve. It's a period in human development that can best be described as an age of mystery and having as much fun as possible. Although the spirit of childhood is to play and pretend, it's during this age period that children will spend a large part of their time physically and mentally growing and developing their minds.

It doesn't matter whether a child's only toy is an old car tire with a stick to guide it or a room full of toys; their only concern is to have a much fun as their mental and physical energy will allow.

As children play, one of many things they enjoy doing is to act as if they are adults. Little girls like to wear their mother's clothing and promenade around the house pretending to be an adult woman.

Little boys will pretend to be a truck driver, cowboy, or a soldier, fighting fierce battles with an imaginary enemy. This is one of many characteristics children throughout the world have in common; that's to have as much fun as they can and for as long as they can.

Children also have a great imagination. When children use their boundless creative energy, they can magically transform themselves into anyone and anything as easily as it is to close their eyes.

One minute, a little boy can become Superman, leaping tall builds in a single bound, and the next they could be riding through a deep forest slaying dragons. A little girl can one minute become a little princess, and the next minute, they can become Supergirl, leaping tall buildings in a single bound.

Children love to play the part of a hero. And it doesn't matter whether the hero is a bad guy or a good guy. For children, a good hero always saves lives or keeps someone from getting hurt. Bad heroes, someone like Robin Hood, a thief who steals from the rich and give to the poor, are heroes that children aspire to imitate.

Laughter is something else children love to do. Depending on the situation, children will laugh until they cry and stop laughing for a moment, think for a second, and begin laughing once again over the same situation.

Laughter for a child seems better than food at times. For many children, even when they are being punished for something they may have done, if they can find something to laugh about, they can survive any parental punishment.

What is the parents' role during this period in the life of their child? In the past, society had a mother or housewife sex-role stereotype in which it was the mother's responsibility to stay at home and make sure the children were fed, clothed, and the house kept clean. The father's role was more laid-back. He would arrive home from work, sit back for a while, eat dinner, and watch television.

In the past, as well as in today's society, many fathers do not arrive home from work and greet their children with a smile and ask them about their day at school. For one reason or another, most fathers of today seem to keep a distance between themselves and their children.

In many homes, the children can see that Dad has the most influence, and he is the breadwinner, provider, decision maker; and above all, he is the disciplinarian. Mom is often the cushion between father and child. Mom is also the children's provider and protector.

However, she will not hesitate to tell the child, "Wait until your father comes home," if they misbehave. After that statement, the children are supposed to drop what they were doing and wait until Dad comes home, not knowing if their father would yell, whip, or threaten them with some kind of later punishment.

Parents are beginning to realize there must be a balance between being a mother or father. Many fathers are now cooking, cleaning, and are involved in outdoor and indoor activities with their children. Many fathers are finding time to assist his children with their homework and are available to answer any questions their children may have.

Many mothers are no longer playing the emotional mental game with her children. If she believes that her children have misbehaved, she will discipline them as opposed to waiting until their father arrives home from work.

Fathers are beginning to take a more hands-on approach to what his children are doing. Many fathers are beginning to laugh, joke, and play with their children without believing that he will be seen as less than a father by doing these things with his children.

Children and Knowledge

During childhood, little boys and girls can obtain a tremendous amount of knowledge about themselves and life in general if they are taught. And when parents do not think they are teaching their children, children are learning from what their parents are saying and how their parents are behaving.

When children are playing, many are acting out behaviors they experience at home. For example, many little boys between the ages of eight to eleven will become *more* interested in little girls. Many little boys will say and do what they have seen their fathers or older brothers do to get their mother's, sister's, or girlfriend's attention.

Boys who have learned to communicate and behave at home will often be gentle with their words and behavior toward other children, particularly little girls. However, there are boys who will chase and tease little girls.

The sad part about these boys is that they will chase and tease little girls until they make them cry. What many little boys are trying to do is get the little girl's attention. In essence, the little boy is trying to tell the little girl that he likes her and will she pay attention to him.

We must remember children do not want to be bad; they are only doing what they have been taught by others. Of course, many parents will tell you that "I will never teach my son to hurt little girls, or teach my little girl to taunt little boys."

Of course, parents didn't directly teach them to hurt or taunt other children. But what about indirectly teaching them how to do hurtful things to other boys and girls? The child had to learn it from someone, and it usually *begins at home*.

If a child's parents constantly argue and fight or if a boy's or girl's favorite television character seems heartless in his or her behavior toward a particular ethnic group or gender, the child will take on that characteristic during play.

Life for little boys and girls isn't all about being bad. Not all children who are witness to negative behavior find it something they would like to do. For example, when children are asked what they would like to become when they grow up, many children will remark, "I want to become a doctor, lawyer, policeman, schoolteacher, or maybe a fireman."

Many children love to dream and talk about becoming someone great and exciting. I have yet to hear a child tell their parents they want to grow up and become a *nobody*, a *loser*, or grow up to steal and harm others and possibly spend the rest of their life in a federal or state penitentiary.

And yet, many children do grow up and steal and harm others and spend the rest of their lives in a penitentiary. We have made this point several times and thought that it's worth mentioning again and again until every parent realizes this fact of life.

Parents must realize that children have rights. And one of those rights is for them to achieve greatness if greatness is what they seek. As parents, it's our responsibility to assist our children with achieving their goals whether their goal brings celebrity status or not.

As parents, we must teach our children to understand the fundamental ideas of life. Qualities such as love, loyalty, courage, self-reliance, truthfulness, genuineness, morality, and healthy self-esteem are all personality traits that will guide children through the difficult times.

Parents must understand their children and provide them with the necessary knowledge and physical skills to be able to manage the difficult days they will encounter. Children must be taught how to use their time and minds to create wonderful and unique ideas so they can get the best out of their lives.

Once the child has completely understood the appropriate teachings of their parents, knowledge and wisdom will be their greatest companions. If you are a parent and you would like the world to become a better place and you would like your child to be someone the world can be proud of, let the change for a better world begin at home.

Exercise

How well do you know your children? Following are questions to assist you with how well you know your children. Apply personal knowledge, as well as information from the chapter, to answer *yes*, *no*, or *NA* (not applicable) to the following questions:

- Do your children misbehave? ___
- Do you know why your children misbehave? ___
- Do you believe children should be punished when they misbehave? ___
- Do you believe children should be physically punished when they misbehave? ___For example, spanked, whipped, or hit in any way. If so, why; and if not, why?

  ____
  ____
  ____
  ____
  ____

- Have you ever used threats to control your children? ___
- Have your children ever been witness to domestic violence in the home? ___
- Has your child told you what he or she would like to become when they become adults? ___
- Are you in a mental and financial position to assist them with their goal? ___
- Do you ever take time to talk and listen to your children's problems or the things they enjoy doing? ___
- Have any of your children ever lied to you? If the answer is yes, what did you say or do? ___

  ____
  ____
  ____
  ____
  ____

- Would you like your children to copy your husband or wife's behaviors when playing with other children? Why?

  ____
  ____
  ____
  ____
  ____

The previous list of questions is to better assess you with what you understand about your children. If you believe that it is necessary for you to learn more about childhood, seek professional assistance for any questions you may have that this workbook does not address.

Adolescence

When we speak of adolescence, there is early and late adolescence. Early adolescence is the ages between eleven and fourteen years of age, and late adolescence is the ages between fifteen and twenty. There are many important changes an adolescent will experience during this period in their life.

Between ages eleven and fourteen, adolescents will experience puberty (sexual maturity). As teenagers grow into their midteens, their thoughts and behavior will become more secretive. Many teenagers will develop their own opinions about certain social and cultural beliefs, which may come in conflict with their parent's beliefs.

Many teenagers will also begin to focus more on their appearance than when they were in their childhood, and their appearance will be of major importance. In a teenager's world, the way one dresses announces, to a large degree, to other teenagers who they are.

Although they will still depend upon their parents for assistance, they will begin to feel a need for more privacy and freedom. This new sense of independence often causes conflict between parents and their children. The most common conflicts that take place between teenagers and parents are staying out late at night, not doing their homework without being told, and dressing in new styles in clothing.

For example, for many teenagers, the things that matter or the fun they will have doesn't begin until later in the evening, hence, the conflict between parent and teenager. Also in many communities across the country, the colors red, blue, and black are colors that stand for membership in a gang of some kind, hence, the conflict with the law.

When most adolescents disobey their parents, it's not because they are trying to create conflict with their parents. Many teenagers disobey their parents because of peer pressure and the need to fit in with other teenagers whether the other teenagers are good or bad.

Of course, all children will not behave in this manner; many teenagers will map out their own path and not rely on others to guide them. However, there are certain teenagers who will test their parents to the limit to see how they will react toward a certain situation and will continue to test their parents to see how far they can go.

In any case, parents must understand that they were teenagers once. And many of the same needs and wants they had as teenagers are now the needs and wants of their teenagers. This is a period, which parents must understand, that their children are making a very difficult transition from childhood to adolescence.

Parents must understand that their teenager will be exposed to new social uncertainties and will need their advice and guidance more than ever. For example, some, but not all, teenagers are exposed to other teenagers who have developed bad habits. Some of those bad habits can be seen in their using of illegal drugs, stealing, lying more than usual, hanging with the wrong group of teenagers, and having premarital sex. These bad habits are real and are waiting for teenagers who have not been made aware of their risks.

Although parents will become frustrated with their teenager's behavior at times, parents must remain alert and closely involved with their teenager's social activities.

Parents who take the time to closely monitor their teenager's social activities can, within reason, keep their teenager from becoming seriously injured in fistfights or auto accidents, running away from home, being incarcerated, inflicting self-injury, committing a homicide, or committing suicide.

Naturally, most of the responsibility of understanding our social environment belongs to the teenager because parents cannot remain with their teenager twenty-four hours a day. In many cases, it doesn't matter how close parents are to their children.

Many teenagers will use every deception at their disposal to make their parents believe they are doing one thing when actually, they are doing something entirely different. Parents must not give in. Parents must remain even closer to their teenager than ever before.

Parents can learn more about their teenager's personality and behaviors outside of the home environment by knowing their teenager's teachers in school, friends, boyfriends or girlfriends, and even the parents of their friends.

Parents should know where their children go (hang out) and what they do when they get there. Parents are usually surprised when they find out there are two people who know more about their teenager's true personality than they do. That's the teenager's best friend and their schoolteachers. Learn more about your teenager because there is a lot to learn.

Any parent who believes in the saying "out of sight, out of mind" is only asking for his or her teenager to find trouble, and believe me, they will find trouble because trouble is everywhere.

Adolescence and Domestic Violence

Any form of domestic violence could cause a teenager to feel emotionally insecure about their future. When a teenager has witnessed threats of violence, intimidation, isolation, and constant emotional abuse toward themselves or another family member, the consequences for such behavior will have a negative effect on his or her mental development.

Many men and women who have experienced previous acts of violence in their home as children speak of forgiving their parents for those dreadful days, months, and years of violence. They also speak of how difficult it is to forget the violence they experienced.

When an adolescent eventually decides to leave home, it should be a source of pleasure to want to be out on his or her own. It also should be a time when an adolescent can look back and have positive thoughts about his or her parents and how he or she was loved and nurtured as a child.

Unfortunately, many adolescents will not allow themselves to think of their childhood or teenage years for fear of the memories of the domestic horrors that once haunted them as a child.

It's distressing to believe that millions of children will have little relief from their nightmares of their past relationship with an abusive parent.

Any parent who is reading this chapter and believe in the motto "spare the rod, spoil the child" must realize that their teenager will someday fight back in some sort of way and bring any sort of physical punishment to a *halt*, particularly young teenage boys.

There are people who believe in "spare the rod, spoil the child." Parents who use physical violence to punish their children do not realize the consequences of such punishment. Teenagers who are whipped will develop one of three attitudes.

They will either become mean (delinquent), timid (abused by others) or (abusers or batterers) and continue the belief that children should be whipped into obedience. No one likes to be hit, and teenagers are not different. When a parent hits his or her teenager, the teenager will feel resentful and will often take revenge by either hitting someone else or will take their aggression out in other ways.

Once again, we recommend professional assistance for any child who was forced to witness the horrors of domestic violence.

Parental Guidance

Although certain aspects of raising a child can be parentally challenging, there are many years of pure satisfaction. For example, watching your children go from infancy to childhood, and enter into adolescence. To be there when your infant begins to crawl, takes their first step, and says their first word are all moments that can often bring tears to the eyes of most parents.

Whether a couple is married, separated, or divorced, parents must be mindful of their equal obligations to nurture their children and give them the basic skills for personal and social survival. This fact of life cannot be emphasized enough, particularly in today's stressful society.

Many Americans continue to hold stubbornly to old, outdated belief systems. For example, "I can only teach my children the way my parent(s) taught me." The problem with this idea is simple; if one or either of the parent's was controlling and abusive, such a statement and their consequent behavior may cause more damage than good.

Are parents continuing to teach their children how to use abusive tactics to control family members? Unfortunately, in some cases, the answer to that question is yes. We would also have to add the question, how would a parent know if they are teaching their children bad parenting skills if they do not know of any other way?

Children not only have the right to be empowered with the essential human survival skills but also be taught how to parent. We must begin to prepare our children from birth for the difficult years ahead.

Many parents are fully aware of the competitive nature of our society. For children to be competitive and become successful, children must be prepared to meet any and all challenges that lie ahead.

There is one other point we would like to make. Children can absorb a tremendous amount of information. They seem to see and hear everything. They learn by watching and listening and do not forget as much as many parents think they forget, particularly when they have been harmed in anyway.

Children remember the kinds of punishments that were handed out by their parents, their personal problems, and the disappointments their parents had to endure. They also remember how their parents always seem to have found some kind of solution to their problems. They remember how their parents worked and struggled to make ends meet.

They remember the days and nights when their parents didn't agree but found someway to compromise to keep harmony in the family. They also remember the criticizing, blaming, yelling, arguing, hitting, and slamming of doors. And later, the long nights of conversations between their parents to keep their family together. Oh yes, children do remember the good as well as the bad.

Self-Assessment

Following are statements to assist you with determining what areas of parenting you believe need improvement. Apply personal knowledge, as well as information from the chapter, to answer *true*, *false*, or *NA* (not applicable) to the following statements. It is important that you answer all statements as accurately and honestly as possible.

1. One of my children is disruptive in school. ___
2. One of my children keeps to himself or herself and cries a lot. ___
3. I know one of my children smokes and drinks alcohol. ___
4. There is domestic violence in my home. ___
5. I believe in "spare the rod, spoil the child." ___
6. I know my children's friends and teachers. ___
7. My children love and respect me. ___
8. If my children are learning from my partner and me, they will become great parents themselves. ___
9. My adolescent boy or girl hangs with the wrong crowd. ___
10. My children are on the right path to becoming respectable adults. ___

The previous list of statements is to better assess you with understanding your teenager. If you believe that it is necessary for you to make any needed adjustments in the way you treat your children, use the information in this workbook, and also seek professional assistance for any questions you may have that this workbook does not address.

Chapter Sixteen

Substance Abuse within the Family

Chapter's Objectives:

1. To provide information concerning chemical dependency
2. To provide information concerning chemical dependency within the family
3. To provide information concerning problems associated with chemical dependency
4. To view parental chemical dependency and how it affects their children
5. To provide the reader with a plan for receiving treatment for chemical dependency

Questions for You to Answer as You Read This Chapter:

1. How can you tell when a family member is abusing alcohol or other drugs?
2. Is there someone in your family who you believe is abusing alcohol or some other drug?
3. Do you believe alcoholism or other drugs can damage or destroy a family?
4. What is the first step to recovery?
5. What are the steps to remaining drug free?

Related Chapters of Interest:

- Parenting Skills
- Communication Skills
- What Is Domestic Violence?
- Anger Management
- A Relapse Prevention Plan

Chapter Sixteen

Substance Abuse within the Family

Substance Abuse

Substance abuse is a major problem affecting families in our society, with no regard for race, culture, or economic status. The abuse of alcohol and other drugs are powerful enemies that can invade a peaceful home or a home already in conflict.

The problems connected to substance abuse is partly or completely responsible for numerous cases of domestic violence, breakup of relationships, increased crime, automobile accidents, illness, and the lost job opportunities in our country.

Our generation is better educated than previous generations on the negative effects of alcohol and drugs. Magazines articles, books, radio, and television are doing their part to demonstrate the negative effects of alcohol and drugs on the family system.

People who are living the nightmare of alcohol and drug use are trying desperately to find all the information they can by attending workshops, reading books, going to self-help groups, and listening to self-help tapes on the subject of the dangers of substance abuse in the family.

Despite all the information that's available concerning substance-abuse prevention, the problem of substance abuse continues to rise.

Although the information is available for those who may need it, many people do not seek out this information. And for many who do read this information do not seem to understand, the message of the dangers of substance abuse and continue to use their drug of choice.

And families that also have had access to the information do not seem to change their ways in terms of dealing with their loved one with the substance problem. This is mainly due to the powerfulness of the disease of substance abuse and addiction of the abuser, which actually takes control of the person's mind and body and erodes their ability to reason with any degree of certainty.

What Is Substance Abuse?

There are many terms that are used to describe alcohol and drug abuse: *substance abuse, drug abuse, drug addiction, alcoholism, alcohol abuse,* and *chemical dependency.*

Any one of these terms that relates to substance abuse occur when the person begins to repeatedly use substances. Let us define some of these terms to gain a better understanding of the drug problem that our society is currently facing.

Substance abuse is when one continues to use a drug, and it is causing a repeated problem in one's life. For example, repeated arrests for driving under the influence of alcohol or repeated firing from jobs due to missing too many days of work as one is out using or recovering from using. This may also be described as drug abuse or alcohol abuse.

Substance dependence is when one continues to use the drug and is, in fact, obsessed with the drug even though the problems related to its use continue and increase over time. The person now develops tolerance to the substance—having to use more and more to obtain the desired effect.

The brain actually adapts to the excessive use of the drug so that when the person stops or decreases the use, withdrawal symptoms appear. The person continues to abuse the drug(s) even though he or she knows it is seriously affecting his or her life and causing increased family, social, legal, health, and/or psychological problems.

The constant consumption of habit-forming substances often leads to many personal and interpersonal problems. For example:

- Depression, anxiety
- Harmful sexual acts
- Fantasies that could injure self or others
- Health problems (such as cirrhosis of the liver and death in extreme cases)

- Financial problems
- Social problems
- Violent behavior
- Employment problems
- Auto accidents

The person now may be spending a large amount of time and money searching for and using the drug of choice. The user may begin to withdraw from parts of his or her life, which once used to be important to him or her.

For example, he or she may begin avoiding spending time with the family or being no longer active in activities that he or she once enjoyed as it would interfere with his or her use. This stage of abuse may also be described as drug addiction, alcoholism, or chemical dependency.

Intoxication

A drug is any substance that affects one's thinking or behavior. Although this would include caffeine in coffee and nicotine in cigarettes, this chapter will focus on the illegal drugs, prescribed medications that are abused, and alcohol.

The following is a list of legal and illegal drugs that are commonly abused as well as the street names that are used for some of these drugs:

- Sedatives (alcohol, barbiturates, tranquilizers; street name: yellow jackets)
- Stimulants (Benzedrine, Dexedrine; street name: crystal, crack, speed, coke)
- Hallucinogens (LSD, STP, mescaline; street name: acid)
- Inhalants and hydrocarbons (household products, glue, paint thinner, gas in whip cream containers, airplane glue, ether; street names: huffing, sniffing, and wanging. Street names: gluey)
- Marijuana (street names: weed, pot, bud)
- Narcotics (heroin, opium; street names: H, snow, sticky, white lady)
- Anabolic steroids (a group of powerful compounds closely related to the male sex hormone testosterone)

> Studies have shown that the most commonly abused substance is alcohol, followed by marijuana, cocaine, methamphetamine, and heroin. These and other drugs inflict serious damage upon American families every year.

Whether it is the first-time use of a substance or after years of use, studies show one of the most common problems of using substances is intoxication. Intoxication is the effect of the drug on the brain when the drug is present in the body. This can occur soon after consuming any substance that may cause a person to become sedated or *high*.

As one continues to use the substances at a rate faster than the body can eliminate it, the drug begins to affect the brain. The more substance in the brain directly leads to increased signs of intoxication. This leads to increasing negative effects on a person's perception, concentration, decision-making abilities, and body coordination, which in turn leads to impaired judgment, aggression, inappropriate sexual behavior, impaired driving, and bad social or occupational functioning.

Unfortunately, many people believe that drinking or using illegal drugs will help them through difficult times. Although this belief may be true for the person without a substance-abuse problem, a moderate amount of a certain substances as a glass of alcohol or the recommended use of a prescribed medication may settle a person's nerves. But once a person overindulges, the alcohol or drug they are using can, at times, instantly change their mood from good to bad and then from bad to worse.

Psychologically, the mood of intoxicated persons can suddenly change from calm to rage within seconds. For example, one minute they can be happy and laughing, and the next second, they can go into an out-of-control rage. One minute they can be calm and easy to talk to, and within seconds, they can become intolerable to be near with. Living under such conditions can be challenging for any family who wants to live and enjoy life.

As you can see, becoming intoxicated can become a disabling and dangerous concern for everyone, particularly when it involves domestic violence, automobile accidents, personal accidents, and unemployment.

Withdrawal—A Symptom of Substance Dependence

It's important to be able to identify the symptoms of withdrawal. Withdrawal can become a medical emergency and also lead to problematic behavior because of the symptoms themselves or the person's overwhelming drive to seek more substance in order to deal with the symptoms or cravings.

When a person has repeatedly abused drugs and then abruptly decreases or stops the use, they most likely will go into withdrawal. The symptoms of withdrawal that are experienced depend on the drug(s) abused.

Depending on the drug, the symptoms may first appear within less than an hour up to several weeks after one decreases or stops using the substance.

The mental and physical symptoms during withdrawal are

- sweating;
- pulse rate greater than one hundred beats per minute;
- trembling hands;
- upset stomach or vomiting;
- auditory hallucinations or illusions (hearing voices or noises that others do not hear and seeing things that others do not see);
- convulsive seizures;
- distress in social, occupational, or other important areas of functioning;
- powerful urges to keep using;

If a person continues to use the drug despite these problems, it's a sign that professional help is needed. Also, one should seek medical guidance to safety withdrawal from habit-forming substances.

The emotional and physical symptoms of withdrawal may lead to problematic and even violent behavior. Withdrawal from substances may be life threatening and should be done under medical supervision.

With medical supervision, people are able to withdraw from drugs while medically dangerous side effects can be monitored and treated. It is imperative to seek medical help if one decides to stop using a drug or suspects or anticipates a problem after using the drugs.

Substance-abusing Parent(s)

Substance abuse is a progressive, destructive disease that affects not only the individual who is abusing the substances but can become extremely disruptive to everyone living in the home.

All that a parent may have initially, as far as expectations for their children, can be destroyed over time by a parent's obsession with using substances. Unfortunately, the substance-abusing parent may not even be aware of how their use is distressing their family.

Most parents have a desire to raise children who will have an excellent personality and healthy state of mind and have the ability to care about others. For a parent to have a desire to raise mentally healthy children is one thing, but to follow through and make that desire a reality is something entirely different.

If asked, most substance abusers would tell you that they have a great sense of commitment toward their family. However, an addict will not tell you that their commitment toward getting high is also great, if not greater than their commitment toward their family.

As previously mentioned, studies have proven in the early stages of substance abuse that the user often has a problem concentrating and controlling their emotions. For someone to be committed to the well-being of their family, they must be able to concentrate enough to control their emotions as well as control their behavior.

When a substance abuser mentally and physically abuses family members, obviously there is a breakdown in their ability to concentrate and to control themselves. The abuser's inability to concentrate and to maintain self-control can be seen in the abuser's behavior while under the influence, which can often lead to immediate danger to their family. For example, driving an automobile while under the influence of alcohol or drugs is a serious threat to everyone inside the automobile. Does the substance abuser realize the danger of driving while under the influence of drugs or alcohol? Sure, they realize the dangers, but they will put their family at risk nonetheless. The irony behind this particular situation is that the family members understand the dangers as well. But they trust, hope, and pray that they make it to their destination and are able to return home safely without a serious accident taking place.

Substance abuse and reckless behavior are common factors. A parent's desire to want the best for their children and a parent's desire to want that next drink or to obtain that next drug high are two entirely different desires.

When an alcoholic or drug user is at their worse, their desire for their drug of choice will come before any other desire they may have. And the substance abuser will often be the last person to notice when their children's personality and state of mind is being affected by their alcoholism or drug addiction.

When many substance abusers finally realize they have a substance-abuse problem, they believe their drug or alcohol problem is their problem and not the problem of other family members, particularly their children. They are certainly the last to realize their children's personality and state of mind has been affected by their alcoholism or drug addiction.

The substance abuser cannot seem to grasp the idea that their addiction affects their children's behavior. A child's behavior can change from being enthusiastic about their family to being unmotivated. Their feelings can change from feeling loved to feeling helpless and unwanted because of their father's or mother's drug or alcohol addiction.

Many addicts have no idea that their children may feel unwanted and helpless because their first concern is getting high. Consequently, their children will continue to feel helpless because they cannot do anything to help their parents.

Many children are aware of the health problems associated with substance abuse. They fear the day that a parent will tell the family that they have a life-threatening health condition as a result of years of alcoholism or other drug use.

If you were raised by parent(s) who were alcoholics or illegal-drug users, how did you feel when you saw one or both of your parents drunk or had passed out from drinking too much or over using an illegal drug? It really does not matter whether it's one or both parents who are addicts; it becomes a family affair.

Furthermore, where is a substance abuser's commitment to their family when they go into a *mental blackout* and continue on their destructive path by committing suicide or committing a homicide or double homicide? After all that has been said, does the alcoholic or drug abuser still think their drug and alcohol problem is still only their problem?

Exercise

Test your knowledge concerning drugs and alcohol abuse to answer *true*, *false*, or *NA* (not applicable) to the following statements:

1. Smoking marijuana can cause lack in concentration, short-term memory loss, distortion in sense of time and space, increase in appetite, anxiety, depression, hallucinations, and psychiatric disorders. ___
2. Drug use is associated with a broad range of problem behaviors. ___
3. People who begin using marijuana will usually experiment with or continue to use other drugs. ___
4. Children who use marijuana are more likely to use other drugs than children who have never used drugs. ___
5. Everyone in the family suffers when a loved one is addicted to drugs or alcohol. ___
6. Drug-related deaths are a waste of one's life. ___
7. A single joint of marijuana yields much more tar than a strong cigarette. ___
8. Billions of tax dollars are spent on stopping the flow of illegal drugs into the country. ___
9. My children would never use prescription drugs belonging to another family member. ___
10. My partner and I have strong commitment toward raising our children. ___

Answers to questions 1, 2, 3, 4, 5, 6, 7, 8, are *true*. The reader must determine if the questions to 9 and 10 are *true* or *false*. Substance abuse is a serious affair and the responsibility of not falling victim to drugs or alcohol is not the responsibility of the seller but of the user.

Disconnecting from Parent(s)

Parents are children's primary role models. Everything a parent says or does will make some kind of impression upon the mental and physical growth of their children. Most children are very intelligent for their age and can recognize when their parents are abusing alcohol or other chemical substances.

When children observe either parent intoxicated or being mentally and physically abusive toward members of the family, such behavior can cause a child to develop unhealthy self-esteem. When a child has unhealthy self-esteem, it places them at risk of *disconnecting* from the addicted parent(s).

As we mentioned earlier, children will isolate themselves from other members of the family and will seek comfort elsewhere. They will have a difficult time finding a logical reason to communicate with someone who is *often* intoxicated. They will also find it difficult to discuss their personal problems with a parent who speaks unclearly and reeks from the smell of alcohol.

Many teenagers resent not being able to turn to their parents for assistance. As a result, many teens will become disrespectful and, in some cases, become physically and verbally abusive toward the addicted parent(s).

Most parents will not accept being disrespected by one or more of their children. As a result, the home will become a *domestic war zone* resulting with child against child, child against parent(s), and parents against each other.

The weapon of choice will be words of cruelty, which will often leave everyone within hearing range a casualty. Consequently, teenagers who have such physical or verbal battles with their parents will begin to search for children in the community who are experiencing similar domestic problems.

When children disconnect from their parents under such conditions, the influence from other children in the neighborhood will be overpowering. Technically, a teenager may be physically living at home; however, mentally, the teenager is on his or her own.

There are ways to tell when your teenager is isolating himself or herself from the rest of the family. Following is a list that will assist with identifying the characteristics of a teenager who has unhealthy self-esteem and is moving toward isolating himself or herself from the family:

Check *yes* or *no* to the behaviors you see in your teenager.

- Complaining about parent's behavior ___
- Fighting with siblings more than usual ___
- Coming home later than usual ___
- Verbally abusing parents and their siblings ___
- Becoming more negative about family situations ___
- Neglecting personal hygiene ___
- Lying ___
- Refusing eye contact ___
- Using drugs ___

- Keeping to himself or herself more than usual ___
- Stealing ___
- Disrespecting parental opinion ___
- Not responding to punishment ___
- Lacking in doing their chores ___
- Refusing to listen to advice ___
- Getting poor school grades ___

If your teenager is acting out any of the above behaviors, do not jump to any hasty conclusions about your child's behavior. Your teenager may be feeling that it's time for him or her to experience life as he or she sees it, at least as far as such thinking would allow him or her to view life. We suggest that you seek professional advice concerning your teenager's behavior.

Teenagers and Drugs

When there are drugs available in the community, teenagers are at risk of using drugs, and this risk increases when there is a substance-abusing parent.

For years, the American people did not want to accept the fact that our children were involved in the use of dangerous drugs. America's parents knew that adolescence is a time of wonder and a time to find their place in life. But many parents would argue with any person that would suggest their child would use or is using drugs.

Many parents forget that they were teenagers at one time and would try anything at least once to fit in with other teenagers. But what many parents do not realize is that teenagers are much different than they were ten or twenty years ago. Teenagers are still as curious as they once were, but the negative side of society has introduced them to new and more dangerous drugs.

Many parents do not realize that if their teenager is using drugs, they were introduced to the drug by a friend, and out of curiosity, they tried the drug to see what would happen. Friends will often tell them that drugs will make them feel good and will reduce stress or depression.

We know many teenagers take drugs to fit in with the crowd, but there has to be other reasons for teenagers to use drugs. Adolescents who had to live a stressful and unhappy life with an abusive or battering parent or parents who use drugs or alcohol feel embarrassed, rejected, angry, depressed, fearful, and helpless. Many adolescents who develop these feelings will often turn to the very drug their parents are using.

Adolescents may experience feelings of embarrassment, guilt, shame, rejection, and anger inflicted upon them by the people who are supposed to love them. Many will believe that *no one loves them* and will become even more depressed or restless.

Substance-abusing parents will find out the hard way that many teenagers will become rebellious in one way or another. Many will withdraw from their family and turn toward their friends for love and acceptance.

Many will do poorly in school and eventually quit school, or they may remain in school and *just do enough* to pass on to the next grade to please their parents. Some adolescents will go as far as to consider committing suicide and often will commit suicide.

It can be very difficult for adolescents to feel any sense of security if their parents appear to be uncaring because of their use of alcohol or drugs.

Only recently have researchers and other professionals assessed the magnitude of substance abuse and the impact this problem has on the lives of children. Following are warning signs of teenage substance abuse.

Physical signs:

- Red and glazed eyes
- Continuous coughing
- Fatigue
- Heath problems

Emotional signs:

- Unhealthy self-esteem
- Mood swings
- Negative attitude
- Poor concentration
- Anxiety

- Depression
- Mentally isolating from other family members
- Easily irritated
- Argumentative

School involvement:

- Negative attitude
- Skipping school
- Failing grades
- Fighting
- Stealing
- Selling drugs
- Hanging out with the wrong crowd

Social problems:

- Getting in trouble with law enforcement
- Selling drugs
- Stealing
- Vandalism
- Rebelling against social norms
- Fighting
- Carrying weapons
- Disrespecting elders

> Many of these warning signs could indicate other problems. Seek professional assistance to determine the causes of such problems and to determine a proper course of action.

These warning signs are great to have as a knowledge base if you are a concerned parent. But what about parents who are alcoholics or drug addicts? What can they say to a teenager to gain their respect if they are abusive and using alcohol or drugs?

I am sure they could say a great deal about not using drugs or alcohol. However, their teenager may view them as being hypocrites. In most cases, their teenager will ignore their parents and will continue to use their drug of choice.

Seeking Help

Substance abuse affects the individual and his or her entire family, but there is help for everyone involved. However, there are reasons people use to not seek help immediately. The substance abuser and the family may be in denial as to how serious the problem truly is.

They may try to take care of the problem themselves rather than seek the help that is required. Or they may seek help for some of the consequences of the substance abuse in the family but avoid admitting the underlying problem of substance abuse itself. For example, the partner of a substance abuser may seek help for their depression and anxiety but be too embarrassed to talk about the substance-abuse issue in the home that is leading to these problems.

Just as one would go to a dentist to take care of a toothache, one would go to specialized help for substance abuse. The initial request for help is a big step for one to take and may be taken with any helping professional as one's doctor or minister.

However, it is best for the substance abuser and the family to eventually seek help from professionals or support groups or both that are specialized in substance-abuse treatment.

There are two types of groups of treatment providers that can assist a person and family with a substance-abuse problem. Our first group of treatment providers are professionals who work in mental health and specialize in the treatment of psychiatric disorders. These are also psychiatrists, psychologists, licensed clinical social workers, licensed counselors, and licensed marriage and family therapists.

The first group consists of individuals who may be recovering substance abusers themselves. They may have read books, studied films, attended workshops, and taken verbal and written tests to become certified substance-abuse counselors.

This group is mostly sought by adults as well as teenagers because the substance abusers believe that they can relate to a person who has been where they have been.

The professionals in our second group may or may not have a license or have earned a college degree but are qualified to provide treatment for substance abuse.

This does not mean that a psychiatrist, psychologist, licensed clinical social worker, or licensed marriage and family therapist has never abused alcohol or other drugs or would not provide them with an excellent treatment plan.

The point we are trying to make is that to be successful in a group or individual treatment program, the substance abuser and the treatment provider must be able to connect with each other, *or it will not work*.

It's important to remember the treatment model used by the first group is designed *to go where the client is*; its design is to assist the addict with understanding that the treatment provider has been there and understands what the substance abuser is feeling and their need to become sober without being assigned a psychiatric label. Also, there are specialized inpatient and outpatient treatment programs, which usually have a multidisciplinary treatment staff that includes doctors, social workers, psychologists, and counselors.

Another source of help is through the twelve-step programs such as Alcoholics Anonymous (AA) and Narcotics Anonymous for the substance abuser, Al-Anon for the loved ones of the alcoholic, and Nar-Anon for the loved ones of the drug abuser.

These programs are made up of people who have gone through living with an addiction and share their experience, strength, and hope with others. One may locate these programs through the Internet or by looking up their number in the telephone book, and someone will help them find a meeting close to their home to attend.

The twelve-step programs have helped many change their lives and remain in recovery. Often, one will go for professional assistance as well as attend the twelve-step program. It's important to remember that not only should the substance abuser receive treatment, but every family member should also receive treatment.

The reason is that everyone in the family has been negatively affected by the addict's behavior in one way or another. For the family to get back on the path of peace and harmony, everyone must receive treatment, which will assist them with finding the right path to family harmony.

The question remains; can therapy help a person with a substance-abuse problem? Yes, therapy can help. There is hope for a substance abuser and his or her entire family. What is important is to take the first step and seek assistance whether through a professional, trusted advisor or minister, or go to a twelve-step-program meeting.

Self-Assessment

Following are statements to assist you with understanding your feelings about the treatment for substance abuse. You should be able to discover whether or not alcohol or illegal drugs are causing your family domestic problems. Apply personal knowledge, as well as information from the chapter, to answer *true*, *false*, or *NA* (not applicable) to the following statements. It is important that you answer all questions as accurately and honestly as possible.

1. My teenagers appear to be happy living at home. ___
2. If my teenager is feeling embarrassed, guilty, ashamed, rejected, or angry, they would talk to us about their feelings. ___
3. I do not like the idea of being labeled. ___
4. I do not know where my teenager is most of the time. ___
5. My teenager seems to be isolating himself or herself from the family. ___
6. My children have never been disrespectful toward my partner or myself. ___
7. I believe my teenager is using some sort of drug. ___
8. My relationship is falling apart because a member of my family is a substance abuser. ___
9. I would know if my teenager were thinking of committing suicide. ___
10. I will look into a program that will assist a member of my family who is a substance abuser. ___

The previous list of statements is to better assess and assist you with understanding your feelings about the treatment for substance abuse. You should be able to discover whether or not alcohol or illegal drugs are causing you personal and domestic problems. If you find it necessary for you or your partner to learn more about chemical dependency within the family, use the information in this workbook, and also seek professional assistance for any questions you or your partner may have that this workbook does not address.

Chapter Seventeen

Codependency

Chapter's Objectives:

1. To assist the reader with understanding the term *codependency*
2. To provide information concerning behaviors associated with chemical dependence
3. To provide information concerning mental characteristics of codependency
4. To provide the reader with a questionnaire to assist with understanding their level of codependency
5. To encourage the reader to seek assistance if they believe they are codependent

Questions for You to Answer as You Read This Chapter:

1. Can you understand the term *codependent*?
2. What are the characteristics of a person who is codependent?
3. Can you explain how a codependent parent can affect the behavior of his or her children?
4. What are problems associated with codependency?
5. What are some methods that may be useful in creating a plan to assist a person who is codependent?

Related Chapters of Interest:

- Substance Abuse within the Family
- Parenting Skills
- Anger Management
- Stress Reduction
- Emotional Abuse

CHAPTER SEVENTEEN

Codependency

Extreme Emotional
And
Pathological Social Dependence

What is *codependency*? Many people use the term *codependency* and do not know its true meaning. The public, as well as many professionals, believe the term *codependency* is too vague to have a single specific definition.

Psychologists and counselors who work in the field of chemical dependency developed the term *codependency*. They define the term as a relationship in which a person has an *extreme emotional and pathological social dependence* on a person who has some sort of an addiction.

In domestic situations, we are referring to a partner or other family member who has an extreme emotional and pathological social dependence toward another family member. In essence, *a codependent person is the person without an addiction.* The person without the addiction becomes obsessed with controlling the behavior of the addicted person.

Although this chapter will focus on the person who is codependent on a person who is addicted to alcohol and other drugs, the concept of codependency can be universally extended into many other addictive behaviors. Among the different types of harmful addictions are

- all categories of drugs and alcohol abuse,
- gambling,
- tobacco,
- sex,
- violence,
- overeating.

To fully understand the concept of codependency, we would like you to understand the terms *addiction* and *addict*. An *addiction* can be defined as developing a habit or becoming obsessed with the consumption of alcohol, legal or illegal drugs, gambling, sex, or violence.

An *addict* can be defined as a person who has a compulsive need to consume habit-forming substances, which is characterized by the level of tolerance, various physiological symptoms upon withdrawal, and by continuing to use the substance despite the negative consequences after consuming the habit-forming substance.

Many psychologists and counselors believe that in order to fully understand the negative effects of being codependent, a person must be able to first identify when his or her partner or other family member has an alcohol or drug problem.

Relationships do not begin as codependent relationships. When two people first meet and, at some point, decide to develop an intimate relationship, neither person may or may not be fully aware of how much alcohol or drugs the other person may be consuming. Usually, when someone is abusing legal or illegal drugs, it's their secret. They will conceal their substance-abuse problem until they decide to make it known or until they are caught abusing the substance.

By the time their partner realizes they are addicted to a certain substance, their partner would have developed caring feelings for the user and will find it difficult to leave the relationship. Therefore, people must be alert to the idea that if a person is using illegal drugs or consuming large amounts of alcohol, there is the strong possibility that they are addicted or could become addicted to the substance.

Subsequently, the nonusing partner must make one of the most important decisions of their life, i.e., to continue with the relationship or not get too emotionally involved with the addicted person.

If their decision is to remain in the relationship, the substance abuser must receive counseling for their substance problem, or the relationship is predetermined to cause a tremendous amount of emotional hardship.

Characteristics of Chemical Dependence

Let us take a closer look at the effects of alcohol and drug dependency and the characteristics of chemical dependence. Although tobacco is the most frequently used drug in the country and has many of the same withdrawal and dependency symptoms as the other drugs, we will focus on the more menacing addictive substances such as narcotic pain killers, tranquilizers, alcohol, sedatives, hashish, heroin, amphetamines, and cocaine.

To determine the level of a person's addiction, we must take a closer look at how much of the drugs the user is consuming and their behavior after consumption.

Following are examples of what one may observe if a person is chemically dependent (for clarity, alcohol is also known as a drug):

- The person who is using will generally consume large amounts of the drug.
- The chemically dependent person will continue to consume more of the drug after reaching a level of intoxication.
- Many chemically dependent people will continue to use the drug until the user is intoxicated or has passed out.
- Many chemically dependent will often continue to consume the drug after frequent hangovers that will cause them to miss work and other normal activities.
- The user denies that they have a drug problem after weeks, months, or years of consuming the drug.
- After weeks, months, or years of denial, the user feels that he or she does not have the ability to stop using the drug.
- A chemically dependent person will often develop a pattern of having various sorts of personal accidents, marital difficulties, financial, and work-related problems.
- Most chemically dependent persons will often have a problem controlling their anger, they will get involve with what is known as periodic cycles of violence that would involve family members, friends, and strangers.
- The user feels helpless in stopping once they have started using the drug.
- When chemically dependent persons go without the substance for a period of time, they can often develop withdrawal symptoms such as upset stomach, trembling hands, headaches, feeling anxiety, sleeplessness, or oversleeping.

The symptoms mentioned above are proven examples that a drug problem exists. If any family member is experiencing any of these problems, seek professional assistance.

Many people do not understand the dangers involved in drug abuse. Some people believe that if they only use illegal drugs or drink alcohol when they become depressed, stressed, or use the substance just for fun or if they only use a small amount of alcohol or a particular drug, they will be okay; and they will be able to stop using at any time.

This is often a user's second mistake; their first mistake was using illegal drugs or drinking alcohol when they are depressed or stressed. Many people suffer from moments of depression and stress every day of their life. And as the depression and stress mount, the user will find himself or herself using the drug more and more to help them to ease their pain.

Many people do not realize at the time, as they continue to use the drug of choice that their body as well as their behavior will begin to change. The user will often experience mood swings, an increase or decrease in their weight, and agitation with heightened moments of anger.

When the body reaches a point in which it can no longer function normally unless it obtains a larger dose of the drug, the person has become chemically dependent.

To truly understand the nature of chemical dependency and how a family can be affected by someone who is abusing drugs, we must understand their emotional state. For many addicts, their emotional state can be summed up in three words: *overwhelming mental pain.* Many addicts believe that by using addictive substances, they can suppress their mental pain.

Studies have shown that alcohol and other drugs can change a person's perception about the world around them. This, in fact, is why many people find themselves addicted to drugs. If they do not like their environment, many addicts believe they can change their environment or *escape* the stress and strain of everyday life or a frightful past by drinking or using others drugs. In this idea lies a tremendous amount of danger.

When a person believes that he or she can change his or her environment (we are not talking about moving from one place to another) by using drugs, he or she must realize that when the high subsides, the environment will be still there. This method to change or escape the realities of stress of everyday life will often lead them into a horrifying future of confusion.

Characteristics of Codependency

A very important point must be made regarding a person who is addicted to drugs or alcohol and codependency. Although a family member may have an addiction, this does not necessarily mean their partner or other family members are codependent. There is a major difference between being concerned for the health and welfare of an addicted person and having an *extreme emotional and pathological social dependence* toward an addict. A partner and other family members can care about the health and welfare of the addicted family member and not destroy the family in the process.

In a codependent relationship, *overly caring* for the addicted person is the primary means through which codependent's cope with the problems created by being in a codependent relationship. People must realize that codependency is not something that happens overnight; it's a process that takes place over time.

Codependency begins when a partner starts to believe that praying to their higher power and begging the addict to stop using is more powerful than the addict's cravings for the drug. Once an addict believes that they cannot live without the drugs, no amount of praying or tears are going to change their mind about obtaining and using the drug.

People must understand that codependency is a *disease*, a disease that lurks in the shadows of a relationship, and is concealed in the behaviors of both the addict and the people associated with the addict.

Family members will go about their everyday life believing everything will be fine, and before they realize it, they will become accustomed to the addict's behaviors and begin to focus more on the addict's problems and begin to ignore their own personal issues.

Eventually, caring for the addict will become so strong that doing so will dominate everyone's judgment, sentiment, as well as behavior. We must also add that when a person truly loves his or her partner, he or she will discover it is extremely difficult to find clarity between caring and codependency.

However, when a codependent becomes aware of where he or she is socially, financially, and mentally in life and finds himself or herself in need for a change, the early signs of codependency become apparent. His or her thoughts and behaviors become clearer regarding their behavior as well as the behavior of the addict.

The codependent can see the relationship turn for the worse because of the instability. The relationship will appear as if everyone is moving forward, but in reality, they are moving backward. The codependent will also realize that they are playing a large role in the family's failure to move forward.

The codependent can also see himself or herself becoming preoccupied with controlling the addict's activities and providing the addict with the necessary means or opportunity to maintain their addiction.

The codependent also comes to realize that his or her partner's drug use, lack of intimacy, and verbal abuse has become problematic but feel helpless to do anything about it.

Consequently, when the codependent begins to experience longer periods of depression, anxiety, or personal or work-related stress, he or she may look toward the caring of the addict to find relief.

Codependents have little or no control over how much care they provide or how long or how often they care for the addict. They are preoccupied with caring, denying their own dependency, and continuing to support the addict even though they have begun to realize the dangers. Eventually, they become mentally numb to the effects of being codependent and continue to support the addicted person.

However, for many people who are codependent, there is an increased awareness of an existing problem, but also a belief that they still have a chance to save the addict and their relationship from personal, social, and economic ruin.

If you are codependent or know someone who is codependent, the following information will better assist you with understanding the characteristics of a person who is codependent:

- Denial: Although the mental pain suffered by the codependent is visible, they will ignore their mental pain for personal, social, and economic reasons.
- Caretaking: Many codependents feel responsible for all family members and believe that they can *save* the addicted person. They will take on all the household responsibilities, make every effort to understand the addict's mood swings, and solve their problems in an effort to bring their family life back to normal.
- Controlling: Many codependents control their partner through the use of emotional, physical, and economic abuse. Through emotional abuse, they will use such statements as "You could never make it on your own," "How can you be so stupid as to use drugs," "No one else will ever want you in that condition," and "You'll never find a

good-paying job." Through physical abuse, they will slap, punch, and kick the addict. Through economic abuse, they will hide family funds, give the addict an allowance, and spend family funds on what they believe is necessary for themselves and not in the interest of the family.

- Enabling: Codependents are also enablers. They will often provide the addict with the necessary means or opportunity to maintain their addiction. This makes it possible for the addicted person to remain in their negative situation and allow the codependent to remain in control of the relationship. For example, a codependent will drink alcohol themselves, but not to the point of becoming addicted. They will lie to cover up for the addict's behavior and give the addict money to maintain their addiction.
- Dependent: Many codependents are dependent upon the addict for some sort of comfort. The codependent may have a strong need to be loved and have a fear of being abandoned. They may also be dependent on the addict's income as well as their companionship.
- Manipulation: They will mislead their loved one, misuse finances and family resources, and abuse their own belief system to maintain their codependency.
- Isolation: They will isolate themselves and their partner from public view to hide the truth of their painful existence.
- Lying: There is continuous lying to cover up the reality that a problem exists.
- Blame: The codependent will find many ways to blame society and the addict for their personal and social failures.
- Irresponsibility: They become unreliable and negligent in many aspects of their personal and social life.
- Personal and social confusion: Unhealthy self-esteem is the key factor in their confusion and their regard for society is at its lowest point.
- Unhealthy self-esteem: Because many codependents take everything personally, they begin to doubt who they are and their ability to achieve, which affects how they view themselves.

If there is someone in your home who is codependent and he or she is feeling major emotional distress, there is a good possibility that there are other emotional issues that need to be addressed. We recommend the person with an addiction and the codependent to seek professional assistance to find a remedy for any emotional problems that may exist.

Exercise

Use the questionnaire below to assist you with determining whether or not you, your partner, or another family member is codependent. (*If you have any questions after answering these statements, seek professional assistance for clarity.*) Apply personal knowledge, as well as information from this chapter, to answer each question that may pertain to you or other family member.

1. The person has a feeling of personal and social confusion. ___*
2. The person has a poor or excessive appetite. ___
3. The person has become unreliable and negligent in many aspects of his or her personal and social life. ___
4. The person feels the need to be withdrawn from others. ___
5. The person is often irritated and easily angered. ___*
6. The person has unhealthy self-esteem. ___*
7. The person has thoughts of committing suicide. ___*
8. The person has thoughts of committing a homicide. ___*
9. The person believes he or she must control the addict's activities. ___
10. The person believes that his or her situation is impossible to manage. ___*
11. The person believes that he or she must tell lies to keep their relationship problems a secret. ___
12. The person shows no interest in outside activities. ___
13. The person has a feeling of anxiety in social gatherings. ___*
14. The person does not trust anyone. ___
15. The person believes he or she must spend most of their time with the addict. ___
16. There are frequent fights with the addicted person. ___*
17. The person has a fear of developing friendships. ___*
18. The person blames the addict for his or her problems. ___
19. The person believes his or her future is hopeless. ___*
20. The person has doubts about his or her mental and physical health. ___*
21. The person believes that he or she must make all the family decisions. ___
22. The person is stressed because he or she believes something terrible is going to happen to the addict. ___*
23. The person has terrible mood swings. ___*
24. The person feels guilty and ashamed of the relationship. ___
25. The person believes the addict will not survive without his or her assistance. ___

> If you have marked *yes* to any question where there is an asterisk (*) next to the question, we recommend that you seek professional assistance as soon as possible.

Although these mental and physical symptoms are related to codependency, answering *yes* to any or all these questions is not enough to determine whether or not a person has an *extreme emotional and pathological social dependence.* The questions are designed to recognize that a problem does exist, and receiving professional assistance is recommended. The keyword in this case is *pathological.* We recommend that a licensed psychotherapist or counselor determine whether or not a person has *extreme emotional and pathological social dependence.*

Solutions for Codependency

One of the most important and yet most difficult aspects of codependency is the reluctance to acknowledge that a problem exists. Once that first step toward recognition has been taken, the codependent partner should begin looking for negative behavior patterns that they would like to change about themselves. The next step would be to understand their choices, i.e., do *I* continue in a relationship that is filled with mental and physical pain, or do *I* find effective solutions to *my* problems? Solutions to the problems are there to be used.

However, to admit that there are serious and debilitating problems that exist in their relationship, the codependent as well as the addict must take an honest look at their past and current situation. Remember, *to admit* that a problem exists and do nothing to put *an end* to the problem will not solve the problem.

Codependents and substances abusers who are able to recognize their negative behavioral patterns should continue to review these negative patterns and discuss making changes in their behavior with a professional counselor or therapist who will assist them with a plan of action.

For anyone who is trying to find a solution to their problem of codependency, they must take into account three important factors. First, many codependents will experience moments of denial, guilt, and fear of being labeled with having a pathological problem. Secondly, many will have a problem facing the amount of work it will take for them to change their lifestyle and return their life back to normal. Finally, and possibly the most important, both partners must find a professional counselor who can offer them the proper assistance that will help both the addict and codependent solve their problem.

As difficult as it may seem, neither partner should give up. If there is a problem finding a professional to whom both parties can feel comfortable with, we recommend that the couple speak to someone who comes highly recommended by others who have succeeded in a particular program that helped them with finding a solution to their problem of codependency.

Following are examples of methods that may be useful in creating a plan to assist a codependent until they can obtain professional assistance:

- Understand that codependency is an illness.
- Learn more about codependence.
- Allow people to take ownership of their personal and social responsibilities.
- Work on obtaining healthy self-esteem.
- Learn to identify your feelings, emotions, and social needs.
- Focus more on individual goals and how to reach your goals.
- Join the local library and obtain self-help tapes on codependency.
- Locate codependent support groups as Codependents Anonymous or support groups for those who are in a relationship with a substance abuser as Al-Anon.
- Make an honest decision to change.
- Understand that you cannot help someone who does not help themselves.

To decide to stop being codependent is the easy part, but to actually stop being codependent will require hard work and determination.

Once a person who is codependent decides to take a serious look at his or her current mental and social status and realize the destructive nature of being codependent, he or she should ask himself or herself these questions: Is this how I want to live my life? Is this lifestyle causing me mental and social hardship? Do I want to change how I feel about myself and change how I view my personal and social life?

If they answered no, yes, and no, respectively, to those questions, making the decision to stop being codependent will not be as difficult as they may believe.

Once a codependent person has taken a long look at his or her situation, he or she should realize that there are no logical reasons or long-term advantages in remaining codependent. To the contrary, he or she will realize that to remain in a codependent relationship is a slow and painful path to personal or social failure.

Self-Assessment

Following are questions to assist with understanding the characteristics and solutions to codependency. Apply personal knowledge, as well as information from the chapter, to answer *yes*, *no*, or *NA* (not applicable) to the following questions. It is important that you answer all questions as accurately and honestly as possible:

1. My partner is codependent. ___
2. I am codependent. ___
3. My children are codependent. ___
4. Do you understand that codependency is an illness? ___
5. Do you think people can be addicted to violence? ___
6. Are your family and friends keeping away because of your partner's drinking? ___
7. Do you believe the relationship can continue under the current circumstances? ___
8. Someone in my family needs assistance with their drug problem. ___
9. Do you understand that it is best to get a professional opinion concerning codependency? ___
10. Do you believe that the use of drugs and alcohol is connected to domestic violence? ___

The previous list of questions is to better assess whether or not you or your partner are codependent. If you believe that it is necessary for you and your partner to learn more about codependency, use the information in this workbook, and also seek professional assistance for any questions that this workbook does not address.

Chapter Eighteen

Aggressive, Assertive, and Nonassertive (Passive) Behaviors

Chapter's Objectives:

1. To define the term *attitude*
2. To understand the effects of maintaining a healthy attitude
3. To define *aggressive*, *assertive*, and *nonassertive behaviors*
4. Review various ways each behavior is expressed and the effect each behavior may have on others
5. To encourage the reader to become more assertive to reach their goals

Questions for You to Answer as You Read This Chapter:

1. What is your overall attitude toward people in general?
2. What is the difference between being aggressive and assertive?
3. How do you feel about people who are aggressive toward you?
4. How do you feel about people who are passive?
5. Can a person experience all these behaviors, and still gain respect from others?

Related Chapters of Interest:

- Anger Management
- Codependency
- Emotional Abuse
- Alcohol and Substance Abuse within the Family
- Parenting Skills

Chapter Eighteen

Aggressive, Assertive, and Nonassertive (Passive) Behaviors

Attitude

The term *attitude* is a concept used in psychology to describe how we judge others, various situations, or things based upon our positive, negative or unemotional view toward people, situations, or things. For example, a person with a positive attitude views life in a constructive and enthusiastic manner. And of course, the opposite can be said for people who view life with a negative attitude.

A person with an unemotional attitude shows little or no remorse toward others. Another familiar term for a person who displays an unemotional attitude toward others would be indifferent or *cold*.

A person can also have an attitude of uncertainty toward a person, situation, or thing; this simply means that a person can have a positive and negative attitude at the same time. For example, a person could have positive feelings for his or her partner and yet have negative feelings concerning his or her partner's behavior.

To understand how we develop our attitudes toward various situations, we must understand that our attitude is based upon what we have been taught socially and culturally. Consequently, what we have been taught affects how we treat ourselves as well as how we treat others. For example, many children who live in a gang-infested environment and are exposed to violent behavior by other gang members will often take on the characteristics and attitudes of their peers.

The same can be said for children who are raised in a healthy environment. When children are well nurtured by their parents, most children will become well-nurturing parents. Of course, there are no absolutes concerning how a child will behave due to their environment.

In many cases, the slightest negative or positive situation will often cause a person to do the total opposite of what others may do in a similar situation. For example, there are children who are raised in a hostile environment, but will keep away from negative influences and go on becoming great achievers. And there are children who were well nurtured by thoughtful and caring parents who become adults who are filled with anger and consequently display deviant behaviors.

Another example concerning learned attitudes would be that most children who witness their parents displaying a positive attitude toward each other, i.e., confront difficult situations with a positive attitude or pursue and achieve major lifetime dreams and goals, will develop a positive attitude toward their future partners, children, and others in society and will also develop a positive attitude toward successfully reaching goals they have set for themselves.

When a person believes in himself and herself and has a healthy outlook on life in general, his or her attitude will often be positive. A person with a positive attitude can usually see beyond the negative in many situations and find something positive and learn from his or her experience. For example, our attitude toward certain situations that have taken place in our relationships, which has caused us mental stress, isn't something that is easily forgotten. However, our attitude toward the person that caused the pain can either make the situation better or worse depending upon how we decide to approach the situation.

A situation that has caused us to feel frustrated or angry must be approached and managed with caution and careful consideration. We can approach the problem with anger or forgiveness depending upon our ability to control our emotions, making the right choice, and understand the consequences of the choice that we make.

As you have probably heard, "For every action there is a reaction." There are many situations in which a person cannot fight fire with fire because of the severity of the consequences. Careful consideration must be taken into account before thinking about retaliating to obtain revenge.

The attitude of many people who live in our society is that "You hurt me; therefore, I must hurt you in return, and whatever happens, happens." Any person who thinks this way is someone to avoid because you never know what they are capable of doing to satisfy their wounded ego. Many people believe that using aggression is the solution to getting what they want and the answer to solving their problems.

We suggest that people must learn to make the appropriate choices and do the right thing. If a certain situation calls for a person to leave their abusive relationship, by all means, leave the relationship if they believe it's *safe* to do so.

If a situations calls for a family to come together to make an important decision that could negatively affect other family members, by all means, bring the family together and discuss the situation to find the right solution to the potential problem.

It is very important to remember that the success of a relationship is basically determined by a person's attitude toward his or her partner and other family members. And based upon one's attitude, a relationship can either be wonderful to be a part of or a total nightmare.

Exercise

The way a person thinks, feels, and behaves is based upon their attitude. How much do you know about your attitude? Because a person's attitude refers to their relatively unique and consistent pattern of thinking, feelings, and behavior, use the list of statements and questions below to determine how you view yourself, others, and various situations that take place in your life.

1. Name three people and three situations in which you must use a lot of patience.

   __________ ______________ ______________

2. Name three people with whom you are angry.

   __________ ______________ ______________

3. Name three people you love being near to.

   __________ ______________ ______________

4. Name three situations that frighten you.

   __________ ______________ ______________

5. If there were three situations in life you could redo over again, what would they be?

   __________ ______________ ______________

6. Name three goals that you have yet to achieve.

   __________ ______________ ______________

7. Name three situations that you know make your family happy.

   __________ ______________ ______________

8. Name three people who have caused you mental harm.

   __________ ______________ ______________

9. Name three people you have caused mental harm.

   __________ ______________ ______________

10. Name three professions you would like your children to enter.

    __________ ______________ ______________

11. Name three situations you could not care less about.

_________ _____________ _____________

12. Name three situations in which you are the most sensitive.

_________ _____________ _____________

13. Name three behaviors you would like your partner to stop doing.

_________ _____________ _____________

14. Name three things you would like to change about yourself.

_________ _____________ _____________

15. Name three people you respect and trust.

_________ _____________ _____________

> The above exercise is not a scientific study, but an exercise for you to take a look the different kinds of attitudes you may have toward certain people and situations in your life. If you cannot determine from the above exercise the kind of person you are, seek professional assistance and show your responses to this list of statements and questions and ask for their professional opinion.

Attitude and Behaviors

Aggression

Although a*ttitude* and *behavior* are connected in terms of a person's conduct toward a certain situation, the two words have two different meanings. A person's a*ttitude* is their inner thoughts and feelings while their *behavior* is an outward expression of their attitude.

Ideally, a person with a positive attitude will often demonstrate normal behaviors, and a person with a negative attitude will, in some cases, demonstrate irregular behavior.

There are three behaviors to consider when we speak of behavior as a result of a person's attitude, i.e., aggressive, assertive, and passive behaviors.

First, let us examine aggressive behavior. What is *aggressive behavior*? *Aggressive behavior* can be defined as behavior that attempts to assert verbal or physical dominance over a person or situation.

When aggressive behavior is used to assert verbal or physical dominance over others, it can be considered as the most destructive of the three behaviors.

The table below reviews various ways that aggression is expressed and the effect that aggressive behavior can have on others.

Characteristics of an aggressor:	Destructive attitude Takes and rarely gives Arrogant Insulting Verbally abusive Emotionally abusive Physically abusive
Aggressor's belief system:	I will take what I want. I give people what I want them to have. I should never feel bad about my aggressive behavior. Kindness is a sign of weakness. Physical strength is the power to success. Do unto others before they do unto to me. I am doing to people what society has done to me. I owe no one anything.
Characteristics of their victim:	Afraid Embarrassed Angry Emotionally abusive Self-doubting Having unhealthy self-esteem Depressed

Aggressive people realize fear is a powerful weapon and believe using aggression is necessary in getting their wants and needs met.

Everyone experiences the feelings of frustration and anger and will react with some sort of aggression from time to time. These feelings and behaviors are normal and healthy and are a part of who we are. However, when people use their aggression in ways that are harmful toward themselves and others, we consider this sort of aggression as unhealthy.

It's sad to say, but many aggressive people enjoy the idea of being in control. And if their power and control come into question, or if there is some sort of threat to their feeling of power, many aggressive people will show extraordinary skill in removing any such threat. Consequently, many aggressive people will go into a rage and become physically violent toward anyone who opposes them.

In marriages or other intimate relationships, this sort of *iron-grip* approach to controlling partners will eventually become too painful for the victim to bear.

Many aggressors believe aggression is the only way to maintain control and to settle disputes. Their truth is the only truth. No matter how dishonest or destructive it may appear, they will go to any lengths to prove that they are a person not to be second-guessed. They will express their disproval by yelling, kicking, throwing objects, or hitting others. In some cases, an attack by an aggressive person can be lethal.

As we have mentioned so many times before and will continue to mention until it's understood, an extreme aggressor is to be avoided whether it's in the home or in public. If you're an aggressive person or you're living with an aggressor, the best thing for you and your partner to do would be to seek professional counseling before someone gets seriously injured.

Assertive Behavior

Being assertive involves being able to express one's feelings and opinions and obtaining what one seeks without denying the personal rights of their partner or others. When people are assertive in their attitude and behavior, they are simply asking for what they want to obtain what they need and avoiding what they do not need or want.

Assertive behavior is the most misunderstood behavior, particularly to an aggressor. An aggressor doesn't like an assertive partner because assertive partners will obtain what they need and avoid what they do not need or want. And for these reasons, an aggressor does not like a partner who will state his or her opinions or openly expresses his or her feelings.

The table below reviews various ways how being assertive can affect others.

Characteristics of an assertive person:	Honest about their needs Direct but not forceful Has self-respect Confident in oneself Healthy self-esteem
How others view an assertive person:	Have a high opinion of them Trustworthy Know where they stand Respected
Assertive person's belief system:	They must protect their rights. Respect the rights of others. Everyone has a right to an opinion. Being violent isn't necessary. They will not accept being abused.

Assertive people realize aggressive behavior is not necessary in getting their wants and needs met. They understand the ideas of negotiation, fairness, and compromise.

Generally speaking, assertive people are self-confident, emotionally honest to themselves, direct, and aware of their feelings and the feelings of others. On the other hand, most aggressors are insecure and believe their personal needs must come first and the needs of their partner afterward.

Of course, aggressors will often declare that they place their partner's needs ahead of their own; however, although aggressors may say that they place their family needs ahead of their own needs, in many cases, they cannot because of their aggressive nature.

Many people who are aggressive believe anyone who is assertive is actually being aggressive, particularly if the assertive partner insists that a certain thing be done. For example, when a partner has been nonassertive (passive) throughout the relationship and decides to become assertive, their aggressive partner will misread their partner's intentions and assume that they are being aggressive. As a result, the aggressor will often become even more abusive, particularly if their partner has been nonassertive throughout the relationship; and the sudden change in their partner's behavior confuses the aggressor into believing he or she is losing his or her power and control.

Nonassertive (Passive) Behavior

What is *nonassertive behavior*? *Nonassertive behavior* is a behavior in which a person is submissive in their behavior. Many people who are nonassertive are nonassertive for various reasons.

Some people are submissive because it's in their nature to be quiet and submissive. And yet, there are people who are submissive because they are afraid of someone or something. In either case, most nonassertive people will hide their true feelings to avoid conflict.

The table below reviews various ways how being nonassertive can affect others.

Characteristics of a passive person:	Untruthful to oneself Self-denying Self-isolated Having unhealthy self-esteem Submissive Unsure of oneself
How others view a passive person:	Lack of respect Someone to be used Mentally lost Cannot be trusted Unintelligent to some degree
A passive person's belief system:	They do not want to make anyone angry. They cannot change who they are. They may like others to take control. They cannot do anything right. If they tell how they truly feel, others may not understand.

How we communicate with others not only determines how we will be treated by others but also tells others how we would like to be treated.

Some of the most isolated and frustrated people are those who are passive and are afraid to ask for what they want from a relationship. Afraid to strike out on their own and become assertive, they constantly fill their life with shallow and aggressive men or women who subsequently abuse them.

How can people who are passive learn to relate more intimately and more enjoyably toward themselves?

When a passive person begins to take an honest look at how he or she truly feels about himself or herself and his or her current abusive relationship, he or she should become more assertive and tell his or her partner that a change must take place in the way he or she are being treated.

What we hope the readers of this chapter will learn is to seriously consider their use of aggressive, assertive, or passive behaviors. Try to understand the importance of these behaviors in the communication process while realizing that the use of aggression will, at times, get them what they want; but more often than not, the use of aggression will get them into more trouble than they can handle.

As for going from being nonassertive to becoming assertive, one will earn respect from others as well as get their needs met. We can only hope that a nonassertive person take the time to focus on his or her attitude and behavior and eventually emerge a more complete person with a full appreciation for who he or she is with the ability to form a deeper and lasting relationship with the people he or she loves.

Self-Assessment

The following statements should assist you with determining whether or not you understand the terms *aggressive*, *assertive*, and *nonassertive behaviors*. See if you can recognize yourself or your partner in the following list. Apply personal knowledge as well as information from the chapter, to answer *true*, *false*, or *NA* (not applicable) to each statement. It is important that you answer all questions as accurately and honestly as possible.

1. The way a person behaves is all about attitude. ___
2. I understand the difference between aggression and assertive behaviors. ___
3. When my partner asks for what he or she wants, he or she is usually assertive. ___
4. When my partner asks for what he or she wants, it's usually aggressive. ___
5. I would like to become more assertive, but it's difficult under my current situation. ___
6. I do not like to be controlled, but I hide my feelings for fear of being verbally attacked. ___
7. My partner is passive and hides his or her feelings. ___
8. It's okay for my partner to be assertive when talking with me. ___
9. I believe that this is a man's world, and it's okay for men to be aggressive. ___
10. If I become more assertive, my partner may mistake my assertive behavior for aggression. ___

The previous list of statements is for you to better understand the terms *aggressive*, *assertive*, and *nonassertive behaviors*. If you believe that it is necessary for you to learn more about aggressive, assertive, and nonassertive behaviors, use the information in this workbook; and also seek professional assistance for any questions you may have that this workbook does not address.

Chapter Nineteen

Anger Management

Chapter's Objectives:

1. To define *anger*
2. To discuss the causes of anger
3. To describe specific coping strategies to reduce the frequency of anger
4. To discuss positive and negative anger
5. To provide strategies to process anger

Questions for You to Answer as You Read This Chapter:

1. How do you feel about someone who always seems to be angry?
2. Why do people respond to a situation with anger when anger may not be the appropriate feeling?
3. How can a person tell when they have an anger problem?
4. How can anger be used in a positive way?
5. What negative behaviors are associated with anger?

Related Chapters of Interest:

- What Is Power and Control?
- Trust and Respect
- Equality in Relationships
- Codependency
- Stress Reduction

Chapter Nineteen

Anger Management

Anger

What is anger? Anger is an emotional response to some sort of real or imagined conflict, injustice, carelessness, shame, or perceived betrayal from others.

Anger can be seen as aggressive or passive. In case of *aggression,* a person who is angry will become verbally or physically abusive toward another person or a thing, whether their aggression is justified or not.

When a person's anger is *passive,* the person will often become quiet and mentally withdrawn, consequently becoming passive-aggressive in his or her behavior toward another person or thing.

When a person becomes angry, his or her anger can change from mild frustration to moderate aggravation to rage, depending upon the person's personality and attitude toward a particular situation.

The physiological symptoms of anger could be anxiety, a rapid heartbeat, shakes, or a headache, depending on the level of frustration or anger.

Frustration is another emotion that should be carefully understood. Frustration is said be the first stage of anger, which can occur in situations in which a person encounters a difficult situation. For example, when a person cannot solve a particular problem or is in a situation in which the person has little to no control over their situation, frustration may occur.

The level of frustration depends largely upon how important the problem is to the person, and the greater the problem, the greater the frustration. Certain people may become frustrated and embarrassed after watching a movie or sport event. Rather than taking the time to realize that the movie or sports event wasn't a personal problem or threat to them, the person will become frustrated and embarrassed, and the person will allow his or her feeling of frustration and embarrassment turn into anger.

Another example is when a person loses his or her job. Believing that he or she is the primary wage earner in their family, his or her frustration becomes so great that he or she returns home and physically abuses his or her partner.

The risk with this sort of behavior is that the angry person will remain angry and displaces their anger on to people inside as well as outside their home. They will attack family members who had nothing to do with the situation that caused them to become frustrated and consequently angry. *We must state the situation didn't cause the person to become angry; the person chooses to become angry.*

There are also people who seem to be angry all the time and will make their anger known to everyone with whom they come in contact. Also, there are people who rarely become angry; and when they become angry, they will process their anger in constructive ways.

Many will settle down by reading, writing, listening to music, taking a short or long walk, taking a nap, exercising, or discussing their problem with someone who will listen and give them honest and appropriate feedback.

Negative and Positive Aspects of Anger

Do you have a partner who seems to be angry all the time? Are they angry with their job, lifestyle, a family member, in-laws, neighbors, and so on? Does it seem that they always have something to complain about?

When you watch them closely, does it seem as if they take pleasure in putting others down? Have you become frustrated and angry with your partner's negative outlook on life? Or are you the kind of person we have mentioned above?

When a person uses their anger to make everyone they come in contact with feel uncomfortable, we call it negative anger. At times, the person with the negative anger appears to be insensitive to the feelings of others and seems to make a habit of making everyone feel uncomfortable.

If we were to take the time to examine the consequences of misplaced anger, we would be overwhelmed with disbelief. Statistics indicate that as a result of negative anger and rage, America's annual violent-death rate continues to climb at an alarming rate. The annual violent-death rate in this country has reached an unbelievable height of thirty thousand homicides and over fifty-two thousand suicides. The reported and the unreported physical injuries due to people who are angry and use their anger to harm others is in the millions.

With the deadly combination of alcohol and drugs, the rising violent-death rate for innocent bystanders has become a disturbing phenomenon in this country. Angry people are creating victim after victim in situations concerning domestic violence because of their inability to control their anger and rage.

Victims of an enraged partner must understand the potential dangers of negative anger and its destructive nature. Awareness of negative anger and rage should be required knowledge in all relationships. Displaying uncontrolled anger is about power and control; the more intense the anger, the more power and control the aggressor expects to have over their victim.

For example, when a family member does something the angry person doesn't like, he or she will go into a rage. The rage appears to seize their mind, and they seem to get a sense of power. And this feeling of power does not disappear until their thirst for obedience or vengeance has been satisfied.

Have you ever wondered why a person with such negative anger would stay in a home if he or she is so unhappy with everyone? Why doesn't the angry partner pack up and find another place to live, a place where maybe he or she can be happier?

There are two answers to this question. First, he or she does not know how to be happy or prefer anger over happiness. In any case, he or she would rather live in the home so that they can sabotage and contaminate the home environment, thus becoming a nuisance to their family's ability to function and become successful.

Secondly, why should the negatively angry partner leave when he or she is being rewarded by other family members, e.g., hot meals, clean clothes, sex, and companionship? The angry partner may be angry and controlling, but he or she isn't stupid, at least not stupid to the point of walking out on a good thing.

People who use anger to control family members realize the power of anger and its power to control. They will do whatever it takes to obtain and maintain control over family members. They are not about to lose those hot meals, clean clothes, sex, and companionship simply because their emotionally abused partner may, every once in a while, tell them to stop the abuse or *get out.*

Victims of a person who is consistently angry must realize that once an incident of anger has ended, the angry person's state of anger returns to a state of relaxed anger, i.e., anger which has not completely gone to a calm state but to another state of anger readiness.

This relaxed state of anger readiness allows a habitual angry person to impulsively, and without provocation, leap at the least opportunity to become enraged once again. Also remember that a person with this sort of anger and rage problem is believed to be incapable of *true love*.

If a person who is consistently angry tells you that he or she loves you, it's not love but an obsession, a dangerous obsession. Victims of a person with an anger problem must understand that anger and love cannot hold the same thought at the same time. Consequently, how can a person love and hate you simultaneously? They can't; either they love you, or they do not love you at that moment. They cannot do both. Some people may want to argue this fact, but it's the emotionally abused victim who must understand the difference between love and hate and how love and hate cannot hold the same space at the same time.

Although most people view anger as a negative emotion, there can be a positive side to anger. If anger is used in a positive way, anger can prove to be a valuable asset. Let's take for example, the lack of family income. Money or the lack of family income seems to be the reason many couples are having difficulty. So let us take a careful look at how positive anger and the lack of income can work to our benefit.

Take, for example, a couple who is angry because of their economic status, and because of their financial situation, they are unable to purchase the fundamental items they need or want for themselves and their family. Instead of becoming angry about their money problems, the couple decides to further their education and seek a better-paying job to satisfy their financial needs. Consequently, the couple would have used their anger in a positive and constructive manner. They would have also learned the values of compromise and patience and would have taught other family members how to use their anger in a positive and constructive way.

When people examine the causes of their anger and learn to process their anger through positive self-talk, the person will realize that anger can be used to inspire them, as well as others, to make a positive change in developing a new and productive outlook on life.

Dangers of Anger and Road Rage

It does not take scientific study for us to understand the dangers of anger and road rage. The media and various television programs describe in detail how some people express their anger toward others while driving on city streets.

When we decide to take a walk or drive an automobile, we are taking a chance that some angry person will come from out of nowhere and plow into us as we are riding our bike, walking, or driving our automobile.

I have taught domestic violence classes for many years, and many of my students have told me that during or after an argument with their partner, their time-out is taking a drive in their automobile.

People must realize that many perpetrators of domestic violence have a serious problem with controlling their anger, and the last thing they should do after an argument is get behind the wheel of an automobile.

People who have left their home in anger have been seen acting out their anger on our city streets by driving recklessly and at incredible speeds, with total disregard for human life. Studies show that there are more than forty thousand automobile fatalities each year; nearly five thousand of those killed by an automobile were walking.

In these figures comes the problem of determining how many were killed as a result of negative anger or road rage. Of course, the solution to this problem is *not to drive while under the influence of anger or rage.* A person must stop and think how quickly an accident can happen when a person is angry or enraged while driving an automobile.

What Are the Causes of Anger?

We mentioned earlier that people become angry because of some kind of injustice. Although people may believe that certain kinds of injustice make them angry, we believe that nothing can make us angry.

We believe that when a situation takes place, based upon one's belief system, some people will become angry or enraged because they believe that they should become angry. Situations are not designed to single a person out to make them angry.

Let us take a simple situation. You're driving along in your car, and someone begins to tailgate you and begin blowing their car horn. They continue to drive closely behind your car for several miles. Was this particular situation designed especially for you so that you could become angry?

There are certain situations in life in which people believe that they are required to become angry or, even worse, enraged. Not so much because it happens to them, but it's a situation in which everyone should become angry.

If a person believes that he is supposed to feel a certain way toward a certain situation, then that's the way he will feel based upon his belief. Actually, it wasn't the situation that made him angry; it was his belief, which suggested that he become angry.

Aside from the fact that we make ourselves angry, researchers have determined that the causes of anger can be related to other factors such as

- psychiatric problems; for example, intermittent explosive disorder, addictive disorders, bipolar disorder, antisocial personality disorder, and borderline personality disorder;
- biological and physical problems; for example, a mental or physical disability;
- social problems; for example, parental abuse, trouble on the job, racial problems, and political concerns
- cultural problems; for example, the race for equality in gender and ethnic concerns;
- domestic abuse; for example, physical, emotional, and economic abuse from a person's past relationships.

Evidence strongly suggests that the pressures and mental tension of living in a hostile environment, particularly a home environment where there is constant abuse, is another reason people become angry. Certain people believe that if they are having a problem with a certain family member and they show anger toward that person, their problem will be solved.

For example, a partner arrives home from work, and dinner has not been prepared. A controlling partner believes that if he or she was to become angry, the person who normally does the cooking will think twice before deciding not to prepare dinner the next time, regardless of the reason for not preparing the dinner.

This sort of anger is used to control and dominate others to get them to do what they want them to do, sort of like a child would misbehave when they do not get their way. And if the parents give in to their child's negative behavior, the child will begin to believe negative behavior is the way to get what they want.

There are so many angry people living in the world; it has become very difficult to leave our home and not encounter some kind of hostility. Some of these angry people seem to take a perverted pleasure in hurting others when they become frustrated or angry. It seems as if they hurt others just to see how much pain they can cause so they can feel better about themselves. If someone were to ask them why are they so angry, they probably couldn't provide you with an answer, at least an answer which would make any sense to someone who has been victimized by an angry person.

Exercise

Are you or your partner angry people? Ask yourself as well as your partner what reasons each of you has for becoming angry. Study the list below and place a check next to the situation *you and your partner have decided* causes either of you to become angry.

_____Selfish people
_____My job
_____Fellow employees
_____People who lie
_____Unpaid bills
_____Bad-mannered people
_____In-laws
_____Merchants who sell you faulty products
_____Slow-moving traffic
_____Lack of finances
_____High taxes
_____People who harm others
_____People who steal
_____Noisy people
_____Rude people
_____Situations that do not go your way

Continue by making a list of other situations that you believe *make you angry*.

____
____
____
____
____

After completing your list of situations, persons, or things that cause you to become angry, ask yourself, is it the situation, person, or thing which causes you to become angry? Or do I cause myself to become angry? Also ask yourself the same question concerning happiness.

Is it situations, people, or things that make you happy, or do you make yourself happy? Or do situations, people, or things simply exist, and I have a choice for them to make me happy or not make me happy?

Many people also have what is known as *hidden anger*. Hidden anger is a repressed feeling of disappointment and resentment that may have been caused by a traumatic event. Every so often, something will trigger thoughts of the trauma; and when a person least expects it, the feeling of anger will appear.

Those who do not realize they have hidden anger will displace their angry feelings upon people who do not deserve to be treated with such negativity.

It's highly recommended that people who become angry and cannot understand why they are angry should seek professional assistance to find out why they become angry, and what they can do to process their anger and not allow their anger to get out of control.

Identifying Behavioral Aspects of Negative Anger

When we meet someone for the first time, we assume that the person is someone who is safe and will not do anything to harm us. Well, suppose they are not safe to be with, how would you know? How do you recognize an angry out-of-control person?

Following are basic steps for identifying the behavioral aspects of negative anger:

- Does the person have a history of getting angry for minor infractions?
- Does the person talk to others in a menacing voice?
- Is the person physically or verbally abusive toward others?
- How does the person react when he or she is told that he or she is wrong?
- Does the person destroy personal property or the property of others?
- Does the person seem to get a sense of pleasure after someone has been injured or killed?
- Does the person have difficulty resisting a "good fight"?

> Although anger is a rational and justified emotion, an angry person does not have the right to physically or verbally abuse others.

People who have a problem controlling their anger must learn to express their anger appropriately and realize it is okay to be angry, but it's not okay to harm others when they become angry. They must understand that everyone has a choice in how they express their anger.

Taking Ownership of Our Anger

When a person becomes angry, it's their responsibility to take ownership of their anger and not the responsibility of the person or thing they believe caused them to become angry.

Taking ownership of one's anger means that angry people acknowledge that they are angry. Once they have acknowledged that they are angry, they must realize that they have a choice as to what to do with their anger.

People must realize that becoming angry is not the problem; it's what we do with our anger that makes all the difference. Each person deals with anger in a manner that is unique to their personality. Learning more about how anger can be used in a positive way can help to save lives as well as relationships that would otherwise fall apart.

As we mentioned earlier, anger, if expressed appropriately, will produce positive results. Below are examples of how appropriately expressed anger can help:

- Often produce positive results
- Will not create arguments that will be difficult or impossible to overcome
- Will not lead to aggressive behavior
- Will often cause people to feel safe
- Will cause others to imitate positive behaviors as a result of their anger

When anger is properly used, anger can often be an asset to positive growth. Obviously, for a person who has been angry all their life, changing such a deep-seated emotion will be extremely difficult. In fact, it will require changing many negative beliefs that the angry person has held.

For example, many angry people believe that anger is an excellent tool for keeping people in line and getting their needs met and as a sign of power. A change in such beliefs is urgently needed if the person is to avoid causing themselves and others further pain and suffering.

Strategies for Managing Anger or Rage

Once a person with an anger problem begins to understand why they are angry and the choices they have to process their anger, their attitude will change. They will be able to relax and focus on what's important and what's not important in terms of how they express their anger.

Following are examples to assist an angry person with understanding their anger:

- Begin with counseling; it is the best approach to learning new techniques on how to manage anger.

- If counseling isn't readily available, read self-help books to learn more about what makes a person angry.
- Learn to identify anger cues, for example, an upset stomach, nervousness, or headaches.
- Learn to take deep breaths and walk away until you have calmed down enough to continue the conversation.
- Learn to understand how to identify your anger and process your feelings so as to decrease your outbursts of anger. For example, use positive self-talk, and talk yourself out of being angry.
- Stop and think about how the fury of your anger affects others.
- Work on developing insights into how others feel and show some compassion for their feelings.
- Become assertive but not domineering toward others, particularly family members.
- Take a closer look at "outdated" traditional beliefs about men and women in relationships.
- Write about your thoughts and feelings in a private journal.
- Redirect negative thoughts and make something positive happen. For example, when you see your children doing something that is harmful to themselves or others, explain to them the consequences of their behavior and advise them on the right way to behave.
- Get involved in a hobby such as painting, drawing, singing, writing music, playing an instrument, or exercising.
- Always talk to someone about how you are feeling. Be sure to choose someone you can trust and who will listen and will not show favoritism.

The previous examples are strategies for managing anger and will reduce the chance for any future outbursts of anger. These strategies can help an angry person discover new ways to deal with their anger.

When we learn to identify and then correctly process our anger, we will begin to see our personal and interpersonal relationships change from unhealthy to healthy. Many people are able to identify their anger without professional assistance; however, for others, outside intervention is necessary.

Self-Assessment

Following are questions you should ask yourself about anger. Apply personal knowledge as well as information from the chapter to answer with *yes*, *no*, or *NA* (not applicable) to the questions that apply to your knowledge concerning anger and its consequences. It is important that you answer all questions as accurately and honestly as possible.

1. Do you believe someone in your family needs help with their anger? ___
2. Are you an angry person? ___
3. Does your partner become physically aggressive when he or she becomes angry? ___
4. Do you become verbally abusive when you become angry? ___
5. Does it feel good to "get even" with people who make you angry? ___
6. Does your partner use anger to get what he or she wants? ___
7. Are you growing tired of your partner's angry outbursts? ___
8. Do you believe that if couples learn more about negative and positive anger, their relationship would improve? ___
9. Would you like your partner to learn more about negative and positive anger? ___
10. Are you or your partner willing to write about your thoughts and feelings in a private journal? ___

The previous list of questions is to better assess negative and positive anger levels. If you believe that it is necessary for you or your partner to seek assistance with managing negative anger, use the information in this workbook, as well as seek professional assistance, for any questions you may have which this workbook does not address.

Chapter Twenty

Stress Reduction

Chapter's Objectives:

1. To define the terms *stress* and *stressor*
2. To understand stress
3. To identify various causes of stress
4. To provide the reader with basic coping strategies that they can use to successfully process and manage stressful situations
5. To encourage the reader seek professional assistance for any stressful situations, which they cannot manage

Questions for You to Answer as You Read This Chapter:

1. What is *stress*?
2. How is *domestic violence* and *stress* related?
3. What causes you stress at home and on your job?
4. How can stress be harmful to your health?
5. What are some of the things you can do to manage your stress?

Related Chapters of Interest:

- Anger Management
- Separation and Divorce
- Alcohol and Substance Abuse within the Family
- Codependency
- A Relapse Prevention Plan

Chapter Twenty

Stress Reduction

Understanding Stress

Everyone feels stress at some point during a given day or week, whether it happens at home and on the job or driving in traffic or shopping in a supermarket.

In this chapter, we will address what is stress, the nature of stress, stress and our health, and techniques for managing situations that cause stress. We will begin by looking at the definition of stress.

What is *stress*? *Stress* can be defined as any personal or environmental situation that causes mental or physical pressure or tension to the point of upsetting the usual mental and physical functions of the human body.

Stress is often associated with situations that people find difficult to handle. People can develop stress as a result of pressure from a personal health problem, family problems, or with problems and various situations outside of the family.

Stress isn't something that just happens for the sake of causing us tension. Stress serves a very important purpose. The purpose of stress is to alert the mind and body to any kind of threat, whether the threat is real or imagined.

A real threat is a threat that actually exists. For example, if someone standing in front of you and they are angry with you, and their hands begin to curl into fists, and you believe that you are about to be harmed, this kind of situation would constitute a real threat.

When we imagine a threat exists, we are assuming that something will happen. If a person was to assume something negative is going to happen to them, they can become stressed. For example, if a partner were to see their mate talking to another man or woman, they could imagine all sorts of negative situations. They could imagine (assume) that their partner is having an extramarital affair or planning to have an extramarital affair. Assuming the worse, the partner becomes stressed. In many relationships, this particular example often proves to be a very dangerous assumption.

When people have high expectations toward a person, situation, or thing, many people will experience a certain amount of stress. For example, watching one's teenager play in a high school sporting event and your son or daughter has the ball with only a few seconds to score or you are watching your favorite sport event and your team has only a few seconds to score, can create a certain amount of stress.

Although these two situations can be considered as moments of stress, they also can be considered as a form of excitement. Excitement in the sense that they want to see their teenager do well, which will cause the teenager to feel good about himself or herself.

The thing to remember about stress is that all stressful situations are not bad for one's health. For instance, a person's stress response can also have a positive effect. Stress can heighten awareness and encourage motivation, which provide us with the stimulation needed to cope with many challenging situations.

Studies have shown that there are people who appear to function better when they are under small amounts of stress. For example, while on the job, there are people who will wait until the last minute to complete an assignment and, while under stress, can complete an assignment without any problem. The same can be said for students in school who will often wait until the last day to study for an exam and, while under stress, will pass their exam.

The amazing aspect about these people is that once they begin working on their assignment or studying for an exam, they will finish their assignment or take their test without breaking stride. However, people who like living on the edge will eventually develop stress-related complications.

Acute and Chronic Stress

When we talk about stress, we are talking about two kinds of stress: acute and chronic stress. What is *acute stress*? *Acute stress* can be defined as mental and physical tension (anxiety) that happens unexpectedly. For example, a parent may be teaching their teenager how to drive, and their teenager nearly runs into another car. At that point, the parent's mind and body will instantly experience mental and physical tension. However, as the teenager begins to follow their parent's instructions, the parent's mental and physical tension will subside. The parent will feel a sense of relief, and consequently, the parent will be relieved of their stress. This is known as acute stress because of its short-term effect on the parent. Of course, the same cannot be said for chronic stress.

What is *chronic stress*? Chronic stress can be defined as mental and physical tension (anxiety) that is always present or frequently recurs, i.e., all day, every day, every week, every month, and so on. For example, living with an extreme controller and being under the constant threat of violence can cause a person to experience chronic stress.

Stressors

What is a *stressor*? A *stressor* can be considered as a person(s), situation, or thing that causes someone mental and physical tension. In today's ever-demanding world, stressors can be found in just about every possible situation. Stressors can be found in our homes as we drive our automobiles, on our jobs, financial problems, and so on.

How do we develop stress? When we are faced with something that appears to be threatening to our mental or physical being, our mind and body react to the situation in the form of mental and physical tension.

A well-known psychologist, Hans Selye, believes that our body goes through three basic changes when we are faced with a real or imagined threat:

- In the initial frightened stage, we react to what is known as the stressor. Our brain produces certain hormones to provide our body with the energy it will need to take action against the threat.
- In the second stage, our mind and body will counteract to the threat. Our hormones provide the energy to our mind and body, and we will either defend against the threat by standing and fighting or running away (fight or flight).
- In the third stage, fatigue occurs. If we were overwhelmed during the fight or could not run fast enough during our flight, the third stage is our other choice. We could have a mental and physical breakdown.

The problem arises when we become totally stressed out. Of course, people who have high thresholds for stress can go day-to-day meeting some of life's toughest threats while others seem to "stress out" over what some people would consider as minor.

People who understand the causes of their stress will often find a solution to the problem. Finding solutions for dealing with your stress can reduce both stress and the negative impact it will have upon your health.

Following are a few examples of frequently occurring stressors:

- An oppressive relationship
- Everyday stop-and-go traffic
- Living under continued threats of violence
- A failing marriage
- Constant employment problems
- Sexual problems
- A disobedient child

> Researchers have proven that what we think and how we feel affects our health. Studies have shown that men and women who had gone through difficult life changes such as separation, divorce, or a job loss have a greater chance of becoming sick than people who have not experienced such changes. Everyone who experiences stress will occasionally develop some kind of symptom(s).

Exercise

Following is a list of what our body may experience as a result of daily untreated stress. Check which symptoms you are currently experiencing concerning stress.

- Poor health ___
- Constipation ___
- Grinding teeth ___
- Upset stomach ___
- High blood pressure ___
- Loss of interest in sex ___
- Fatigue ___
- Tension headaches ___
- Weight loss ___
- More rapid heartbeat ___

Following is a list of changes that take place in our behavior as a result of daily untreated stress. Check which applies to your current behavior.

- Dodging responsibilities ___
- Crying ___
- Overeating ___
- Undereating ___
- Aggressiveness ___
- Substance abuse ___
- Physically abusive ___
- Verbally abusive ___

Following is a list of changes that take place in our mind as a result of daily untreated stress. Check which applies to your current mental state.

- Anxious ___
- Poor concentration ___
- Argumentative ___
- Easily frightened ___
- Impatient ___
- Suspicious ___
- Forgetful ___
- Inability to make up your mind ___
- Negativity ___
- Sleeping problems ___

You must remember that prolonged unrelieved stress can lead to many kinds of illnesses. If you are experiencing stress for any reason and cannot seem to cope or find a solution to the problem, seek professional assistance.

Learning to Cope with Stress

How can we cope with stress? To understand how to cope with various problematic situations in our life, we must be able to identify what our stressors are. Once we know what our stressors are, we can develop methods to cope with the problem until we can solve the problem.

Problems come to us in the form of information; once we have received the information, we will process the information and then respond. The information in which we receive must be adjusted so we can change the method in which we respond.

Adjusting the information we receive simply means that we must make sure that the information we received is correct. This takes understanding and *self-control.*

If the information we have received is not correct based upon an assumption, then we must make the right adjustments so that we can gain a true understanding of what we have heard or seen. This will help a person to not overreact before finding out the facts and consequently saving themselves needless stress.

Learning to solve problems is a gradual process, which involves self-awareness and having a realistic understanding of one's environment. Understanding one's environment simply means that the person must learn more about themselves as well as the people they come in contact with and situations that take place around them.

A person must learn more about their family and job environment. What does each person expect from them, and what are their demands? Also, remember that most of us have stressors that are self-imposed. Specifically, we expect less from others and too much from ourselves; this can be mentally and physically exhausting. With all the various situations that take place in one's life, we must develop skills to cope and eliminate unwanted stressors.

A person's primary concern with developing the skills necessary to reduce stress is to realize that they are having a problem with stress. Once the person has come to this conclusion, they must obtain the knowledge necessary to cope with their stress until a solution has been found to solve their problem. There are men and women who find themselves torn between aggressive confrontation and compromising when it comes to coping with their problems. Some will use aggressive confrontation to cope with their problems by causing someone else stress.

Those who are stressed over a certain situation will use compromising to find a solution to their problem. To compromise means to find a middle ground in a stressful situation. For example, using the three Ws, we ask ourselves, *what* stresses me, *when* am I the most vulnerable to becoming stressed, and *why* do I allow certain situations to cause me stress?

When we can determine what, when, and why a particular person, thing, or situation stresses us, we can set our boundaries. For example, if it's one's partner who stresses us, and we know why and when he or she stresses us, our compromise will be based upon negotiating some sort of peace agreement and not become confrontational.

What many people fail to realize is that the problems we have, whether they are on the job or in our home, will eventually work themselves out if we learn to compromise.

In some cases, compromising is nothing more than making a slight adjustment in a certain area of our thinking process to win the battle against stress. Remember that there are some battles in life that are not worth fighting.

The following are examples of battles that are not worth fighting or situations that can be avoided

- Job demands. You have been given extra work, and you have eight hours on the job. You can only do your best and leave the rest until tomorrow.
- Fellow employees are constantly rude toward you. Put them to the side and speak with them about their rudeness. It's better than arguing and fighting with them and being labeled as a troublemaker and losing your job.
- You are late for work more than usual. Driving to work knowing that you will be late can cause stress. This can turn out to be a terrible morning if you do not think about the traffic that surrounds you. Most accidents are caused by people trying to make up time. Slow down because you may not make it to work if you get into an accident.

- Interacting with rude and angry people in public. What are you going to do with someone who likes to fight? In such a case, let law enforcement deal with such people, and you simply walk away.
- Neighbors can be very stressful at times. What can you do when one of your neighbors is playing their music loud or if their dog is constantly barking? Do not sit for hours and even days stressing over their loud music or their dog barking; first, calmly go and ask them to turn the music down or tell them the problem you are having with their dog barking. If they do not comply with your request, call law enforcement and find out what you can do about the noise.
- Someone tailgating you. What's the point of stressing over someone tailgating? Simply move out of their way.
- Financial problems increasing. Stop buying unneeded items, and plan a budget and stick to it.

These are minor stressors that can be avoided if we realize at the time of the stress that we have choices we can make to avoid becoming overly stressed. Take a moment and think about the choices you have in any of the above situations or situations not mentioned above. Make clear to yourself what your reaction will be if a certain situation arises.

Stress is unique in the sense that it affects each individual differently. In order to determine your threshold for stress, you must find the medium between what makes you feel comfortable and what makes you feel uncomfortable. Try to determine your threshold for stress.

Begin by

- studying your thoughts after a stressful situation;
- understanding your feelings after the situation;
- recognizing your body's reactions before, during, and after the situation;
- not overreacting toward the event;
- taking several deep breaths and holding them for five seconds; and exhaling slowly.

Think of other ways to avoid "stressing out" during a stressful situation, and discuss them with your partner, or seek professional assistance.

Researchers have identified basic coping strategies that people use to successfully process and manage stressful situations:

- Use self-control to avoid sudden outbursts of anger.
- Develop skills to remain calm during a crisis.
- Learn not to take on more than you can handle.
- Take time to understand your mental and physical limitations.
- Do not go on a blaming spree, blaming others for your stress.
- Try putting the stressors out of your mind until you completely understand everything involved in the stress.
- Put things in perspective with the most important things first, from the easiest to the most difficult.
- Understand the time frame that you have available to you to work through a situation. (Remember, many problems can solve themselves by simply leaving them alone.)
- Use a method called self-talk to process any moments of tension.
- Discuss the problem with someone who will listen and be useful and assist you with the problem.
- Be assertive: stand up for yourself if you feel that you are right.
- Learn to apologize when you are found to be in the wrong.
- Use prescription medication prescribed by one's doctor for anxiety.

> From time to time, we must be reminded that personal problem solving is not always easy to do. The most difficult aspect of this process is to "stand back" and look at situations as unemotionally as we can.

Problematic Stressors

What stressors should a person dispose of first? First, find out what stressors bother you the most. We recommend that you start on any problematic stressful situations at home. Shift to your job and eventually move to situations in your external environment such as driving in traffic, noisy neighbors, and so on.

Take each category (home, job, and external environment) and decide what is most important, and schedule time to work on every detail of a particular problem. For example, abusive behavior should be your first priority. If you or your partner is abusive, learn to stop the abuse. If you have a problem deciding whether or not you are abusive, ask your partner and your children, and they will surely tell you if you are abusive or not. If your partner is abusive, you shouldn't have to ask anyone; it would be obvious. While you are working on disposing of situations that cause you stress, you can learn to relax.

Following are suggested methods of relaxing:

- Always have something to do.
- Exercise, go bowling, dancing, biking, cycling, or join a softball team.
- Listen to your favorite music.
- Clean your vehicle, read a good book, or write a journal.
- Make sure you are getting enough sleep.
- Avoid using sugars, caffeine, and nicotine.
- Watch a good comedy.
- Try laughing some unimportant issues off.
- Do not self-medicate; stay away from alcohol and illegal drugs.

Do not wait until it is too late seek professional assistance if you find that you cannot work through your stress alone.

Self-Assessment

Following are statements to assist you with understanding your stress. Apply personal knowledge, as well as information from the chapter, to answer *true*, *false*, or *NA* (not applicable) to the following statements. It is important that you answer all statements as accurately and honestly as possible.

1. I understand what causes me stress. ___
2. Learning to control my thoughts will help me with my stress. ___
3. Muscle tensions, rapid breathing, rapid heartbeat, anxiety, and shakiness are some of the ways our body let us know that we need to relieve the stress. ___
4. I use my feelings and emotions to help me to solve my problems. ___
5. I will attempt to compromise if it will solve the problem. ___
6. Prolonged, unrelieved stress can lead to accidental injury, insomnia, migraines, and serious illness such as alcoholism, depression, and cancer. ___
7. I understand that learning to solve my problems will help me with my stress. ___
8. Eating right is important; caffeine, refined sugars, starches, and junk food create false energy and will cause the body stress. ___
9. An exercise plan can help me feel healthier and less stressful. ___
10. Getting professional assistance for my stress can help reduce the negative effects of stress. ___

The previous list of statements is to better assess your understanding of stress. If you believe that it is necessary for you to learn more about the dangers of stress, use the information in this workbook, or seek professional assistance for any questions you may have which this workbook does not address.

Chapter Twenty-one

Self-esteem

Chapter's Objectives:

1. To define the term *self-esteem*
2. To assist the reader with gaining an understanding of having healthy and unhealthy self-esteem
3. To assist the reader with determining their level of self-esteem
4. To provide information that will demonstrate the importance of having healthy self-esteem
5. To assist the reader with understanding that healthy self-esteem is the result of how well we treat ourselves

Questions for You to Answer as You Read This Chapter:

1. How is my self-esteem?
2. Why it is important to have healthy self-esteem?
3. How do people develop unhealthy self-esteem?
4. What can a person do to improve their self-esteem?
5. Do you know how your children feel about themselves?

Related Chapters of Interest:

- What Is Domestic Violence?
- Communication Skills
- Anger Management
- Codependency
- Love and Commitment

Chapter Twenty-one

Self-esteem

Healthy and Unhealthy Self-esteem

One of the most important topics in counseling sessions and group meetings is the subject of self-esteem. Most people like to refer to a person's self-esteem as being "high or low." However, there is greater relevance to consider self-esteem as being healthy or unhealthy, in terms of its role in providing a positive or negative effect upon the human mind and body.

What is *self-esteem*? *Self-esteem* is how much a person likes, accepts, and respects himself or herself as a person. Self-esteem is measured by the degree of self-confidence, faith, and pride a person has about themselves. Self-esteem can influence one's personality, their ability to love themselves, and their capacity to care for and love others.

In professional settings, one's self-esteem reflects on one's ability to accomplish important goals and utilize their individual sense of morality (right and wrong). For example, a person can be said to have healthy self-esteem when they have self-respect and take pleasure in doing what's right for themselves as well as for others.

Healthy Self-esteem

People with healthy self-esteem are more confident, caring, cheerful, and friendly than those with unhealthy self-esteem. A person with healthy self-esteem takes pleasure in finding a purpose in life and in reaching out into the unknown and finds a way to reach what other believe to be unreachable.

Those with healthy self-esteem do not dwell on their imperfections but accept both their strengths and weaknesses and strive to achieve an inner peace.

When a person has a positive attitude, any weakness they may have become of lesser importance, and this allows them to remain focused on their strengths. A positive attitude also allows them to feel good about themselves and work on any weaknesses that may interfere with their *inner harmony*.

Also, people with healthy self-esteem are valued by people who may have unhealthy self-esteem because of their pleasant and optimistic attitudes. People like to associate with others who feel good about who they are and have dreams and aspirations.

Unhealthy Self-esteem

To a large degree, unhealthy self-esteem is a way of thinking and behaving that has become irrational. Unhealthy self-esteem can cause certain types of depression that could easily cause people to believe that other people are better than they are. Such a belief is not spiritually based since no one is better than any other person. Being yourself makes you special. A person may not be rich, intellectual, or the most attractive person in the world, but this matters not.

The best thing that we can do for ourselves is to make the most of the mental and physical attributes that we possess. Bringing negativity into our belief system affects who we are and our ability to achieve and will eventually cause negative situations to develop. This is an accepted law of nature.

Many controllers know the power of healthy and unhealthy self-esteem. Controllers use unhealthy self-esteem as a popular method to dominate and control others through the use of sex, social status, finance, or physical ability. If a person continuously uses sex, wealth, social status, or physical ability to dominate others, one's self-esteem can be affected.

Controllers who are unhappy with themselves typify the saying, "When I feel miserable, I want the world to feel miserable, and if I am suffering, I want the world to suffer."

Controllers labor at turning happy situations into sad ones. Controllers demonstrate a lack of ability to assist others in achieving their goals, particularly those who are closest to them, like family members. Not all families are so structured, yet even having a few families affected by someone who attacks another person's self-esteem is too much.

Leading sociologists and psychologists believe developing or having unhealthy self-esteem is about how a person views himself or herself and the world around him or her. Sociologists and psychologists believe that the thinking processes that guide a person to develop unhealthy self-esteem are based upon having little or no faith in one's mental or physical abilities.

There are people who have unhealthy self-esteem because they believe other people fail to appreciate them for who they are as a person; therefore, they feel unwanted and unloved. A person with unhealthy self-esteem may believe that no one cares about them, when in fact, the opposite is true.

To assume the belief that no one cares or one cannot do anything right and to be told by someone you love that you are useless can become devastating to a person's mental health.

A person with unhealthy self-esteem must realize that if they ignore people who put them down and search for those who care about them, they will realize that there are millions of people who care about them and their well-being.

Following are some mental affects of having unhealthy self-esteem:

- Feeling helpless and irritable with feelings of guilt and anger
- Difficulty in concentration
- Loss of hope and energy
- Loss of appetite
- Experiencing difficulty sleeping
- Loss of sexual drive
- Constantly making mistakes
- Difficulty in communicating with others

Exercise

How do you feel about yourself? Describe yourself by answering the following:

- I feel good when______________________________

- My greatest fears are______________________________

- I become disappointed when I cannot____________________

- I know people care about me because____________________

- I love myself because______________________________

- I have problems loving myself because____________________

- My life is filled with______________________________

- My feelings about my current job are______________________________

- When I am alone, I feel______________________________

- I believe someday that I will______________________________

> The previous list is to better assess you with determining your level of self-esteem. If you believe you would like to learn more about healthy and unhealthy self-esteem, use the information in this workbook and also seek professional assistance for any questions that you may have concerning self-esteem not addressed by this workbook.

Situations in Life

Some people believe in the grand design of life, which simply means that all life on this planet must experience both good as well as the bad with no exceptions. For example, for several days or so, everything is great or at least satisfactory; everything seems to be going the way we want them to go. All of a sudden, nothing seems to go the way we planned. What happened?

We will use all our power of reasoning to make sense of what went wrong. We will question ourselves, and then we will question others. Maybe we will figure out what went wrong, and maybe we will not.

Problems in which we can determine a solution in a matter of seconds can give use the strength to move on, and yet there are some situations that we will never understand unless we ask for assistance.

There are certain problems that do not have an immediate answer and sometimes will work themselves out without any additional involvement from us.

If we cannot resolve a problem, remember that there are situations in life that we can change, and there are those that we cannot. Most importantly, we must not allow any situation that we cannot change to negatively affect our self-esteem.

For situations that we cannot change, we must get assistance or move on to another situation where changes can be implemented. We must remember that there are situations in life that will cause us to feel sad and even helpless, but we must continue to feel good about who we are. And we must be careful not to give in to depressing days and depressing nights and allow difficult situations to work themselves out.

Remember, the burden of completing a goal or assignment doesn't fall entirely upon you. *If you ask for help, you will receive help.*

As human beings, we will at times encounter extremely complicated situations in which we cannot seem to comprehend. At such time, many of us will call upon *our higher power* to assist us through such difficult times. Does calling on a higher power work? We believe that in order for a high power to continue when you can no longer endure is a matter of belief.

We should not become all the more frustrated when we ask *our higher power* for assistance, and our immediate request is not received. The important factor is that we are not afraid to ask for help when we feel the need or feel discomfort in having even expressed a need for help.

All humans are vulnerable to attacks from negative influences in our environment over which we have no control. All we can do is learn from these experiences and be prepared when they revisit. The alternative is to ignore the problem and continue to allow it to negatively affect our self-esteem.

How many times must a person get thumped on the head before realizing that he or she is being attacked? For some, it takes only once, and for others, it depends largely upon how they feel about being thumped.

People who associate themselves with good, happy, and caring people will often become good, happy, and caring persons themselves. People who associate with those who are uncaring, mean, violent, and untrustworthy can and often develop these dreadful traits.

Living in a fast-paced society filled with stress and instability can make a person vulnerable to developing negative attitudes about everything and everyone around them. We cannot allow our environment to control our thoughts and behaviors. Consequently, the choice to be happy or unhappy is ours and not the condition of our environment. The relationship between our fast-growing unpredictable society, the development of unhealthy self-esteem, and violent behavior in domestic situations has been the topic of numerous sociological and psychological studies.

We are in agreement with the results of previous studies conducted by leading sociologists and psychologists. They have confirmed that abusers and batterers, who have unhealthy self-esteem, are a contributing cause of domestic violence. Although the environment may or may not be a contributing factor in how we think, we ultimately have the final say in how we react.

Given that we are capable of controlling our emotions, making the right choices, and understanding the consequences of our actions, we should be able to make the right decision during any given any situation.

Abusers and batterers have choices and should understand the consequences of those choices. Abusers and batterers who suffer from unhealthy self-esteem will often put unnecessary stress on their partner and children. Abusers are not coerced to abuse or batter their partner or children; it is a conscious choice.

Abusers and batterers may or may not understand or care to understand the consequence of their children continuously living under conditions of stress. Whether the abuser or batterer understands or not, the facts are that constant stress by parents, siblings, teachers, or peers can lead a child to self-destructive tendencies.

If abusers and batterers take the time to learn more about relationships and spend less time fighting and yelling, they *should* understand why so many teenagers have thoughts of running away from home or committing suicide to escape the mental pain caused by being abused and battered.

> This fact has been stated previously in this workbook, and we decided to revisit this issue due to its utmost importance.

A fast-growing society may be related to the development of unhealthy self-esteem, but it is not reason enough to use abusive behavior to enhance the self-esteem of a controlling individual.

Following is a list of negative situations many children face daily, which could cause them to develop unhealthy self-esteem:

- A troubled childhood
- Memories of being sexual abused
- Lack of affection
- Unwarranted threats of punishment
- Relationship problems
- Having no plans for the future
- Being the target of practical jokes and or teasing by peers or both
- Poor appearance (clothing or physical or both)
- Having combative parents
- Substance abuse in the family

> Many children with unhealthy self-esteem experience these situations on a daily basis. Children are not as mentally strong as adults; therefore, many think with feelings and not with logic. Most children do not even consider why a parent is abusive; they are more attuned to how they are feeling as a result of the abuse.

How to Build Healthy Self-esteem

There is nothing more powerful or sustaining in difficult times than having healthy self-esteem. Self-esteem and finding self-fulfillment are the central points of how we feel about ourselves. This is most important when day-to-day situations in our lives appear discouraging and unrewarding.

Living in an environment with obstacles that impede our progress toward reaching our goals can dampen our spirit. Continuing development and maintenance of healthy self-esteem may seem very difficult to achieve. For example, frustration occurs when a person is involved with situations that cause them to take two steps backward for every step they take forward or when two pennies are taken from three pennies earned. Maintaining a healthy self-esteem under such conditions may seem impossible, but it's not impossible.

Maintaining a healthy self-esteem pertains to how we love and care about who we are as a person without being overly concerned about how others believe we should feel about who we are. Equally important is remembering that everyone is not going to love us as much as we love ourselves or going to treat us fairly.

Once a person has reached a level of complete self-respect and self-fulfillment, it cannot be taken away unless they allow it to be removed. A person with healthy self-esteem will not allow anyone or anything to deprive them of such a precious and magnificent personal treasure.

All of us have the ability to define who we are and make a conscious decision as to whether or not we like what we have discovered about ourselves. If we decide to change how we feel about ourselves, we must look deep within ourselves to make the necessary changes and move forward. Gaining a better understanding of our level of self-esteem does not take magic but rather an honest evaluation of what we like and dislike about ourselves.

The mechanisms that guide a person to having healthy self-esteem are learning self-control, keeping in good physical health, making good use of their time, having a continued success, and having *faith* in oneself. Another method of developing healthy self-esteem is to monitor what we say positively and negatively about ourselves.

For example, avoid personal attacks such as calling yourself stupid or clumsy after an accident or if something does not quite turn out the way you wanted it to. You must never stop trying if what you are seeking to achieve is worth the effort. When a situation becomes difficult, take a mental time-out by thinking about something positive in the past or present. Also, do a self-assessment on paper to allow evaluation of the areas you need to work on.

People need to feel good about themselves and their life's development. Striving to achieve is a sure way of maintaining healthy self-esteem. Failures will happen as no one is perfect, so simply understanding the mistakes made and trying again are ways to reach your goals.

Everyone feels sad and depressed at times, but you cannot give up. In the grand design, success follows failure. The perception that some people seem to do everything right the first time is an error. Somewhere in the process to achieve goals, there have been failures, but they never stopped trying.

Self-Assessment

Following is a list to better assess your understanding of healthy and unhealthy self-esteem. Apply personal knowledge, as well as information from the chapter, to answer *true*, *false*, or *NA* (not applicable) to the statements that apply to your knowledge concerning self-esteem. It is important that you answer all statements as accurately and honestly as possible.

1. I have a healthy self-esteem. ___
2. I have unhealthy self-esteem, and I would like to learn more about gaining healthy self-esteem. ___
3. I do not care what people think of me. ___
4. I allow others to determine how I feel about myself. ___
5. It is important for parents to be aware of their children's self-esteem. ___
6. Substance abuse can destroy healthy self-esteem. ___
7. Self-esteem is something that can be healthy one day and unhealthy the next day. ___
8. I know having healthy self-esteem can help me reach my goals. ___
9. People can be sad at times and still have healthy self-esteem. ___
10. People care about me, and I care about people. ___

The previous list of statements is to better assess your understanding of healthy and unhealthy self-esteem. If you believe that it is necessary for you to learn more about self-esteem, use the information in this workbook, and also seek professional assistance for any questions you may have that this workbook does not address.

Chapter Twenty-two

Conflict
Resolution

Chapter's Objectives:

1. To explore the term *conflict resolution*
2. To address the issue of domestic conflicts
3. To discuss the idea of personal opinions during domestic conflicts
4. To address the idea of negotiation and fairness
5. To discuss solutions to settling conflicts

Questions for You to Answer as You Read This Chapter:

1. How often am I in conflict with my partner?
2. What causes conflicts in your relationship?
3. What are good methods to settle disagreements?
4. Does everyone have a right to express his or her opinion?
5. What's negotiation and fairness?

Related Chapters of Interest:

- Communication Skills
- Anger Management
- Codependency
- Trust and Respect
- Love and Commitment

Chapter Twenty-two

Conflict Resolution

A Difference of Opinion

What is *conflict resolution*? *Conflict resolution* is a means to resolve the difference of opinions, belief and ideas of two or more people or groups. In domestic situations, conflict resolution emerges when both partners explore ways to find a positive solution to their problem(s), in which both parties will find acceptable.

Most conflicts are the result of people having difference of opinions. First, let us define the term *opinion*. What is an opinion? An opinion is a thought that a person holds to be true. Whether an opinion is true or not is what usually causes conflict.

Whether a person has a different opinion than someone else or whether the truth of their opinion is questionable, they still have a personal right to have an opinion. In a relationship, a conflict usually arises when one person is not allowed to completely voice their opinion, and the other person in the conversation attempts to impose their opinion on their partner.

Whether it's a marriage or a relationship with friends or extended family members, it is almost guaranteed that when two people find a subject to discuss, a difference of opinion will occur. Individual diversity is very important and can be the basis for obtaining new ideas; it is how the diversity in ideas is handled that is important.

Inviting others to share opinions expands our knowledge base, but when a partner absolutely refuses to listen to their partner's opinions, there is a breakdown in communications, usually resulting in a fierce argument.

If you have ever been in a verbal domestic war of words, you know people can become physically and emotionally abusive. There are couples who don't like to argue with each other, and there are people who seem to get a sense of enjoyment from arguing. This is particularly true with people who like to be in control.

All of us have encountered people who seem to think they have the answer to every possible question. If you know such a person, the best thing to do is disengage in a conversation with them after a certain amount of time because they will drain every ounce of your mental energy to prove to you that they are right.

People who know how to communicate with their partners, realize that a disagreement doesn't necessarily have to be a discussion gone badly. There can be positive outcomes in domestic disagreements without either person becoming frustrated because they were proven wrong in their opinion.

It's important to remember to manage your thoughts and feelings and not try to change someone's belief(s) once they have made up their mind about a certain subject. If you are speaking with someone who respects your opinions, respect theirs as well.

Never allow a discussion to turn into a competition or allow a conversation to get out of control because you want to prove the other person wrong.

If you know for a fact that you are right, why argue? A great day or weekend can be completely destroyed because one partner or the other believes he or she must prove his or her partner wrong. Most people dislike being told they are wrong when they believe they are right.

For the sake of maintaining harmony during a discussion, let us review a situation in which two people have differing opinions. Let us take for example a discussion in which both partners are right in their opinion, but neither partner is willing to take the time to consider the other's perspective.

They may be saying the same thing but are using different words and are approaching the subject of discussion from different angles. If they were good communicators, they would be able to listen and understand what the other person is saying, and there would not be a need to challenge the other person's opinion.

In a discussion about a particular family problem, approaching the problem from different angles can be beneficial to obtaining a solution. Couples must realize that many family problems do not come with only one answer.

Many family problems are like multiple-choice questions in which there are four possible correct answers to the question, one being better than the other three. Seeing the perspectives of others allows several reasonable possibilities and can be a great asset to finding the best possible solution.

Once a problem has been solved, it will be much easier to move on to the next without believing that you must revisit the same problem again. However, should the same problem return, the couple can resolve the problem with less effort.

Controllers must come to the realization that no one knows everything, and no one is right all the time. Actually, when there are multiple factors involved in a particular problem, there are only a few people who are *right half the time*; so it would be in the best interest of all concerned to get a second opinion concerning difficult situations that may cost the family time, money, and unnecessary stress.

Having a partner who believes he or she knows it all is difficult at best. Anyone who believes that he or she knows everything is a foolish person, who usually understands less than any person in a discussion. Most relationships cannot withstand a mind-draining know-it-all. Some listeners soon come to the conclusion that it's useless to speak their mind and believe that saying nothing is best to keep the peace.

While remaining silent may seem to be the right thing to do, even that approach has its drawbacks. People who simply sit and listen while their partner rambles on and on with no meaningful outcome will eventually reach their limit and explode in anger or rage. In some cases, the silent treatment may result in a physical altercation and may cause a fight to the death over an issue of little or no importance. This resulting reaction may have a more disastrous effect, so what was gained by keeping silent?

People do not want to be proven wrong every time they speak about a subject, particularly when they have the facts to prove their case. For example, if a couple has a child with a serious cough and a slight fever, the controlling parent will argue that it's *just* a cold, and the child will be okay. The other parent believes it could be something more serious, and the child should be taken to a physician. Who is right, and who is wrong in this case? Both partners could be right, but why take a chance with the health of the child when there is no risk involved in obtaining assurance?

The proper thing to do would be to take their child to see the family's physician, yet the controller doesn't listen to reason, calling his or her partner stupid for overreacting while the child remains ill. Why does this happen? Why do couples fight each other to the point of becoming physically and emotionally abusive?

Is it because of the struggle to have or maintain power and control over their partner? Or could it be due to a list of possibilities such as a lack of communication skills, trust and support, lack of respect, resentment issues, past or current physical and emotional abuse, anger problems, financial problems, or incompatibility? The answer to that question could be any or all of the above.

In addition to the possibilities mentioned above, many couples have a tendency to forget about the love they have or once had for each other and the responsibility that goes along with loving someone. When this happens, it seems as if the relationship has taken a turn for worst, and the result is every man or woman for himself or herself.

The Causes of Domestic Conflicts

Along with what has already been mentioned, living in a mentally demanding social environment often produces stress. Job demands, changes in technology, and social changes are situations that have placed a tremendous amount of stress on relationships. Most people who work in high-pressure positions will unintentionally bring their stress into the home and unload their feelings of frustration and anger on unsuspecting family members.

Many people, men in particular, have not taken time to learn about their feelings and how to work through frustrations that are a result of overwhelming job demands, technology, or social changes. When either partner brings problems home without sitting down and discussing their concerns with their partner, conflict becomes inevitable. Job demands, changes in technology, or social changes aren't the only reasons there is conflict in the home. Numerous other reasons can cause domestic conflicts:

- Lack of communication skills
- Little or no spousal trust
- Complete lack of respect
- Spousal alcohol or drug addiction
- Lack of money to pay household bills
- Different beliefs about raising their children

- Disagreements over financial situations
- Lack of intimacy or sex in the relationship
- Lack of parenting skills
- Communication with their children
- The sort of punishment parents may or may not use toward their children
- Failure to understand the need for personal time for either partner
- Conflicts over child care and medical care for the family
- Resentment
- An extramarital affair
- Either partner having anger issues

Any of the situations mentioned above does not necessarily mean that one partner is trying to control the other; rather it means that solutions for reducing stressful situations with the relationship should be pursued.

In a *reality-based relationship*, couples must understand that life is filled with temptations, problems, and vices. For example, a reality-based couple should avoid temptations or vices, which cause their family disruption. If a problem should arise, both partners should be able to sit down and respectfully find a solution to the problem. If the problem is a habitual vice, such as drugs or alcohol, couples should be able to discuss methods to solve the problem and seek professional assistance to facilitate working through their problem(s).

Exercise

Following are a series of statements and questions to determine the level of conflict in your home. Apply personal knowledge, as well as information from the chapter, to answer *yes*, *no*, or *NA* (not applicable) to the following statements or questions. It is important that you answer all questions as accurately and honestly as possible.

1. Do you and your partner argue more than ____once a week ____three times a week ____every day of the week?
2. Name several situations during which you and your partner argue about the most.

   ____
   ____
   ____
   ____
   ____

3. Do you have a problem admitting having been found to be wrong? ____
4. Does your partner have a problem admitting it when he or she is found to be wrong? ____
5. Have you or your partner ever used threats or intimidation to control a conversation? ____If the answer is yes, name the kinds of threats and the methods of intimidation that your partner used.

   ____
   ____
   ____
   ____
   ____

6. Have you or your partner ever used threats or acts of intimidation to control what they other say or do? ____If the answer is yes, name the kinds of threats and the methods of intimidation that you or your partner used or currently uses.

   ____
   ____
   ____
   ____
   ____

7. Name several negative consequences that could affect children who witness daily and weekly bouts of arguing or fighting between their parents.

8. Describe how an average argument begins in your relationship.

9. Describe how the argument ends.

10. Describe how it would feel to not argue and fight with your partner.

The previous list of statements and questions is to better assess your understanding of conflict in your relationship.

The Family Negotiation Process

What is *negotiation*? *Negotiation* is the process of two or more people coming together to arrive at an agreeable decision. When you are involved in any discussion with regard to transactions, arrangements, bargaining, agreements, coming to terms with settlements, meeting someone halfway, or signing a contract, you are in the process of negotiating.

Family negotiations focus primarily on cooperation without upsetting or embarrassing the other person. There should not be a one-dimensional approach where someone is exploited or left out of the negotiating process. Family negotiations balance the wants and needs of those involved in the negotiation process toward reaching a resolution that will satisfy all involved.

Since life is highly competitive, most relationships could not survive a hard-bargaining partnership. A *hard-bargaining partnership* is a relationship in which one partner or the other is a take-no-prisoners opportunist. This kind of partner will use any means necessary, to obtain the upper hand to take control of the negotiation process. They will use flashy words, play mental games, and use put-downs to manipulate their partner into doing things their way.

Many couples will say that they do not care who makes the decisions as long as the results are successful. It would be great if one person in the family had all the answers all the time, but no one is capable of having all the right answers all the time.

What's Important during Negotiations?

The main factor in negotiations is to believe at the end of a discussion that everyone is treated fairly. That is, everyone believes that everyone gain something from the negotiations process. Many people would call it a win-win situation.

It is essential to learn what's important and what has no discussion value during family negotiations. Learning to compromise is another major factor in family negotiations. Learning to compromise can teach a person to abandon ideas that are not important and retain ideas that are important to reach a common goal or maintain stability in a relationship.

In a sincere effort to negotiate for something, it must be worth the effort and time involved. Constantly quarrelling over who will cook, wash the dishes or clean the house can prove to be a waste of precious mental energy and can create an undue amount of stress. Causing a partner or other family member to become stressed over situations with little to no value in maintaining a happy home environment is obviously not worth the time or effort.

Since the goal of negotiation is to seek a balance and reach a resolution that meets everyone's wants and needs, to ensure that this happens, couples must join together and plan reasonable guidelines for each person's involvement in the negotiation.

Basic Guidelines for Negotiations

Guidelines are designed for people to reach certain goals, and setting guidelines for negations is no exception. Keep in mind that guidelines are used by open-minded people who want to reach some kind of settlement. A controller, on the other hand, has his or her own set of guidelines and would feel threatened if approached by his or her partner to set new guidelines. Controllers make no effort to understand the importance of peaceful negotiations in family situations.

Most controllers enjoy using the *old-school* approach of "it's my way or the highway." This approach is another form of psychological and emotional abuse.

Apart from a partner who is an extreme controller, many controllers will listen to reason if they believe that their partner is serious about making changes and if their previous ideas for solving a problem aren't working.

Following are basic guidelines that will prove useful during negotiations with your partner:

- Make your point clear and valid without quarreling.
- Avoid verbal attacks.
- Avoid making demands.
- Avoid I-warn-you statements.
- Stick to the issues at hand.
- Listen to what the other person has to say without interrupting.
- Be willing to compromise.

> One sure way of solving conflicts is through effective communication through fair negotiations.

Following are three basic steps to remember when engaging in communication with your partner:

Step 1: Understand all aspects of the issue at hand and listen to what your partner has to say. After carefully listening to what your partner has to say, go over their main point and the facts that support their point. For example, the family is spending too much money on unimportant items; bills are not being paid on time, and the cost of late fees are the issues being discussed.

- What is the main point in your partner's subject matter?
- How important to the family is your partner's issues?
- What facts does your partner have to support their issues?
- What steps should you take to resolve the problem or what steps should you take not to create a *fight*?

Step 2: Assess your partner's main point and the information you can identify in their argument.

- Bills are not being paid on time, or too much money is being lost to late fees.
- More attention should be paid toward less unimportant items and more toward paying bills.
- Develop a budget to prevent loss of hard-earned money.

Step 3: Draw an honest conclusion regarding the importance of your partner's argument.

- I realize that my partner is right about our financial situation.
- I believe that my partner is out of line when it concerns how I spend my money.
- I admit, in part, that my partner is right about our financial problems.

> There are many day-to-day personal and domestic problems to be encountered. The bad news is that many couples do not have the skills or ever take the time to learn how to resolve their problems. The good news is that all problems have some kind of solution.

Couples must learn that problems in relationships can be solved with patience, logic, and reasoning, which are the basic laws of nature. However, many people do not use basic logic and have not developed patience to settle their differences; they would rather rely on their feelings to make decisions.

Consideration of feelings in the resolution of a problem may work in some situations but will never work in all situations. Consideration of one's feelings in the resolution of certain problems may include an immediate reward, but the long-term effects of their decision may cause a larger problem. For example, it's Christmas, and there is a conflict over being in debt, and we feel great that it's Christmas, and we want our partner and children to have a good Christmas. Consequently, the decision was made to think with our heart, and expensive gifts were purchased for everyone. The short-term immediate goal has been accomplished in that their partner and children are happy, but now, the family is deeper in debt. Thinking logically, what could have been done to avoid the long-term problem?

Another example shows a partner is feeling angry about something that has taken place in the relationship. Anger has resulted in a graduation from ignoring a partner into physical contact. The problem is now greatly complicated with added frustration, anger, and resentment as well as the possibility of police intervention. Thinking logically, what could have been done to avoid the long-term problem?

In the process of having one's needs met, there are times when a couple must be able to compromise through negotiations. Couples must believe they can communicate with each other without feeling as if one or the other have been denied a personal right or have been outsmarted.

A couple must also understand the difference between what their family *needs* and what a family *wants* during negotiations. For example, a family may want a new car but cannot afford the expense. The need for a car is evident, yet buying a new car is not realistic at this time. Consequently, buying what the family needs and can afford would be the best solution.

Fairness

What is *fairness*? In a relationship, fairness is marked by honesty free from selfishness, injustice, or favoritism. Great and lasting relationships are built upon good communication, love, trust, respect, and fairness. Any deficiency of any one of these qualities may result in conflict.

When a person believes that he or she hasn't been treated fairly, there is usually retaliation that results in conflict. For example, the weekend has arrived, and both partners have had a long and tiring week on their job. One partner would like to spend a quiet weekend at home, and the other partner would like to go out with friends. How would the couple decide whether to stay home or go out without arguing and fighting? The obvious solution would be to compromise.

They will have to decide whether to spend the weekend together or go separate ways. In either case, fairness has tremendous implications with regard to each person believing that they were treated fairly.

In the world of reality, can a couple treat each other fairly in *every possible situation* without showing any signs of selfishness? Sure, it's possible if we decide not to include the small and seemly unimportant situations. Situations such as drinking the last glass of orange juice or leaving the top off the toothpaste are insignificant situations. Such situations aren't reasons couples separate or divorce. However, when a partner believes they are being used repeatedly or disrespected, separation or divorce is inevitable.

Success or failure in resolving conflict is basically about being treated fairly. It's realistic to believe that some conflicts that take place in relationships are really good for the growth of the relationship if managed correctly. However, we must remember that in cases where domestic violence is involved, the victim may find it nearly impossible to find resolution following circumstances of physical or emotional abuse.

A partner who has been abusive must remember serious conflicts cannot be resolved overnight; it takes time and effort to discover what has been lost when someone has been abused by their partner.

Self-Assessment

Following are statements to assist you with understanding the idea of fairness in your relationship. Apply personal knowledge, as well as information from the chapter, to answer *true*, *false*, or *NA* (not applicable) to the following statements. It is important that you answer all statements as accurately and honestly as possible.

1. I understand the basic idea of fairness. ___
2. Fairness carries with it the notion of equality. ___
3. Inconsistent behavior is not fair to my partner or the children. ___
4. I teach my children about fairness. ___
5. I am only fair when others are fair toward me. ___
6. I do not think that it is fair for my partner to withhold sex or money from me when I upset him or her. ___
7. I want to be fair, but it's hard after having a past in which everyone was out for what they could get from me. ___
8. I am fair only if my partner is fair. ___
9. Good communications, trust, and fairness are the most important aspects of a relationship. ___
10. Self-interest and favoritism are considered as being unfair. ___

The previous list of statements is to better assist you with understanding the term *fairness* in your relationship. If you believe that it is necessary for you to learn more about fairness and the ability to compromise in your relationship, use the information in this workbook, and also seek professional assistance for any questions you may have that this workbook does not address.

Chapter Twenty-three

Separation and Divorce

Chapter's Objectives:

1. To discuss the basic idea of the rise and fall of a relationship
2. To discuss reasons couples separate and divorce
3. To discuss feelings during a separation
4. To discuss coping strategies during after separation
5. To encourage anyone involved with separation or divorce to seek professional assistance when necessary

Questions for You to Answer as You Read This Chapter:

1. Do you believe couples can remain married for life?
2. What feelings people may experience during separation?
3. Why do couples separate or divorce?
4. What are reasons professionals give for the increase in separations and divorces?
5. How difficult would it be for you to separate from your partner if you find it to be necessary?

Related Chapters of Interest:

- What Is Domestic Violence?
- What Is Power and Control?
- Communication Skills
- Anger Management
- Trust and Respect

CHAPTER TWENTY-THREE

Separation and Divorce

The Beginning of a Relationship

Take a moment and think back to a time when you were alone and had a kind of deep painful need to love someone and be loved in return. How did it feel waiting for someone to enter into your life? Some people would feel afraid, abandoned, and insecure that they will never find anyone. And others may experience loneliness, a little concern, yet remain secure.

In either case, one day, you meet someone who has a good personality, is physically attractive, economically secure, and enjoys sex. You believe that this is the person that you have been searching for all your life. The feeling of being alone no longer exists, and the feeling of excitement is overwhelming. You believe that you can respect, love, and trust this person forever.

Can you remember how you craved such a relationship, particularly the need to be loved and be able to love someone so deeply that it does seem real? But it is real, at least while you're experiencing this wonderful feeling of excitement.

Then there is talk of moving in together and someday getting married. The two of you speak of wonderful plans for the future. There are future discussions regarding vacations, buying a new home, cars, and possibly having children. All the right things are being said, and both of you feel as if you're on a ride to Fantasy Island.

What is either not realized or accepted during this time of bliss is how difficult and confusing a marriage can be at times. The couple must realize that a healthy relationship requires continuous caring by both partners. It requires good relationship skills to rise above the long days and nights of the same monotonous routine, uncertainties, and the numerous distractions that will arise, both inside the home and outside the home.

Distracting and ill-advised behaviors of one's partner, such as staying out late with friends, drinking, drug use, dishonesty, and continued arguments over bills and other things occur as a result of these unwise behaviors.

These situations as well as other negative situations will take place, such as insecurities from previous relationships may surface causing tears to precede sleep. Despite all this undisclosed information, the couple decides to live together and eventually get married.

After a few months or even a few years, things begin to fall apart. Responsibilities, personalities, and behaviors that weren't present or at least recognized during the dating stages of the relationship have begun to appear. It's beginning to seem as if one person has begun to carrying more of the household responsibilities. They have become the family's nurse or doctor, psychotherapist, cook, waitress or waiter, and housemaid. Arguments erupt over unimportant situations, and one person has become controlling.

The person being controlled cannot seem to understand what went wrong in the relationship, and it becomes apparent that the relationship has taken a turn for the worst. The couple begins to realize that marriage isn't a ride to Fantasy Island after all; instead the marriage has turned out to be a day-to-day struggle to survive.

The closeness and the lovemaking have all but become a chore, if not vanished completely. Communicating with each other has become difficult, secrets are being kept, and the idea of unselfish compromise has disappeared. Although the couple is still living together, the couple feels confused and once again lonely. As time continues to pass, the person being controlled becomes even more confused, and this confusion turns into frustration and eventually into resentment.

Overburdened by a sense of failure, resentment, and anger, the arguments become more intense. Verbal disputes over situations that would otherwise have previously gone unnoticed in the beginning of the relationship take on large proportions that proceed into accusations of unfaithfulness and more arguing. At this point, trust has been lost, and the breakdown in communication is complete. Without the ability to communicate and trust each other, the relationship has no foundation and is on the verge of collapse.

The relationship experiences a total loss of value, and the home turns into a physical and emotional theatre of hostilities. At some point during the continued domestic conflict, one or both of the partners come to a decision to separate or get a divorce. What either partner does not realize is the feelings involved and the process of separation or divorce can become overwhelming.

When a couple decides to separate or divorce, the process can be very painful. Obtaining advice and advisement on a mental or legal level is necessary but time-consuming and stressful. Taking the pain and moving forward with the process, one or both individuals realize that a marriage and family therapist may provide them with information that will save the relationship. That is, if both parties are willing to listen and take action to make the relationship work. If not, a good attorney can assist the couple with the legal issues with separation and divorce. *From love to divorce*, oh, what a ride that can become!

Exercise

The following exercise is for you to provide reasons why you believe your relationship will succeed or fail.

Apply personal knowledge from your current and previous relationships to answer the following questions and statements.

- What have you learned about your partner's personality and behavior that wasn't present during the dating period of your relationship?

  ____
  ____
  ____
  ____
  ____

- Name several wonderful and unforgettable experiences you and your partner have experienced during your relationship.

  ____
  ____
  ____
  ____
  ____

- Name several unpleasant and unforgivable experiences you have experienced with your partner during your relationship.

  ____
  ____
  ____
  ____
  ____

- Give several reasons why you believe that your relationship will succeed.

  ____
  ____
  ____
  ____
  ____

- Give several reasons why you believe your relationship will not succeed.
 ____
 ____
 ____
 ____
 ____

> Once you have answered the questions and have responded to the statements, ask yourself two questions: Should my partner and I obtain some sort of family counseling before going through with a separation or divorce?" And is my relationship with my partner beyond repair?

Mistakes vs. Negligence

It is a simple fact that *no one is perfect*; therefore, everyone makes mistakes. In all situations in which something has gone wrong, there needs to be a clear distinction between a mistake and negligence.

What is a *mistake*? A *mistake* can be considered as an unconscious act caused by a failure to notice or misunderstanding a particular situation. A mistake can be forgetting to perform a simple action such as stopping by the supermarket to purchase something for dinner. This can be interpreted as an honest mistake. The solution to this mistake would be to get back into the car and go to the supermarket and buy the forgotten dinner.

Negligence, on the other hand, is any conscious action that results in negative consequences for oneself or others. For example, driving while under the influence of drugs and alcohol is not a mistake but a conscious act of negligence. Other examples of negligence are being emotionally and physically abusive, leaving young children home alone, failure to take proper care of one's health, and having an extramarital affair. None of these situations is a mistake but a conscious act, which could result in someone being seriously injured.

As far as mistakes are concerned, mistakes may seem innocent enough, yet when repeated over and over again, problems can arise. For example, repeated mistakes can cause frustration for those who have to endure someone else's mistakes or have to continuously clean up someone else's mistakes. Constantly having automobile accidents, forgetting family members' birthdays, forgetting to pay bills, and constantly not supporting the needs of the family can eventually drive a family apart.

Repeated mistakes can drive everyone crazy, particularly family members or fellow employees who have to constantly experience someone else's mistakes.

What happens when a person constantly makes mistakes on their job? Usually, they will not keep their job very long. The same can be said for a relationship in which a partner constantly makes particularly costly mistakes. If a partner believes they are having a difficult time living with someone who constantly makes costly mistakes, what can they do? What would you do under similar circumstances?

The reason most people live together or decide to get married is because they're in love. However, two people can be in love with each other, but the constant progression of mistakes will sooner or later take a toll on the relationship. At some point, someone will suggest a separation or divorce not to hurt anyone's feelings but to keep from developing emotional and physical problems due to stress.

Those affected by these constant mistakes could easily become frustrated, angry, or even enraged at the person who is making the errors and become emotionally or physically abusive or both.

Hoping that either partner would be innocent of abuse is idealistic; yet living with someone who constantly makes mistakes is difficult, even if the couple loves each other. Numerous attempts to find a solution to the problem may not be possible, and a decision must be made one way or the other. Either family members learn to live with an abundance of mistakes or seek a resolution to their problem through counseling, separation, or divorce.

Building a healthy relationship is far more complicated than loving a person and needing to be loved. It takes a tremendous amount of patience, communications, a healthy attitude, trust, respect, *divine intervention*, and more. Having and maintaining a healthy relationship is a challenge that must be accepted with this commitment and enthusiasm in order to be successful.

Money, Money, Money

Many people believe money or a lack of money is a major issue with couples separating or filing for divorce. Realistically, money plays a large part in how some people view themselves and how they view others. Many people believe that money is a measurement used by others to determine a person's character and their ability to succeed. And still others relate money to power, a tool to control, and in this, they are absolutely right. Money is power, and people use money to control others. However, most people do not use money to control others but primarily to purchase the things they need and like.

Sensible people believe in the *power of love* and not in the power of money, knowing that love cannot be measured in dollars and cents but rather by the content of their partner's heart. They realize that money cannot buy love. If a person marries for money and not out of love for a person, he or she will usually find himself or herself alone, angry and broke.

Marrying someone because they have money is asking for trouble. Anyone who has large sums of money or the potential to earn large sums of money isn't stupid. They know that they are being used and realize the person they are about to marry is marrying for money and not for love. From the beginning, the relationship is questionable. And when the person with the money becomes bored with their relationship, he or she will become aggressive or passive-aggressive to the point of ending the relationship. Emotional abuse is a common outlet in this kind of situation.

There are people living in our society who believe money *means absolutely everything*. In this pursuit, they will do just about anything to obtain it, using it for both good and horrible things and will do almost anything to keep it. Having money is important, but not to the exclusion of family. When a person values money over family, some sort of negative response from their partner is inevitable.

The same can be said for a person who marries for money. They aren't in love with the person; they're in love with the excitement of obtaining their partner's money. This kind of attitude toward money and the person they claim to love will result in manipulation and deceptive behavior.

Some people choose to marry with nothing to offer but looks and sex. Those who use their looks and sex to marry for money may emerge from the relationship with the money they were seeking, only to leave their partner emotionally exhausted.

Basically, the same thing can be said for people who marry without proper funds to support their relationship. This person gives the other person the impression that they have money or have the ability to earn large sums of money when in fact, they do not have any money and aren't capable of maintaining gainful employment. This person who marries for looks and sex is another type of con artist.

Lying about having adequate funds to support a family may work for a short while, but the lack of adequate family income will wear thin. Eventually, one partner will want more from the relationship than empty promises; and one day, the negative attitude will appear, and the relationship takes a turn for the worst.

The relationship will become a daily verbal battle over what they can and cannot afford. The relationship can further deteriorate and will come to a point when having enough money will not be enough to save the relationship. The verbal battles will have taken its toll—all *for the sake of money*.

Separation and Divorce

The rate of separation for couples who live together but aren't married is unknown. Due to the tremendously high rate of couples moving in and out of relationships, this particular statistic concerning unmarried couples living together and separating will most likely remain unknown.

However, the average marriage in America lasts between four to six years, and more than 25 percent of marriages will end in separation, and more than half of all marriages will end in divorce. Generations of the past believed that marriage was something to be respected and was held sacred. Today, marriage has taken on a new meaning, a new and frightful purpose.

Marriage for many people is simply an opportunity to have a sex partner, to relocate from an economically deprived country, to get away from parents; and yet others live together because they have a child or desire to have a child. These aren't the only reasons relationships fail; usually, personality clashes and financial problems are also obstacles which couples cannot seem to overcome.

Personality clashes and financial problems top the list of reasons for the failure of relationships. The failure to understand or notice a person's *true* personality or to understand the importance of money management at the beginning of a relationship often results in arguments, verbal abuse, and, in many cases, physical abuse. Before moving in with someone, try very hard to look beyond all the promises made and focus closely on his or her behavior. The best time to study someone's behavior is when something doesn't go quite the way he or she wanted. Considering the way he or she treats others during bouts of anger can be another clue that should tell you about a person's personality and how he or she reacts under stress.

In terms of verbal abuse (name-calling), never call your partner or allow your partner to degrade you by name-calling. Yelling, being called fat, stupid, lazy, and other names is a sign of disrespect and will only get worse if this tendency to call one a name is not stopped the very first time it happens.

Many abusers and batterers will minimize the situation and blame their partner when they use verbal abuse by using statements such as, "You didn't say anything at the beginning of our relationship when I yelled and called you an idiot, lazy, or crazy, so why are you making such a big deal out of it now?" Or they will blame the victim by saying, "I was only joking with you" and "Can't you take a joke?"

The use of verbal abuse is another example of being cruel for the purpose of taking control or resuming control of a conversation or the relationship in general.

Many abusers do not realize it, but the first episode of verbal abuse was actually the beginning of the collapse of their relationship. Once abusers believe the relationship is collapsing, some abusers believe that if they use physical abuse, they will frighten their victim into submission; and he or she will remain in the relationship.

Although verbal abuse can be hurtful, receiving a slap or punch in the face is absolutely unforgivable. In situations in which a man or woman has been physically abused, how could either do anything but file for a divorce? How many slaps across the face will it take before the victim realizes that a real problem exists in their relationship? The worst thing a man or woman can do is to accept being physically abused. Believing that one day everything will be okay and things will get better once the batterer *cools down* is nothing more than wishful thinking.

What the victim should do is take a marriage or relationship *reality check* before someone becomes seriously injured. The moment their partner becomes verbally abusive, the days of best friends, trust, and respect, are long gone. At some point in the relationship and to the astonishment of the abuser or batterer, the victim will decide to bring an end to this agonizing period in his or her life and decide to move on.

Following is a list of reasons that professionals give for the increase in separations and divorce:

- People are getting married before they are mentally prepared.
- People are getting married before they are financially prepared.
- Women are no longer willing to tolerate domestic abuse.
- Many women no longer fear the financial hardships of separation or divorce.
- Married couples are no longer concerned about social opinion regarding divorce.
- Women do not want a dictatorship-type relationship.
- Unfaithfulness (cheating) on the part of either partner is not tolerated.
- Couples grow apart because their financial, social, mental, and sexual needs change.

The reasons that many people separate or divorce are too numerous to mention in this workbook. However, a good way to find out why people separate or divorce is to ask yourself what would have to happen for you to separate or divorce from your partner.

Exercise

Following is a list of questions and statements for you to determine whether any situation mentioned above apply to you and your relationship:

1. What are reasons you would separate or divorce from your partner?

   ____
   ____
   ____
   ____
   ____

2. What positive effects would separating or getting a divorce have on your children?

   ____
   ____
   ____
   ____
   ____

3. What negative effects separating or getting a divorce will have on your children?

   ____
   ____
   ____
   ____
   ____

4. Describe any problems you may have with your partner once you have separated or divorced.

   ____
   ____
   ____
   ____
   ____

5. Give several reasons why you would not separate or divorce from your partner.
   ____
   ____
   ____
   ____
   ____

> It has been said that separation or divorce can be one of the most stressful periods in a person life. We have to agree with that statement. A couple who actually cares for each other and have children may split due to having grown apart for one reason or another. Separation or filing for a divorce takes a mental toll on everyone involved, particularly children.

Feelings during Separation and Divorce

People experience many kinds of feelings during a separation or divorce: from anger, betrayal, and disappointment to various degrees of depression and joy.

People who were and are currently victims of domestic violence will tell you that they feel a sense of relief as well anger at the time of their separation or divorce. They feel relieved because the violence has ended and angry because they allowed it to happen and continue as long as it did. For many victims of domestic violence, there are very few day-to-day situations in which feelings can be generated with such intensity as the feeling of being free from physical and emotional abuse.

Survivors of abuse should consider separation or divorce as a time for celebration. Both feelings of sadness and joy may be felt as memories of their past emerge, causing the person to reflect upon what they have experienced. The joyful memories will resurface and remain longer as the victim realizes that he or she is no longer under daily inspection by someone else's control, but they are in control of their own life and destiny.

Positive Self-talk

What is *positive self-talk*? *Positive self-talk* is a positive conversation a person has with himself or herself concerning day-to-day situations. Positive self-talk is an excellent way to keep a person focused on maintaining healthy self-esteem and moving forward with their life.

Like most mental tools used for mental growth, self-talk is a process that involves guidelines or sequenced steps for it to be effective. The following are instructions to help you develop positive self-talk and will help you to remain focused on the task at hand:

- Your self-talk must be reality based. For example, "I live alone or with my children, but I am not lonely."
- What you are telling yourself about the situation during self-talk should never be negative. Use the positive suggestion, "I am strong, and I know what needs to be done to make my home a better place for me and my children" instead of "I am too weak to do this by myself."
- Believe in yourself. For example, "I am a good person, and there are people who care about me."
- Identify your feelings whether they are bad or good. For example, "Some days, I will feel good about my situation, and other days I feel bad. That's life."
- Be realistic about how you are feeling. For example, if you are feeling sad, tell yourself that you're feeling sad; however, include positive motivation as well, like "I will work through my sadness, and things will improve."

Remember, positive self-talk is about being realistic and developing self-confidence. Do not overwhelm yourself. Take one day at a time, keep it simple, and let life do the rest. Some people would say, "Do your best, and allow your higher power to take over when you have done all that you possible could."

Affirmations

What is an *affirmation*? An *affirmation* is a statement that confirms and supports what you believe to be true. An affirmation is an important step in the process of understanding. *Let there be no mistake in what you believe to be true and what is actually true!* Learn to use affirmations to guide you in your quest for doing the right thing.

Following are realistic affirmations:

- I know what I would like to do in this situation; I will allow my positive feelings to lead me.
- My life is my responsibility, and it will get better each day.
- There is a sense of pleasure to be gained from learning to be patient.

- I must take my time and work hard at achieving my goals, and I have the time and the skills necessary to do the work.
- It will be great to have someone in my life, but for now, I can make it on my own.
- I have the ability to make positive things happen.
- I have had some great times in my life, and great times will continue.

> If you do not understand where to begin, start with learning to be patient with yourself and others. Many people have traveled the road you are currently traveling. Many have been successful, and so will you. Once you have reached your destiny, many pleasures of life will be waiting.

Self-Assessment

Following are questions to assist you with understanding certain aspects of separation and divorce. Apply personal knowledge, as well as information from the chapter, to answer *yes*, *no*, or *NA* (not applicable) to the following questions. It is important that you answer all questions as accurately and honestly as possible.

1. Do you believe that verbal abuse can be the beginning of the end of a relationship? ___
2. Do you believe your relationship could last for twenty years or more after being verbally or physically abused? ___
3. Would you realize it if your relationship was at risk of separation or divorce? ___
4. Would you have any difficulty living with a person who *constantly* makes honest mistakes? ___
5. Do you believe that money has a great deal to do with having or not having a successful relationship? ___
6. Do you understand the importance of positive self-talk? ___
7. Do you ever use positive self-talk? ___
8. Do you ever say good things about yourself? ___
9. Do you understand the idea behind using affirmations? ___
10. Do you ever use affirmations? ___

The previous list of questions is to better assess you with maintaining a healthy state of mind if you are considering separation and divorce. If you believe that it is necessary for you to learn more about separation and divorce, use the information in this workbook, and also seek professional assistance for any questions you may have that this workbook does not address.

Chapter Twenty-four

The Impact of Divorce on Children

Chapter's Objectives:

1. To discuss the idea of divorce and separation
2. To view separation and divorce from the minds of children
3. To define the term *using the children* as a tactic of abuse
4. To discuss the negative effects of using children as a tactic of abuse
5. To discuss steps to take after a separation or divorce

Questions for You to Answer as You Read This Chapter:

1. Do you have thoughts of separating from or divorcing your partner?
2. How does a separation or divorce affect children?
3. How are children affected after being used during a separation or divorce?
4. Do you understand the steps involved to keep your family together?
5. Are you able to recognize and understand what your children may be feeling after a separation or divorce?

Related Chapters of Interest:

- Parenting Skills
- Communication Skills
- Anger Management
- Economic Partnership
- Economic Abuse

Chapter Twenty-four

The Impact of Divorce on Children

Separation and Divorce

When two people meet and eventually get married, they do not ever consider the possibility that one day they will separate or divorce. On the contrary, many couples who decide to live together or get married believe entirely in what their partner has told them about the future of their relationship and believe that they will live happily ever after.

Unfortunately, many relationships don't last forever. Why don't relationships last? What happens? Is there any one person to blame?

Some couples believe they must separate or file for divorce because one partner has outgrown the other (which could mean many different things), and others may say that they could not get over being called nasty names, or they cannot justify being physically abused by their partner. In either case, the battle for separation or divorce has begun.

Unfortunately, for the children, many of the battles that take place during a separation or divorce resemble footage from some of our most horrifying war and monster films. Like soldiers in a combat zone, couples will charge at each other yelling and screaming. There are fistfights, stabbings, shootings, kidnappings, and even homicides. In relationships that resemble monster films, someone can be stalked or scared half to death in honest fear for his or her life.

Thanks to some kind of divine intervention, this doesn't happen in all separations or divorces. However, society has come to realize that something must be done to stop domestic violence and the mental and physical effects domestic violence has upon the victims. Society is beginning to understand the nature of domestic violence and is creating new laws to hold perpetrators accountable for their abusive behavior. People must understand the importance of finding the right person with whom to develop a relationship, or society will never be able to put and end to the continuance of separation or divorce.

According to census figures, the percentage of unmarried couples in U.S. households has increased dramatically, and the average age at which marriage takes place is higher than at any time since the turn of the century. Currently, the rate of first-marriage divorces indicates that six out of ten first marriages end in divorce. Studies show that more than twenty million children live in single-parent homes, and factored into this figure, seventeen million children live with their mothers.

Certain aspects of society have negative views concerning couples who separate and divorce, but what about the couples who are involved in the decision to separate or divorce? How do individuals feel about having to leave a relationship they thought would last throughout their lives?

Many individuals who find themselves in the mist of a separation or divorce feel a sense of relief. The sense of relief comes from the fact that the domestic war is finally over, and everyone can now live in peace. There are men and women who claim they are much happier after leaving an abusive relationship.

On the other hand, there are also individuals who have difficulty accepting the fact that their marriage is over; and in many cases, they feel sad, alone, and helpless. Many individuals become saddened because their idea of living a long and happy life with their partner and children has come to an end.

Many may feel alone because of the quiet in their home life, without the presence of a partner to exchange ideas and feelings. Many feel helpless because they believe that they cannot make it on their own and fear that they may not find another partner.

For many individuals who choose to leave their home, anxiety over loss of daily contact with their children or limitations in seeing or visiting their children make their lives a living hell. Although many parents have the opportunity of visiting their children after a separation or divorce, many will often feel disconnected from their family. The feeling of being a disconnected parent can become a painful experience.

Many parents who find themselves in this kind of situation will often turn their frustration into deep feelings of resentment toward their ex-partner. Negative attitudes are never an answer. Consequently for men and women who harbor resentment, the war isn't over, and once again, children are caught in the crossfire of parental conflicts. Although the physical abuse may end, the mental abuse continues.

Studies also show that men and women who were abusive toward their family when they were together often have a difficult time connecting with their children after separation or divorce. It's not that the parents do not want to connect with their children; it's that children may have difficulty connecting with an abusive parent. Children do not forget the days and nights that their parent's were yelling and fighting each other, and most children do not want to revisit such a traumatic past.

Parents Divorcing from a Teenager's Perspective

A great deal of thought and study has gone into learning more about the impact of divorce on children. What does a child think, and how do they really feel about the separation or divorce of their parents?

During and following a separation or divorce, there are a number of changes that children have to accept. Sooner or later, parents *who are aware of their children's feelings* will notice the impact of not having their mother or father at home. What parents must realize is that children's emotional pain will vary with each child's age, gender, maturity, and psychological development. The common factor during this time in a child's life is that all children need to know whether or not both parents will be supportive of each other and whether or not both parents will continue to be part of their lives.

During a separation or divorce, most children believe they could be abandoned at any time after the divorce because one parent cannot carry the mental, physical, and financial responsibilities without assistance for the other parent.

Many parents do not believe children think in terms of mental and physical responsibilities, but children are more aware of what's going on within their environment than parents believe. Studies have shown that the following examples would apply to most children who are involved with their parents being separated or divorced.

- ♦ Child abuse and domestic violence can be more harmful to a child than their parents getting a divorce.
- ♦ Children can *cope* with their parents getting a divorce if done properly.

- Although getting a divorce may be the right thing to do, divorce does not necessarily benefit a child when one or both parents abandon responsibility for their child's social and emotional development.
- Many teenagers believe that their parents need to listen to their opinion before divorcing their mother or father.
- Some children cannot understand how their parents can "just stop loving each other" particularly if there wasn't any known physical abuse.
- Many children internalize and take responsibility for their parents' divorcing.
- Children often feel abandoned and may believe that both parents may leave them.
- Children suffer even more because of the single-parent status. (Attention currently received is now only half of what they were receiving before the divorce.)
- Parents do not have to love each other to raise healthy children.

When parents are considering separating or filing for a divorce, rarely can they anticipate all the factors that children will experience during and after separation or divorce. Many parents believe that children cannot comprehend the idea of divorce; consequently, children are left to assume that everything will be all right.

When parents make the decision to divorce, children are expected to accept and deal with their decision. Except in cases involving spousal or child abuse, it is unlikely that children will feel good about the situation and continue with their personal lives without distress.

Children do not have the same coping skills as adults, but children can understand changes that affect family dynamics. As a result of these life-altering decisions, children will develop certain behaviors, and even adolescents will have problems and demonstrate symptoms.

These symptoms may include the following:

- Isolating themselves from other family members
- Becoming angry with one or both parents
- Becoming angry with society
- Displaying negative behavior
- Blaming themselves
- Abusing drugs or alcohol

- Becoming rebellious
- Physically harming themselves and others
- Becoming irresponsible
- Having thoughts of committing suicide
- Being impatient and quick to anger
- Breaking social and family rules
- Becoming more depressed
- Developing unhealthy self-esteem
- Having difficulty setting and reaching personal goals
- Having difficulty forming lasting relationships

> If you are divorced or are in the process of getting a divorce, try putting your feelings aside for a moment and consider what your children may be feeling. If you can recognize one or more of the symptoms mentioned above, seek professional assistance to help the family through this painful period of adjustment.

Both parents must learn to speak to their children about the family being divided. The parent leaving the home (usually the father) should inform the children that he will continue to be a part of their lives. He should also inform his children that he will provide for their well-being and will always be there for them should any need arise. Children need to be informed as to what is happening to their family. Why should children be kept guessing as to where they are going to live or how financial needs will be met?

Following a separation or divorce, most children do not become happy because they have lost a parent, and now they will receive more attention, and more money will be spent on them. Most children realize that they will receive less than before, particularly if the family has financial difficulties, and the parent who has custody of the children must focus on day-to-day and week-to-week survival.

For one reason or another, many adults believe that children should not be made aware of the family's financial situation. In some cases, that may be true, but children have expectations that need to be addressed. If parents explain the family's financial situation, most children can better accept limitations as to what they cannot buy and learn to better manage what they already have.

There is also the issue of children connecting with an abusive parent after a separation or divorce. Most children find it difficult to connect with an abusive parent following a divorce. They will find it difficult to trust that the abusive parent will not continue their abusive behavior during visits to his or her new home. Whether or not the parent receives legal custody or visitation rights, the parent must provide their children with a sense of safety. If abusive behavior continues, the child will refuse to visit.

Some parents, out of guilt, allow their children to do whatever they please during visitation. To keep a child in their favor, the parent allowed their children to eat all sorts of junk food, play with any game they please, watch television for hours, or just hang out with friends and get into mischief. Parents must understand that most children will take advantage of any opportunity presented if allowed, particularly when it relates to hanging out and eating junk food.

Additional complications arise with consideration of the visiting parent's new girlfriends or boyfriends. Parents must understand that their children must develop a liking for any new intimate relationship the parents have with another person in their own time, and not upon demand from the parent.

Children, like previous partners, view such relationships as a replacement of the other parent. Children will question what role this new person will play in their lives. With the development of new intimate relationships, it is essential for both parents to keep a *positive* and *respectful* open line of communication with their ex-partner.

Positive communications means that there isn't any verbal abuse or threats to harm the other partner, and *respectful* in the sense that each partner respects the other partner's *space* and realize that their ex-partner has the right to find another partner if they choose to do so without fear of being harmed. The idea of an ex-wife or ex-husband finding another partner can become a frightful thought for many couples who separate or divorce, but life continues, and both partners must understand this fact.

Using the Children

For purposes of having an immediate understanding and recognizing how children are manipulated in domestic disputes, we define the term *using the children* as a power and control tactic used by controllers to gain and maintain control over their partner or other family members.

Using children in situations during a separation or divorce is contrary to the idea of caring and nurturing children. The physical and emotional problems presented during many domestic disputes are bound to affect children. Some parents are so bitter toward each other that they do not realize the consequences of their behavior and how their behavior has negatively affected their children.

The following are examples of how children are used to control one's partner or ex-partner:

- Children are used to emotionally abuse a partner. For example, statements such as, "You will never see your children again."
- A partner may threaten to take away or kidnap the children when they get the opportunity.
- Children are used to relay abusive messages. This can be especially harmful if the message contains negative information about the child.
- Children are turned against the other parent. For example, telling the children personal husband-and-wife situations that should be left to adults.
- Name-calling is used to manipulate the partner or to make the children feel guilty. For example, "You're just like your mother or father," "You cannot do anything right," or "Our child is handicapped because of you."
- Using visitation rights partner behavior to harass causes the children distress. For example, tracking a person's personal life, i.e., boyfriends or girlfriends.

> No one likes to be manipulated, not even children. It must be understood by both parents that children are not to be used as weapons of domestic warfare.

Any of the above behaviors can do more harm than good, particularly to children. It has been accepted by many in society that some men and women are too vindictive to realize that there are silent victims before, during, and after a separation or divorce.

The stereotype of divorced parents is that they get a perverted sense of pleasure through revenge inflicted when the children are used against their former partner. If children are being used by a parent, the aftereffects can be devastating to the child's development. It is the parent's responsibility to make sure that they are aware and responsive to the feelings of their children.

Children must believe that their home is a safe place, and their safety will never be compromised for any reason. If partners become upset with each other and if they find it difficult to work out favorable solutions to their problems, they should seek professional consultation.

Following is a list of ways parents can avoid manipulating children during domestic disputes:

- Direct and honest communication between parents and between parents and children
- Discussing with children issues with the intent to turn them against the other parent
- Refusing to put children in the position of making decisions regarding truth or deception on any subject
- Acknowledgment of abuse toward either partner without denial as the children were there, and they saw what happened
- Helping your children to adjust to environmental changes
- Making no changes in household rules to turn the children against the other parent once the separation is complete
- Not flaunting of new relationships in front of the children, which will bring distress to the other parent
- Never using power and control tactics to solve any issues

Children can recover from a divorce or separation easier when they do not have to choose sides or experience constant mental tension between parents. Children will learn to accept what has happened and continue to move in a positive direction in their lives if they are not involved in parental conflicts.

Exercise

The following statements are designed for couples to understand the effect separation and divorce has on children.

1. When I first met my partner, I thought he or she was

2. I am thinking about divorcing my partner because he or she

3. My children feel they are caught in the middle of my separation or divorce because

4. Children constantly exposed to domestic violence can be more harmful to them than their parents getting a divorce because

5. List any change in your children's behavior during and after the separation or divorce.

____
____
____
____
____

6. How can a parent help their children cope with separation or divorce?

____
____
____
____
____

7. Explain the statement that parents do not have to love each other to raise healthy children.

____
____
____
____
____

8. I have used my children against my ex-partner by

____
____
____
____
____

9. My ex-partner has used my children against me by

____
____
____
____
____

10. If I had to separate or file for a divorce, my children would welcome the change because

____

____

____

____

____

Answering the above statements will enable you to determine if your separation or divorce have affected your children. This workbook provides insight and generates discussion. For additional advisement, seek professional assistance.

Steps to Take after a Separation or Divorce

When we stop and reflect on any situation, we will realize that we have choices. Having choices and making the right decision doesn't stop after a separation or divorce.

Following the decision to separate or divorce, there are steps one can take like the following:

- Seek professional advice from someone qualified to give advice on the subject of separation and divorce.
- Come together as a family to discuss the family's situation.
- Allow your children to have their own opinions about the separation or divorce.
- If you make a promise to your children, keep your word.
- Beware of any behavioral changes from your children during and after the separation or divorce.
- Be careful to watch your children's behavior with regard to drugs or alcohol.
- Never displace your frustrations and anger on your children.
- Reassure your children that both parents love them and will be there for them.
- Listen to your children and watch for suicidal tendencies.
- Keep your children safe from arguments or any abusive behavior between you and you ex-partner.

- Never make negative comments about the other parent.
- If you feel emotionally overwhelmed, seek professional assistance.

Your children have been a part of the collapse of your relationship from the beginning. They have heard the arguments and seem to have survived. Children may seem to have survived the painful arguments and fights, but if you were to take a closer look, you will see that your children are suffering as well as the victims of the domestic abuse.

Children have the same feelings as adults and, in some cases, are just as intense as their parents with the limitations of maturity and perspective. When couples decide to separate or divorce, parents must take into account the feelings of their children. If a child has experienced an abusive parent, they realize that life will not be the same; but at least, there is the possibility of peace in the home.

Self-Assessment

Following are questions to assist you with understanding the impact separation and divorce has on children. Apply personal knowledge, as well as information from the chapter, to answer *yes*, *no*, or *NA* (not applicable) to the following questions. It is important that you answer all questions as accurately and honestly as possible.

1. If you are still married, do you believe your relationship will last beyond five years? ____
2. Are you currently in the process of separating or filing for divorce? ____
3. If you were to separate or divorce, do you believe that your life would be much happier? ____
4. Are you a devoted parent? ____
5. Do you understand how a child may feel after experiencing a fight between their parents? ____
6. Do you understand the term *using children*? ____
7. Do you understand how children could blame their parents for the failure of their marriage? ____
8. Are your children old enough to mentally survive the harsh realities of separation or divorce? ____
9. Do you believe that many children need therapy after a violent separation or divorce? ____
10. Are you afraid that your children will be taken away from you? ____

The previous list of questions is to better assess your thoughts and feelings concerning a separation and divorce. If you believe that it is necessary for you to learn more about this period in your relationship, use the information in this workbook, and also seek professional assistance for any questions you may have that this workbook does not address.

Chapter Twenty-five

Setting Reachable Goals

Chapter's Objectives:

1. To discuss the importance of setting goals
2. To encourage the reader to set reachable goals
3. To discuss expectations and desires
4. To discuss setting guidelines to reach goals
5. To describe obstacles that may stand in the way of reaching personal goals

Questions for You to Answer as You Read This Chapter:

1. How important is setting goals?
2. What goals have I completed in the last five years?
3. What is a major goal that I have yet to complete?
4. What problems do I have with reaching my goals?
5. What is my worse fear about setting goals?

Related Chapters of Interest:

- Codependency
- Self-esteem
- Communication Skills
- Economic Partnership
- Stress Reduction

CHAPTER TWENTY-FIVE

Setting Reachable Goals

What Is a Goal?

What is a goal? A goal is something that a person plans to achieve within a given amount of time. Every day of our life, from the moment we awaken until we go to sleep at night, we are working toward completing some kind of goal.

A typical day for most of us is filled with small goals. For example, when we leave for work, our main goal is to arrive safely, and once we arrive, we have assignments to complete for that day. When our workday is over and we return home, our goal is to prepare dinner for our family and to help our children with their homework and so on.

These are day-to-day goals that don't require much effort. However, when we become interested in working toward seriously improving our health, finances, family relationship, and relationship with others, or planning a family vacation, we must take our time and decide what are the necessary steps needed to complete these goals.

Setting Goals

The first step to reaching a particular goal is deciding what goal really interests us, i.e., what goal will improve our situation, whether it be mental or physical. Let there be no mistake; setting goals is extremely important to our mental and physical health as well as to our financial prosperity.

To live every day and not have a dream or idea of living a better life can become very depressing, especially when we want the best for ourselves and our family. An excellent example of a goal that would change how we feel about ourselves would be a goal worth achieving. For example, we spend a lot of time on our jobs. Therefore, it may be time to begin developing a plan to improve our employment situation, such as extra training or attending a university or college to get the necessary skills needed to advance and earn more income as well as earn the respect from fellow employees. Reaching such a goal would certainly strengthen one's self-esteem.

Positive and Negative Aspects of Reaching One's Goal

When we have an idea as to what we like to achieve, a great deal of consideration must go into the positive and negative aspects of making change, particularly if it's a major change.

It's extremely important *not to give up what you currently have* before reaching one's goal. For example, do not leave your current employment for a job in which you have not been hired or without having adequate funds to support your family until you find new employment.

Also, remember not to begin a new project out of spite, stubbornness, or blind determination. Being spiteful and stubborn takes a great deal of mind energy—energy you do not need to waste. The pathway to reaching goals has a logical order and must be followed. For example, all goals should begin with a *strong desire* to want to succeed.

Most people want to improve their life, but they do not have the desire or the self-discipline to follow through on what they have started. Another problem many people have is doing things their way and not the right way. A lot of us like to skip over what we believe to be unimportant. In most cases, this can prove to be our second mistake in reaching our goals, and we call this second mistake taking *shortcuts*.

Shortcuts to reaching one's goal can often prove to be not so short, and eventually, the person will have to go back and complete what they missed before they can continue moving forward toward completing their goal. For example, a person decides to go to college, and the instructors give the student homework.

However, the student decides not to complete his or her homework and pays someone or has his or her partner or friends do his or her homework for him or her. When he or she receives his or her degree and finds employment, he or she does not have the knowledge to perform the job with any degree of consistency. Most likely, he or she will fail at the job.

Consequently, what have they gained by taking a shortcut? And who suffers from this person's inability to perform their job? The public suffers.

When it comes to establishing a realistic plan of action and actually reaching one's goals, there are certain rules that must be followed. In working toward your goal, you must *stick to a plan.*

Exercise

Following is an exercise to assist you with determining changes you want to make in your life or discovery of something you have always wanted to do but never got around to doing:

1. Name several things about yourself you would like to change. For example, lose or gain weight, decrease stress, work on your self-esteem.

   ____
   ____
   ____
   ____
   ____

2. Name several things about your employment situation that you would like to change. For example, find a different job, improve a current job, or start a business.

   ____
   ____
   ____
   ____
   ____

3. Name something about your current relationship you would like to change. For example, improve your current relationship, separate, or get a divorce.

   ____
   ____
   ____
   ____
   ____

4. Name something that you have always wanted to buy but never had the opportunity. For example, buy a new car, home, or take a trip to Europe.

   ____
   ____
   ____
   ____
   ____

5. Name something about your personal finances that you would like to work on. For example, getting out of debt, earning or saving more money.

____

____

____

____

____

Find one or two situations from this exercise that you have always wanted to change, but were postponed or never were able to do for some reason. Once you have decided upon something you would like to achieve, begin by making a plan to reach your goal.

You must learn to follow a step-by-step guideline to complete your goal. Following is a list of steps to review for setting and accomplishing your goals:

- Start with several realistic goals. You can begin by selecting something easy to achieve or discovering one of your greatest ambitions. For example, buying a new home or car, stopping drinking, losing weight, stopping smoking, or choosing a new profession.
- Carefully write three or four goals that would give you the greatest satisfaction. From this list, select one goal you would most likely to achieve.
- Once you have selected your goal, develop a step-by-step, workable schedule toward reaching your goal and, above all, *do your homework.*

For example, how much money and time is involved; where you would like to be in three, six, and twelve months regarding your goal; and what routine you would have to give up while working toward achieving your goal (watching television, going out on weekends, talking on the telephone for hours at a time, and so on).

- Take responsibility for your goal and everything that takes place on the pathway toward achieving it. If you miss a day or something happens that is out of your control, make no excuses.
- Simply learn to accept what you cannot control and continue doing the best you can. Lingering over negative outcomes can be an obstacle that creates doubt of your abilities.

- Try not to depend on others to do your work. A little help from others is fine, but do not expect them to complete what you should be doing.
- Always keep your focus on completing your goal.
- Always think positive and focus on the end rewards.
- Do not stress over difficult situations. Find someone who has completed the same goal that you are currently working on, and ask them for assistance.
- Keep away from negative influences. For example, people who like to party or people who have negative things to say about what you are trying to achieve—they could prove to be your first worst enemy. The second worst enemy is taking on too much at one time.
- Once you have completed your goal, take time out to feel good about reaching your goal, and then reset your goals.
- With patience and willingness to endure moments of frustration, you will grow to a level where you can enjoy one of life's greatest pleasures, and that is a sense of achievement.

With patience and determination and by "keeping your eye on the prize" and maintaining patience and determination, you will achieve your goal(s).

Realistic Expectations and Desires

Success begins with realistic expectations and desires; these are the keys to success. If we find something that we would like to achieve, it must be something within our mental and physical capabilities. We can dream of being successful in a certain area, but is it realistic? If what we want to achieve isn't realistic, the mental and physical journey can become extremely difficult and agonizing. Selecting a goal that's within our limits allows the journey toward reaching that particular goal to be as rewarding as actually reaching the goal.

A person craving to achieve is deemed a person with a strong desire. When we have a hunger or a burning feeling deep inside of us to accomplish something, many of us will not stop or allow anyone or anything to get in the way of finishing what we have started.

Having realistic expectations and desires are only part of our quest to achieve. There will be good moments and bad ones, and both require mental preparation to survive failures and to achieve success.

Those who have accomplished goals realize that the more difficult the goal, the greater the reward. We also remember that goals cannot be reached without planning. In life's grand design of experiencing the good with the bad, working hard for what you get and then struggling to *keep it* is also included.

Approaching goals with flexibility and understanding allows progression from one problem to the next. Therefore, approach your goal with the understanding that there will be small problems to work through before moving on to the next problem. With patience and understanding, small problems are nothing more than a minor part of a larger solution toward reaching your goal. While you may have a strong desire to achieve your goal, you also must maintain self-discipline and self-determination.

Following are more guidelines to assist you with completing your goals:

- Always think about the feeling of accomplishment you will have once you have completed your goal.
- Ask for help when you need it, but do not depend on others to do your work for you.
- Believe in yourself.
- Keep good notes on what has to be done, and do not put off until tomorrow what you can do today.
- When you become frustrated, take a time-out.
- Remember, you are doing something you have always wanted to do, and it will take time. Become comfortable with that fact, and then time is on your side.

Our imagination can keep us moving toward our goal, but we must beware of self-imposed obstacles. For example, negative self-talk like "I cannot do anything right" and "I know that I will fail" can delay progression.

Keep your mind focused on the rewards of your labor. Whether your goal is to return to school or to improve your relationship, desire and performance is the key. Quite simply, do your best to obtain and become the best.

Self-Assessment

Following is a list of ideas concerning self-control and self-determination. Apply personal knowledge, as well as information from the chapter, to answer *true*, *false*, or *NA* (not applicable) next to the statement that is appropriate to your behavior:

1. A person can do anything that they set out to do when he or she is prepared. ___
2. Completing goals takes determination. ___
3. A person must know his or her strengths and weaknesses before starting any project. ___
4. I do not have the energy to start a new project at this time. ___
5. My partner is very supportive. ___
6. I'm easily distracted. ___
7. I work better with a team. ___
8. Being able to make personal and social adjustments is important to completing my goals. ___
9. I will continue to evaluate my achievements. ___
10. I will not allow anyone to stop me from reaching my desired goals. ___

The previous list of statements is to better assess your understanding of setting goals, self-control, and self-determination. If you believe that it is necessary for you to learn more about setting goals, self-control, and determination, use the information in this workbook; and also seek professional assistance for any questions you may have that this workbook does not address.

Chapter Twenty-six

A Relapse Prevention Plan

Chapter's Objectives:

1. To define *relapse* as it relates to domestic violence
2. To discuss why people relapse
3. Be able to identify warning signs before a relapse occurs
4. To discuss three major points to remember concerning relapse
5. To encourage men to read this chapter very carefully

Questions for You to Answer as You Read This Chapter:

1. What does it mean to relapse?
2. What are the various early-warning signs to relapsing?
3. What are some interpersonal problems that can cause a person to relapse?
4. What are some social pressures that could cause a person to relapse?
5. What support systems are available to assist a person from relapsing?

Related Chapters of Interest:

- What Is Power and Control?
- Substance Abuse Within the Family
- Anger Management
- Stress Reduction
- Conflict Resolution

CHAPTER TWENTY-SIX

A Relapse Prevention Plan

What Does It Mean to Relapse?

What does it mean to have a relapse? In terms of domestic violence, to relapse means to return to the previous act of emotionally or physically (or both) abusing their partner or other family member after a period of time.

Although women are known to be mentally and physically abusive toward family members as well, studies confirm that a very large percentage of the reported cases of domestic violence are committed by men.

We have learned that men who abuse or batter their partners realize the suffering they have caused their partner's and other family members. Many of these abusers believe that if they show remorse for their abusive behavior and promise that they will never abuse their partner again, their partner will forgive them.

Many abusers and batterers will try anything to convince their victim that they will not harm them again. Some abusers and batterers will get down on their hands and knees and cry for forgiveness. Many will go and talk to the victim's mother, father, the victim's closest friends, or a counselor; and other abusers will go to church to prove to the victim that they have changed. During this phase of the cycle of violence, the abuser or batterer actually believes he or she has changed and will not abuse his or her partner again. However, the slightest incident could cause the abuser or batterer to ignore the promise he or she made to the victim and return once again to becoming abusive.

Usually abusers relapse because of their inability to control their emotions and a strong need to regain control over their victim. Under these circumstances, the victim can rest assured that there will be more relapses in the future due to the abuser's or batterer's unpredictable personality.

The problem with the second, third, even fourth time that an abuser or batterer relapses is that the battering and emotional abuse often increases to another level of abuse. For example, the violence may escalate from shouting as loud as they can to spitting, pushing, and hitting; and in some cases, a homicide may be committed.

When an abuser or batterer states that he or she will kill their partner if he or she does or doesn't do a certain thing, many victims foolishly believe that their partner is incapable of *really killing them*. They do not take the threat of possibly being killed seriously enough to do what it takes to remove themselves from the home.

Facts do not lie. The FBI files on serious crimes are a testimonial to the terrible crimes many couples commit against each other and are apparent when an abuser or batterer kills his or her partner. We cannot mention the fact enough that every threat to human life must be taken seriously.

In my domestic violence classes, I have asked students over the years, "Is there anyone in the class who has ever had thoughts of committing a domestic homicide?" With a forgiving smile, at least two or three would admit having thoughts of *killing* their partner in their past or current relationship. However, they would immediately state that although they have thought about killing their partner, they would never do such a thing; and in their defense, they would state that "it was only a thought."

Although a person cannot be convicted based upon what they think, I believe that anyone who would have such thoughts needs professional advisement beyond what they are receiving in a domestic violence classroom setting. Continuing with the same line of questioning, I inquired, "Is there anyone in class who is currently thinking of killing their partner?" No one would answer that question.

Certainly, if anyone had answered yes, I would have been obligated to contact the proper authorities. As an instructor, I had to use all my professional skills and, keeping within the context of the weekly instruction, rid them of such homicidal ideas.

Why do Abusers and Batterers Relapse?

Why do abusers and batterers relapse? A quick and honest answer to that question is a simple: because they choose to relapse and not because someone *forced them.* An abuser or batterer can have a relapse at any time, particularly those in the role of being an extreme controller.

Men and women who have battered and abused their partner earlier in the relationship may go fifteen, twenty, and even thirty years and have never relapsed. These people made a choice to change or deal with the consequences.

Those abusers and batterers who relapse should be proof enough that they have a violent nature. Abusers and batterers who watch violence on television through movies and sports cannot seem to separate the violence they watch in movies and sports from the violence they inflict upon their family members. For example, there are men who would tackle their partner as if they were on the football field, throwing and punching their victim as if they were in a prize-fighting ring, or shooting their victims as if they were playing a part in gangster movie.

Substance-abuse treatment programs often call a relapse by an ex-addict, a *mistake or a learning experience.* Relapsing in terms of domestic violence *is not a mistake and certainly cannot be considered as a learning experience* for the abuser or batterer. If anyone should learn from the abuse, it should be the victim.

Many abusers say that they feel bad afterward, and actual tears run down their face as proof of their remorse. If the abuser feels bad about punching and kicking their partner, how should the victim feel?

Many counselors believe that when a person relapses, they have allowed their emotions to take control of their behavior. We believe that a person who has the physical strength to harm others is driven by their physical strength and their desire to maintaining or regaining control over their victims. The abusers' and batterers' strong desire to control their victims overpowers their ability to think rationally.

There is no acceptable reason, whether it be their emotions or physical strength, for someone to slap or punch their partner in the face. For example, one man is five feet five inches tall, weighing ninety-five pounds; and his partner six feet tall, weighing more than 250 pounds. What are the odds of this man wanting to get into a physical confrontation with his partner? People who are bigger and stronger have the option of using or restraining from using physical strength in regard to becoming abusive. Most men have greater physical strength than their partner; yet it is their physical strength, attitude, and their beliefs toward their partner that determines their behavior.

An abuser's negative beliefs concerning women are a major factor in whether or not he will relapse and become violent once again. An abuser or batterer must change his or her belief system in order not to relapse.

Following are examples of the negative belief system that many abusers and batterers hold toward women:

- Men are stronger and women are weaker.
- Men should have the last word.
- A father is the enforcer.
- If a woman believes that her partner will not hesitate to strike her, she will do as she is told.
- Women shouldn't have male friends.
- Jealousy is an act of showing love.
- Women are manipulators.
- Don't do as I do, do as I say.
- Women should not criticize men or tell them that they are wrong.
- Women are only after what they can get from men.

These are only a few of the negative beliefs men hold toward women that are not made clear at the beginning of a relationship.

Warning Signs

Victims, as well as abusers and batterers, can identify early-warning signs before any abusive behaviors occur. Once the victim and the abuser or batterer recognize and understand these warning signs, relapse can be prevented. It must be very clear to victims of domestic violence that men or women who are extreme controllers (dominators) aren't interested in learning about warning signs. They cannot handle the idea of not being in control, particularly, a person that patrols a home like a watchdog, waiting for someone to get out of line, so they can prove that they are a force to be feared and respected.

The following is a list of early warning signs of a possible relapse:

- Denies that a problem exists after swearing, yelling, or making any sort of unnecessary physical contact
- Blames family members for his or her problems in life
- Blames family members for his or her anxiety or depression
- Displays negative changes in his or her attitude toward their partner's friends and extended family
- Appears innocent, yet their behavior upsets family members, for example, with threatening looks and gestures
- Has friends who batter and abuse their partners
- Is mentally and physically stressed
- Abuses alcohol and other drugs
- Keeps to himself or herself
- Complains about not getting enough sex
- Demands to have sex and will perform the sexual act even though their partner isn't interested in having sex
- Believes that being verbally or physically abusive is necessary to get things done
- Believes they have all the answers
- Acts without thinking
- Makes idle threats
- Becomes easily frustrated or irritable
- Harbors resentment from the past

> These warning signs are part of a process that often occurs long before a person relapses and may be based upon certain situations that may have happened days and even weeks prior to relapse.

If the abuser believes that he or she has been insulted during a particular discussion weeks ago, has difficulty on the job, or hasn't had their sexual needs met for days or weeks, his or her resentment toward a partner builds until one day, he or she explodes into a rage.

There Are No "Mistakes," Only Relapse

Abusers and batterers will give their victim many excuses for relapsing. For example, an abuser or batterer will often say, "When I pushed, shoved, cursed, or hit you (meaning their partner), I made a mistake, and I apologize." What abusers and batterers fail to realize is that there are no mistakes when the abuse is a pattern of violence.

People can make mistakes, but *a mistake is an unintentional physical or mental error*. People who understand the difference between right and wrong may *choose* to do wrong; and therefore, it is not a mistake. The facts concerning relapses are simple. If a person relapses, they either did not work hard enough at not relapsing, or they intended to cause mental or physical harm. There are no accidental relapses.

Also, beware of the term *I'm sorry*. Many abusers and batterers believe that they can abuse their partner as long as they tell the victim that they are sorry and that all will be forgotten. The words *I'm sorry* will not heal a black eye or broken bones. The words *I'm sorry* are not designed to heal the mental pain or the broken bones of the victim but to heal the wounded *ego* of the abuser or batterer (Read the chapter on ego defense mechanisms.)

Relapse Prevention Plan

The purpose for developing a relapse prevention plan is so that an abuser or batterer and the victim can become aware of the potential for violence in their relationship. People who really care about the success of their relationship will develop the skills necessary to make the relationship prosper.

One of the major steps in any plan of action is to think about being successful without consideration of failure. For the relapse prevention plan to be successful, the abuser or batterer must think optimistically about the future of their relationship and not think about maintaining or losing control over their partner.

The problem that many controllers face is the fear of giving up control over their partner because they do not want to be perceived as being weak. In many cases, abusers and batterers believe that they may fall victim to being controlled by the person they are controlling. Controllers must give up such fears, or making positive changes in their negative behavior will be very difficult to accomplish.

The first step in any relapse prevention plan is to acknowledge that you have a problem. It's not just admitting that you have a problem; it's acknowledging over and over again in one's head that a problem truly exists.

Next, an abuser or batterer should sit down and make a personal list of their negative behaviors. The list brings an awareness of their past abusive behavior toward their partner.

The abuser or batterer should read his or her list every day as a preventive reminder not to do negative things to people they care about. An abuser or batterer often uses anger as an excuse to hurt others.

Taking the time to think through their choices and the consequences of their behavior that accompanies anger will help facilitate change in negative behavior toward their partner and other family members.

Men and women who have abused their partner and other family members in the past must learn why they were abusive in the first place. Using the five Ws—who, what, when, where, and why—may help bring an awareness of how abuse starts. This may seem difficult for an abuser or batterer to do because of the guilt and shame involve. But an abuser or batterer must remember why this book is being read in the first place—as a positive step to stop domestic violence.

Following are questions for an abuser or batterer to answer. The abuser or batterer must apply personal knowledge as well as information from this chapter and other chapters to answer each question honestly. However, we would like to caution any abuser or batterer who decides to complete this exercise. If he or she writes the truth about physically or emotionally abusing his or her partner, and his or her partner reads what he or she wrote, it may cause the victim more pain. Therefore, it would be in their interest as well as in the best interest of their partner to discuss this exercise with a counselor.

We believe that the abuser or batterer may or may not understand his or her motives behind his or her abusive behavior. The same can be said for the victim; he or she may or may not understand the real reason for being abused or battered by someone he or she loves.

Exercise

The following questions are designed to put the abusers and batterers past abusive behavior into its proper perspective:

- Who have you physically and emotionally abused in the past? For example, your partner, children, or pets.

  ____
  ____
  ____
  ____
  ____

- What have you done to each person? For example, pushed, hit, yelled, or threatened in any way.

  ____
  ____
  ____
  ____
  ____

- When are you most likely to become abusive? For example, in the morning, after work, or while watching a sporting event.

  ____
  ____
  ____
  ____
  ____

- How often are you abusive? For example, every day, once a week, or once a month.

  ____
  ____
  ____
  ____
  ____

- Where are you when the abuse occurs? For example, are you at home, in the car with friends, or in public?

____
____
____
____
____

- Why are you abusive? You're not seeking to justify your behavior by answering this question; you're seeking to find reasons not to repeat your abuse.

____
____
____
____
____

- What can you do differently? For example, learn better communication skills and learn how not to use violent behavior to make a point.

____
____
____
____
____

After you have written down your responses, go over your answers, and try to think about how you were feeling when you were abusing your partner. And most importantly, what was your motivation *then,* and what is your motivation *now*, whether or not to repeat the same abusive behavior?

Exercise

What can an abuser or batterer do to prevent future relapses? First, they can focus on self-control in situations that may trigger a relapse. For example, when abusers and batterers begin to feel irritated, angry, or overly stressed, they must take a time-out. When they take a time-out, they must decide how to best utilize their time-out. They can decide whether to take a walk, take a drive in their automobile (however, not when they are angry or irritated), work on a hobby, listen to music, or read a book.

They must find something to do to relieve their anger and stress. These skills must include learning how to relax, how to communicate effectively, respecting their partner, and restraining any urges that would cause them to relapse.

Fill in the blank spaces with the appropriate feeling or idea about yourself. Determine what is true, not true, and what you're not sure of concerning yourself and your relationship.

1. I have an anger problem. ___true ___not true ___not sure
2. I am a controller. ___true ___not true ___not sure
3. I have emotionally and physically abused my partner. ___true ___not true ___not sure
4. I will never physically or emotionally abuse anyone again. ___true ___not true ___not sure
5. My partner is my best friend, and I can talk with her about anything without fear of becoming abusive. ___true ___not true ___not sure
6. I am committed to becoming a loving husband and father/wife and mother. ___true ___not true ___not sure
7. I will learn to relax and communicate effectively and learn how to hold any urges that would cause me to relapse. ___true ___not true ___not sure
8. My relationship cannot be restored. ___true ___not true ___not sure
9. I will learn more about gaining healthy self-esteem. ___true ___not true ___not sure
10. I will seek professional assistance to help me with my anger. ___true ___not true ___not sure

The previous list of statements is to better assess your determination not to relapse. If you believe that it is necessary for you to learn more about relapse prevention, use the information throughout this workbook, and seek professional assistance for any questions you have that this workbook does not address.

NOTE TO A CONTROLLING PERSON

How many times have you promised that your partner will not be harmed again, only to repeat the same behavior a few minutes, days, weeks, or months later? This vicious cycle can create emotional pain that family members will carry with them for the remainder of their lives. Why would your partner remain in an abusive relationship in which cruelty has been a way of life?

The feelings of being exploited by someone they love or loved causes a tremendous amount of pain. Victims who are currently in an oppressive relationship will remain in the relationship for various reasons. Yet many victims will eventually grow tired of being abused and realize that one day they must put an end to their agony by walking out and never returning.

Self-Assessment

Following is a list of ideas, feelings and behaviors you must understand so as not to relapse. Apply personal knowledge, as well as information from the chapter, to answer *true*, *false*, or *NA* (not applicable) to the statements that apply to the changes you have made in your behavior.

1. I must not shout at my partner to control her or him. ___
2. I must understand that my partner does not like being controlled. ___
3. I understand why it is important to remain free from abusive behaviors. ___
4. I will take responsibility for my feelings and behaviors. ___
5. I will constantly examine my belief system and make the necessary adjustments. ___
6. I have learned that I cannot control someone else's life. ___
7. I have learned that irritation and frustration can often lead to stress and anger. ___
8. I am learning that maintaining a healthy relationship takes a lot of effort. ___
9. I understand the consequences of relapsing. ___
10. I will continue to seek new methods of controlling my frustrations, irritations, and anger. ___

The previous list of statements is to better assess your feelings and behavior before a relapse occurs. If you believe that it is necessary for you to learn more about relapse prevention, use the information in this workbook, and also seek professional assistance for any questions you may have that this workbook does not address.

Recommended Reading

Abbott, Franklin. Ed. *Men and Intimacy: Personal Accounts Exploring the Dilemmas of Modern Male Sexuality Freedom*. CA: Crossing Press, 1990.

Al-Anon Family Groups. *Al-Anon Faces Alcoholism*. New York: Al-Anon Family Groups. Alcoholics Anonymous. New York: AA World Services, 1984.

Beanie, Melody. *Codependent No More: How to Stop Controlling Others and Start Caring for Yourself*. New York: Harper/Hazel, 1987.

Berkeley, C. Kathleen. *The Women's Liberation Movement in America*. Connecticut, London: Greenwood Press Westport, 1999.

Blackstone, William. *Commentaries on the Laws of England*. 4th ed. Eds. James Dewitt Andrews and Thomas M. Cooley. Chicago, IL: Callahan, 1891.

Brown, Stephanie. *Treating the Alcoholic: A Developmental Model of Recovery*. New York: John Wiley and Sons, 1985.

Bradshaw, John. *Creating Love: The Next Stage of Growth*. New York: Bantam Books, 1992.

Chiriboga, D. A. and M. Thurnher. "Marital Lifestyles and Adjustment to Separation." *Journal of Divorce, no.* 3 (1990): 379-390.

Corey, G. and M. S. Corey. *Groups: Process and Practice*. 2nd ed. Monterey, Cal: Brooks/Cole, 1982.

Edelman, Ric. *The Truth About Money*. New York, NY: Harper Business, Harper Collins Publishers Inc.

Engel, Beverly. *Healing Your Emotional Self: A Powerful Program to Help You Raise Your Self-Esteem, Quiet Your Inner Critic, and Overcome Your Shame*. Hoboken, New Jersey: John Wiley & Sons, Inc., 2006.

Erikson, E. H. *The Life Cycle Completed: A Review*. New York: Norton, 1982.

Evens, G. W., S. Carrere, and M. N. Palsane. "Type A Behavior and Occupational Stress: A Cross-cultural Study of Blue Collar Workers." *Journal of Personality and Social Psychology*52, no.5 (1987): 1002-1007.

Fenwick, Elizabeth and Tony Smith. *Adolescence: The Survival Guide for Parents and Teenagers*. Great Britain, 1994.

Galassi, Merna Dee, John P. Galassi. "Modifying Assertive and Aggressive Behavior through Assertion Training." *Journal of College Student Personnel*19, no. 5 (September 19, 1978): 453-56.

Gottman, John M. and Nan Silver. *The Seven Principles for Making Marriage Work: A Practical Guide from the Country's Foremost Relationship Expert*. New York: Three Rivers Press, 2000

Guthrie, W. K. C. *Socrates*. Cambridge: Cambridge University Press, 1971.

Harrell, Keith. *Attitude Is Everything: 10 Life-Changing Steps to Turning Attitude into Action*. New York: Cliff Street Books, 2000.

Heyman, Richard. *How to Say It to Teens: Talking about the Most Important Topics of Their Lives*. Paramus, New Jersey: Prentice Hall Press, 2001.

Lenson, Barry. *Good Stress, Bad Stress: An Indispensable Guide to Identifying and Managing Your Stress*. New York: Marlowe & Company, 2002.

Miller, Alice. *For Your Own Good: Hidden Cruelty in Childrearing and the Roots of Violence*. New York: Farrar, Straus, and Giroux, 1990.

Martin, Del. *Battered Wives*. Rev. ed. San Francisco: Volcano Press, 1981.

Myers, David G. *The Pursuit of Happiness*. New York: William Morrow, 1992.

Pence, Ellen and Michael Paymar. *Power and Control: Tactics of Men Who Batter*. Duluth, Minn: Domestic Abuse intervention Project, 1979.

Pheiffer, Vera. *Total Stress Relief: Practical Solutions That Really Work*. London: Piatkus Books, 2003.

Provine, R. R. and K. R. Fischer. "Laughing, Smiling, and Talking: Relation to Sleeping and Social Context in Humans." *Ethology*. Vol. 83 (1989): 295-305.

Roths, Michael S. *Freud: Conflict and Culture*. New York: Alfred Knopf, 1998.

Schaef, Anne Wilson. *Co-dependence: Misunderstood—Mistreated.* San Francisco: Harper & Row, 1986.

Schmid, Joyce. "Alcoholism and the Family." *Treating Alcoholism*. Edited by S. Brown. San Francisco: Jossey-Bass, 1995.

Steinglass, Peter, Linda Bennett, Steven Wolin, and David Reiss. *The Alcoholic Family*. New York: Basic Books, 1987.

Tifft, Larry L. *Battering of Women: The Failure of Intervention and the Case for Prevention*. Boulder, CO: West View Press, 1993.

Walker, Lenore. *The Battered Woman*. New York: Harper and Row, 1979.